Lessons *for* Leaders

Building a Winning Team
From the Ground Up

HOMER RICE

LONGSTREET PRESS
Atlanta, Georgia

Published by
LONGSTREET PRESS
2140 Newmarket Parkway
Suite 122
Marietta, GA 30067

Printed in the United States of America

1st printing 2000

Library of Congress Catalog Card Number: 00-105059

ISBN: 1-56352-632-8

Jacket and book design by Burtch Bennett Hunter

DEDICATION

When I think of dedicating *Lessons for Leaders*, I immediately turn to my family. I have been blessed to be married to my childhood sweetheart, Phyllis Wardrup of Middlesboro, Kentucky, for more than fifty years. Her encouragement throughout my career gave the inspiration that pushed me forward. Our marriage produced three lovely, outstanding daughters: Nancy Hetherington, Phyllis Ingle, and Angela Miller. Our daughters have always been special to me.

I also must look back to my parents, Dr. and Mrs. Samuel C. Rice. Their support in the early years started me on a positive path to success. My older brother, Robert Cecil Rice, as a model student-athlete, influenced my career. Many coaches, teachers, and associates through the years influenced my life as well. Last but not least were the thousands of student-athletes with whom I had the privilege to be in contact – and to see them go on and become successful in their careers. That is what it is all about. Receiving the good from others and giving back to others. *Giving* is the most satisfying feeling a person will ever experience. It has been for me.

ACKNOWLEDGMENTS

When I retired from Georgia Tech in May of 1997, Georgia Tech's President Wayne Clough challenged me to write a book on my seventeen years as Director of Athletics of the Georgia Tech Athletic Association. He asked Dr. Robert McMath, Vice Provost for Undergraduate Studies, to assist me. Dr. McMath provided me with an astute young graduate student, Haven Hawley, to work with me on the manuscript. Haven earned her undergraduate degree in journalism from Baylor University, worked in publication production for several years, and is now a doctoral candidate in Georgia Tech's history of technology program. An avid athlete and youth soccer coach, she enthusiastically took on the project of helping me tell the story of the Total Person Program.

I began handwriting and sometimes using a tape recorder to put my thoughts together. The key to finishing was writing and taping each day. Whether at home, flying on Ron Allen's Delta airplanes, in a waiting room, or any other place, I forced myself to work – sometimes for an hour or so, sometimes for just a few minutes. The discipline to approach the task every day was the key. After developing one part of the story, my long-time assistant Ann Harrell began typing to get a clean copy. The pages were then passed to Haven, who edited and miraculously put the words and phrases into order. Once the first draft of the manuscript was completed, I asked Bob Harty, Georgia Tech's Executive Director of Communications and Public Affairs, to look over the material. It had his blessings. Then it was time to approach a publisher.

My other books went through New York publishing houses, but during a casual luncheon with my friend Bill Reynolds of the architectural firm Smallwood, Reynolds, Stewart and Stewart, I mentioned the book I was working on. He recommended an Atlanta company that had published a Civil War history involving his ancestors, as well as a recent bestseller, *The Millionaire Next Door,* and other successful books. Scott Bard, president of Longstreet Press, was the contact, and the publishing company became interested. Next, John Yow, senior editor, began the editing process, and we were in business. It certainly was a team effort to produce this book, which, hopefully, will provide readers with lessons that can positively affect their lives. Thanking these people isn't enough: I salute them, because without their vision and hard work, *Lessons for Leaders* would never have gone into print.

TABLE OF CONTENTS

Foreword   By Grant Teaff IX

Chapter One   REFLECTIONS 1

Chapter Two   WHAT WENT WRONG? 25

Chapter Three THE FIRST FIVE-YEAR PLAN
               (1981-1985): PURSUIT OF
               (ACC) RESPECT!. 39

Chapter Four   THE SECOND FIVE-YEAR PLAN
               (1986-1990): SEEKING
               NATIONAL RECOGNITION!. 79

Chapter Five   THE THIRD FIVE-YEAR PLAN
               (1991-1996): WORLD
               ATTENTION! 115

Chapter Six   RETIREMENT AND THE
               FUTURE 149

Afterword   GEORGIA TECH: A
               HISTORY OF INTEGRITY 169

Appendix A   THE STUDENT-ATHLETE
               TOTAL PERSON PROGRAM 173

Appendix B   ORIGINS AND DEVELOPMENT
               OF THE ATTITUDE TECHNIQUE
               PHILOSOPHY. 179

Appendix C   THE BANQUET PROGRAM. 187

Appendix D   A PROCLAMATION. 191

Index 193

My dream, and thus my goal, was to follow my high school coaches into their world and their profession. To become a football coach and educator consumed me. Being from a small west-Texas town and, frankly, having very little athletic talent never once deterred me from setting my ultimate goal to be a head football coach in the famous Southwest Conference. I learned early on that I would have to be innovative and seek knowledge from every source available to me.

I was fortunate to become a head track coach on the college level at age 23. By my twenty-sixth birthday, I was also the head football coach at McMurry College in Abilene, Texas. My methods of learning were trial and error, clinics, and books on football.

In 1963, a young assistant football coach at the University of Kentucky wrote a book entitled *The Explosive Short-T*. The author, Homer Rice, had been a very successful high school coach and was now moving up the ladder within our profession.

The Explosive Short-T offense developed by Homer Rice and described in his new book used the quickness of the T-formation, the deception of the short punt, the role of the blocking back in the single wing, and many elements found in other successful offenses.

The book was well organized, extremely informative, and thorough in its approach to the offensive philosophy it described. The basic fundamentals of organization, information, and thoroughness found in Homer Rice's first book can be found in all of his accomplishments and aptly describe the man himself.

Homer Rice had been one of the most successful high school coaches in America. His offenses broke record after record, and he was beginning to be recognized throughout the nation as an individual with great leadership ability and outstanding integrity.

I truly admired Homer Rice as a man and a football coach even before I had the privilege of knowing him personally. Out friendship has endured coaching in the same conference and serving on numerous NCAA and AFCA committees. I, along with the rest of the nation, marveled at his ability to achieve success on every level of coaching and in the world of athletic administration.

Lessons for Leaders is a book that every leader should read. Every aspiring coach will learn from this book how to get where he wants to go. Every athletic administrator or CEO will find an outline that will assure success in his or her chosen field.

There are leadership lessons from the first page through the last page of *Lessons for Leaders*. Notice the concept of the "we" instead of "I" in each of the five-year plans. Dr. Rice teaches a desire to dream big dreams, combined with a willingness to do the work that will lead to missions fulfilled.

Selecting the right team will guarantee success, and Homer Rice, over the years, has always attracted outstanding athletes, coaches, and individuals willing to give their time, their energy, and their finances to a higher purpose.

Lessons for Leaders is a history book and a how-to manual for when you want to get something really big done. Homer Rice's life has taken him on a fortunate journey to serve many institutions, but the most important part of his journey is his service to young people. The Attitude Technique philosophy developed and taught over the years by Homer Rice has reached thousands upon thousands of students, coaches, and administrators. An academic course that he now offers at Georgia Tech entitled "Leadership Fitness – Striving Toward the Total Person/Total Success Concept" teaches students to live life as positive, self-motivated persons, developing a successful plan for their entire lives. The complete and fulfilling life is what Homer Rice and *Lessons for Leaders* are all about.

This book is a must-read if you want to be successful *and* if you want to serve others.

Grant Teaff
Executive Director, American Football Coaches Association

AUTHOR'S NOTE:

During the process of writing my story for *Lessons for Leaders*, I relied on memory, research, and other people's recollections of the facts. To the best of my knowledge, all the facts are accurate – except on the few occasions where I have indicated that a little storytelling beyond the facts might be in order. To paraphrase a theatrical phrase for my own ends, I will claim that this book is based on a true story but that I haven't changed the names to protect the innocent.

My only regret is that I am certain I missed several wonderful people with whom I made special contact throughout my career and at many events. This book is about helping leaders to apply lessons of success to their own careers. For those unmentioned in my narrative, I hope the knowledge of having played an unnamed part in helping others to put those lessons into practice is enough.

Lessons *for* Leaders

CHAPTER ONE
REFLECTIONS

The banquet room at Atlanta's Grand Hyatt overflowed with family, friends, and associates. So many of the people who had meant so much to me during a career almost a half-century long. As I glanced at the head table and caught a glimpse of Ray Bardill, my first quarterback on the 1951 Wartburg Central High School football team, the floodgates of memory opened wide.

Coming home from my service in the U. S. Navy at the end of World War II, I began focusing on what would become my career. My college coach, "Swede" Anderson at Centre College, invited me to join him as he moved to a university in Texas. I was bold enough to believe that I could handle a head job in my first year, however, and I turned him down. Little did I know what lay ahead!

Phyllis and I were married August 12, 1950, and after I finished my undergraduate degree the next year, we headed for Wartburg, Tennessee, where I had accepted the job of head football coach at Wartburg Central High School. There I would begin a 47-year coaching and administrative career. Soon after, our first daughter, Nancy Kathryn, was born. With a baby but no automobile, we started my first job with the whopping annual salary of $2,700.

Wartburg was so small, we joked, that the sign welcoming visitors passing through on Highway 27 had 'Welcome' printed on both sides. The school had only 50 students.

In August before the 1951-52 school term, I called the first practice. Only seven applicants appeared. I was devastated. How could I coach 11-man football with two-thirds of that number? Before the first practice, I had met with the principal, John Dillon. I asked to see the locker room and was ushered into a small room, just 10 by 12 feet. A small box in the corner contained the equipment. Nails on the wall served as lockers. Just producing a team with the required football gear to compete in the first game was going to be a challenge.

They didn't expect much of the season, I was told, because they had never won more than four games before. I began recruiting mightily to find enough players for us to even start a game. One week before our first contest at the start of September, 11 players' names appeared on the roster. I was so happy I ran all the way home to the small duplex we rented, cutting through a cornfield shortcut I'd found, and hugged Phyllis when I arrived. We could play the first game!

One problem remained. We didn't have enough equipment. The boys had their own brogans, onto which we nailed cleats. Mothers sewed numbers on blue jerseys for their sons. But we still didn't have enough shoulder pads, helmets, or pants.

Racking my brain for ideas about where to get some equipment for the boys, I remembered that Petros Prison, the state penal farm near Wartburg, at one time had a football team. It was worth asking about, as I had no other possibilities. Paying a visit to the warden, I explained my dilemma and asked if they had any football equipment stored away. They did. But the warden was noncommittal and requested that I come back the next day.

When I appeared again as he had asked, he agreed to let me borrow the equipment for a trade: I could use the prison's property in exchange for coaching the prison team. The men needed recreational activity as they prepared to be released back into society. The warden had what I wanted, so there was no way out of making the deal. I agreed to his terms. Now I was head coach of two teams: Wartburg Central High School and Petros Prison. And from that dual appointment, two stories have to be told.

The Wartburg Story

I found that on the high school team I was not only the head coach but the assistant, trainer, and equipment supervisor. This job was solo! After football, I coached both the boys and girls basketball teams, then went on to direct all the spring sports. It was a one-man show for the entire sports program at that school.

I began the football season by whipping the team into action for its first game. Although our numbers increased during the season, only 14 boys made up the playing squad. And each of those 14 had a special characteristic that required special coaching attention.

Quarterback Ray "Bubby" Bardill had been in a hunting accident the year before that blew off part of his leg. He hadn't been expected to walk again, to say nothing of running and participating in football. But he wanted to play. I designed a doughnut-type pad to cover the damaged area of his leg. He not only played but became an All-District Quarterback. One of our ends, Don Terry, had only one eye. We designed our pass patterns so Don received throws on his good-eye side only. We joked that our offensive practices were 11 on 3.

Most coaches count the field during football games to make sure only 11 players are present for the kick-off. But I simply had to glance at the bench. If I saw three boys there, then 11 were on the field.

Preparing for our first home game presented a traumatic experience. We didn't have a regular football field and had to play in the school yard. I asked the teacher who ran the shop class to make a wooden goal post for the team. We only needed one because at the other end the field ran into concrete. When a team scored and wanted to kick for the extra point, we maneuvered to the end of the field where the lone goalpost awaited. We had many more problems to solve, but the fact that stands out is that the team won its first game. Then they won a second. And they ended the season undefeated. A miracle!

Perhaps. I knew from experience I could find success in any situation. Each player on the team performed a role in making that success possible. They learned to perfect their particular assignments and techniques, taking charge of what lay within their own hands. Lowell Lowe became highly effective at his halfback position, and Paul Langley stood out as defensive tackle. Ralph Goodman and others made this team a highlight in the school's history. Years later, in a local newspaper, writer Brian Langley investigated whether the

1951 Bulldog team was the "greatest team ever."

> Paul Langley, Lowell Lowe, Don Terry, and Ray Bardill were
> the key players on the 1951 team that went 8-0-1. They defeat-
> ed the likes of Oneida by 20-12, Sunbright 15-0, Coalfield,
> Oakdale, and others. The only blemish on the team's record was
> the 0-0 tie with Huntsville. There were only three teams that
> scored on the Bulldogs all season.
>
> Coach Rice recalled the Huntsville game, played on the
> Bears' home field. "We scored four or five times and they (the
> referees) kept calling them back. I knew right away they were
> not going to let us win the ball game, but on the other hand, I
> knew they (the Bears) were not going to score on us."
>
> The '51 team was crowned Morgan County champs and will
> be remembered by many as the greatest team in Morgan County
> history.
>
> "It (the 1951) season was a very special team for me. What I
> remember most about those kids is how hard they worked and
> how well they played on the football field," Coach Rice recalled.

Quarterback Ray Bardill went on to earn a Ph.D. and become a consultant to the U.S. Congress before accepting a dean's position at
Florida State University. Ray's courage in coming back from his leg
injury to fulfill his dream of playing football inspired me as a coach.
In return, he shared with me his story of how I played a role in
encouraging him to reach for his goal.

> I was 16 years old in the fall of 1951, wrote Ray. Over the pre-
> vious nine months, I had been hospitalized for seven weeks, had
> a skin graft on my upper right leg, been told I might never walk
> again without a limp, and that I'd certainly never be able to play
> football again. Despite all of this, I found myself reporting for
> football practice at Wartburg Central High School in August of
> that year. I told our new coach, Homer Rice, about my physical
> situation and my determination to play football again.
>
> I will never forget his response. He had both a deadpan and
> a compassionate expression on his face as he told me that he
> would give me a chance to play football. After he looked at the
> wounded leg, he told me he would wrap the leg with a donut-cut
> sponge to protect the wound. I don't know if Coach Rice ever

really knew how much his response that day influenced my life.

That year Wartburg Central went undefeated for the first and only time in the school's history, operating out of the split-T while the rest of Tennessee high school football followed the Bob Neyland single-wing formation. No one could stop our offense. Every practice and every game, Coach Rice talked to me about football as he wrapped my leg with the sponge. I had an opportunity to get to know a man of deep honesty, integrity, and caring. He had a great football mind. He was a true leader. Coach Rice wanted to win — very strongly — but he also wanted to win within all the rules. His practices were grueling and very demanding. He took a group of green young boys from Morgan County, Tennessee, and molded us into an efficient young football team.

Coach Rice left Wartburg at the end of the 1951-52 academic year. Wartburg High School sports have never been the same since that year. Coach Rice was an inspiration to all the young boys who played for him. I still get calls from students who were in high school that year. It was a dream year! The specific philosophy that still inspires me may be summarized in the talk Coach Rice told us before the last game of the football season. He said, 'Play your very best tonight because you will never forget this year. It always will be a memory for you.' It's true. I have never forgotten the Homer Rice year. I never will!

The Wartburg season provided its own kind of drama, but High school was just one of the two teams I coached. The prison team had its own story.

Petros Prison Story

As time has passed, the story has picked up many humorous anecdotes. Some are only partially true — especially one that I used many times to enliven my public speaking engagements. The tale became so popular that people requested it at banquets, speeches, and other public events. Each time I added a little more until the story practically became a novel. But what follows is at least *based on* a true story.

When I arrived to coach the Petros Prison football team, it was during the time when prisoners wore chains and the standard black-

and-white striped uniforms, including a matching cap with no bill. Guards brought the prisoners out into the yard for the start of the first practice. I talked with the men, explaining that we could only practice on certain days because I coached the local high school team. We would have early morning practices so I could get to school on time to teach during the day. I told them I taught civics. They gave no response. Then I added that we would have an election for a captain to run the team when I could not be present. A tough looking man stepped forward and informed me, in front of the squad, that he was the captain. I quickly agreed.

The warden didn't tell me why these men were sent to this prison. Personally, I didn't want to know. I found out later that my captain had robbed a candy store at age seven, landing in a reformatory school for young boys. Released at age 17, he robbed several service stations and wound up back in prison. He was a bad actor, always causing trouble. He'd been told he would never be released from prison and would spend the rest of his life inside prison walls.

This was the man who one day approached me with an unusual request. He asked for permission to see one of my high school football games. He had never seen an actual game, he said, and he wanted to experience a true game. I thought to myself, "The warden will never let this man outside."

The captain went on to tell me, "The warden believes in God, and he will let me go if you ask him." His statement overwhelmed me. I was so impressed with his sincerity that I decided to convey the request to the warden. The warden shocked me by agreeing. He only stipulated that the captain wear his prison uniform and ride in an armored vehicle to the game, with a rifle team present in the event he tried to escape.

When he arrived at the field, I put a coaching jacket on him. His cap went into his pocket. He wouldn't be conspicuous. During the game, he walked back and forth on the sideline, watching every play. He was completely immersed in the game. And from that day on, he was a changed person. I'll never know how, why, or what changed his attitude from the tough character he displayed in prison that first day to the gentle, positive man he became.

He later earned parole with good behavior and moved to Florida, where he became a model citizen and leader in his community. He married, raised a wonderful family, and turned into a successful businessman. No one knew his past. He changed his life to a positive direction. I knew that if he could do that, it was possible for any one to change his attitude and life.

As the years passed, it was interesting to stay in contact with this highly successful and changed man. I moved up the coaching profession, climbing that so-called ladder, and made my debut as the head football coach with the NFL Cincinnati Bengals. Every now and then, I heard from my friend. During one game against Don Shula's Miami Dolphins in the Orange Bowl, apparently Howard Cosell made a derogatory remark about my coaching abilities in his commentary on ABC's Monday Night Football. The next day, I received a phone call. My friend wanted to see how I was doing. He was concerned about the remark on national TV. "Coach, I'm coming out of retirement," he told me. "There's going to be one less sportscaster."

Three weeks later, the Bengals again played on ABC's Monday Night Football, this time against John Madden's Oakland Raiders. Howard Cosell appeared to have had a change of heart. He now called me the "gentleman coach" and made other flattering remarks. I never knew the details, but as I progressed through my career I knew I had a friend with his hand on the sports media. I assume they understood the message: Instant elimination!

Looking back, I often remark that the prison job turned out to be the best coaching position of my entire career. First of all, we had all home games. I never had to worry about sending towels back after a game. Second, I had no problems from the alumni. When they came back, they were always a help: I simply inserted them back into the lineup. Third, whenever I heard the sheriff's siren, my reaction was quite different from that of other citizens. "I hope they pick up a tight end," I would think. Finally, I never signed a contract. They couldn't fire me, but I could quit any time I wanted. The unusual benefits of coaching a prison team gave me lots of good laughs and great material.

But back at Wartburg, the successful season had caught the eye of several schools, and I received offers for other coaching positions. I was always amazed at the number of offers through the years. Phyllis and I seemed to have decision after decision to make, usually at Christmas. From among those first offers, we chose to move to Spring City High School in Spring City, Tennessee, where our daughter Phyllis, named after my dear wife, was born. Another undefeated season, and then two in a row followed at Spring City, as did more outstanding players. Quarterback George Perry reminded me years later that in front of the squad I reprimanded him by saying, "George, you have a million-dollar arm, but a ten-cent brain." In the end, he led the team to many victories.

We picked up friends with each move. At Wartburg, we made the acquaintance of Ray Bardill's parents and remained close for many years. The A. M. Hullings became our friends in Spring City. Our next move was to a place where I already knew many people. My own alma mater, Highlands High School in Fort Thomas, Kentucky, called me home to coach in the greater Cincinnati area. My former coach, Ewell "Judge" Waddell, had become the superintendent of Fort Thomas schools. Coach Waddell was a father figure for me, and he'd profoundly influenced my life and career choice. I was his pick for the high school position he'd left.

We completed our family in Fort Thomas with the birth of our third daughter, Angela. In a selfish streak, I'd always thought I'd have a son who might someday play for his dad, but that was not to be. What I had was even better. My three lovely daughters always cheered for me, whether my team won or lost. My family cheerleaders encouraged others in the stands who could always see our daughters yelling and cheering for their dad. And because of their arrangements with the two biggest players on the team to raise me to their shoulders and carry me off the field at the end of a game, the fans always got the impression that players loved me even in defeat.

Well, you can't expect a storyteller to tell the truth all the time, can you? That last part was an exaggeration, of course. But it leads me to a story about a time early in my high school coaching career when my team was down at halftime. I jumped on the biggest player in the room and challenged him by saying, "If I was as big as you, I would be the heavyweight champion of the world!" He looked back at me and said, "Coach, what's keeping you from being the lightweight champion?" That simple question helped me define my goal of helping people to achieve their individual greatness, which later resulted in the Student-Athlete Total Person Program.

At Highlands we had many good years, winning several state titles and going undefeated in the last 50 regular season games. During those years, Phyllis and I became close to Gloria and Clem "Boonie" Fennell. While I coached on the field, Boonie became caretaker of our families at both home and away games. We each had three children. Their sons, Clem and Kent, and daughter, Jenny, were a match for our own three daughters, Nancy, Phyllis, and Angela. Boonie always complained that I had the easier task while he fought the battles of the "clan." It was later my pleasure to return to Highlands High School to present Boonie with an award for his continued support of his high school football program.

Meanwhile, eighty miles south of Fort Thomas, I spent hours discussing technical football with Head Coach Blanton Collier of the University of Kentucky, nearby in Lexington. We became very close, and I learned much from the gentle giant of football, who was perhaps the best teacher the game has ever known.

I first met Blanton Collier when I reported to the Great Lakes Naval Station for boot camp during World War II. I had an opportunity at Great Lakes to try out for the baseball team, coached by Bob Feller, who had gained fame as pitcher for the Cleveland Indians. I made the team, but during practices I found myself looking across the field where the football team worked out under the skillful coaching of Paul Brown. Ironically, the bat boy for the baseball team was Paul's son, Mike. Mike was about 10 years old at the time. I asked him to take me to football practice and to let me meet his father if possible. Paul had coached Ohio State University to a national title in 1942 before he joined the Navy during World War II and became head of the Great Lakes sports program.

Unbeknownst to me, a sailor took notes on the football scrimmages from outside the field's fence. Coach Brown had the sailor brought inside, and he turned out to be Blanton Collier, a high school coach from Paris, Kentucky. Paul brought Blanton to practice and later made him a member of his coaching staff. The day I came to visit practice, Blanton recognized me as the quarterback from Highland High School. To my good fortune, both of these men would become my mentors in the coaching profession. We lost contact during the war, but while coaching later back at Highlands I renewed ties with Blanton at Kentucky and with Paul with the Cleveland Browns, spending time with both as I began my own coaching career.

After the war, Paul Brown took his coaching staff, including Blanton, to Cleveland. The Cleveland Rams eventually moved to Los Angeles in the National Football League, but Paul and other investors bought the franchise in the American Football League and

*formed the Cleveland Browns. Paul Brown and Blanton Collier
teamed up for championship after championship at Cleveland, until
Blanton returned home to coach the Kentucky Wildcats. Blanton
replaced Coach Bear Bryant, who left Kentucky for Texas A & M
and, eventually, his home at the University of Alabama where he
had played the opposite end to All-American Don Hudson.*

I made trip after trip to Cleveland and Lexington to visit with Paul
and Blanton. After spending several years at Kentucky, Blanton
returned to the Cleveland Browns, where he eventually became head
coach after Paul Brown parted ways with Art Modell, majority
stockholder of the Browns. Blanton went on to win a world championship on a team that featured Jim Brown. Bernie Shively, the athletic director at Kentucky, contacted me about the head position left
vacant by Blanton's departure. Bernie, an All-Big-Ten lineman from
Illinois, had coached my older brother, Robert Cecil Rice, at
Pineville, Kentucky, in the late 1930s. My brother was an outstanding player and captain of the team that claimed a conference championship under Head Coach Walter Grabuck. I merely served as
team mascot, attending every practice and running onto the field
with the team on game day in my football suit. From age six on,
football was ingrained in me!

Coach Shively had left Pineville for the University of Kentucky
to coach under Ab Kirwan. Ab in turn moved forward to become
head of the graduate school at the University of Kentucky, and his
son Brit was later named president of the University of Maryland
and an active member of the ACC. In the early 1940s, Bernie Shively
was appointed head coach and recruited me to play at Kentucky
after my senior year at Highland High School in Fort Thomas,
Kentucky. I ended up opting for Georgia Tech, as will be explained
later, but Uncle Sam's plans called me into the Navy during World
War II. As director of athletics at Kentucky, Bernie called again, asking me to come to Lexington to talk with "the committee" about the
head football job. The congenial gathering included Kentucky's
president, Frank Graves Dickey, chairman of the University of
Kentucky Board, Dr. Ralph Angelucci, and W. L. Matthews Jr., dean
of the law school and faculty chairman of athletics. I'd been contacted by several small colleges and been offered assistantships from
large colleges because of my success at Highlands, but Kentucky was
quite a different proposal. This was the first major university to call

about a head coaching position.

I grew up in Kentucky, staying in the state to pursue my undergraduate degree at Centre College in Danville. And here was the state university calling for me. Dr. Angelucia compared me to Paul Brown. He noted that Paul had gone from the successful Massillon High School program to the campus of Ohio State University. I'd be making a similar move if they extended the offer, which wasn't certain yet. For some reason I lacked the self-confidence I'd thought I would feel about such an opportunity. The coaching aspect didn't concern me, but recruiting collegiate players was something I'd never done. Unsure about whether I was prepared for all the tasks that a head coach had to have mastered, I rejected the offer, thanking the Kentucky officials but explaining that I didn't feel ready to make such a giant step.

President Dickey then asked me to consider filling out the top assistant's job. After considering the proposal, I replied that I would be interested only if the new head coach specifically wanted to work with me.

Returning home to Fort Thomas, I prepared for our football team's annual banquet. We had captured another state title, with quarterback Roger Walz named to the All-State first team. I had invited Charlie Bradshaw, the top assistant at Alabama under Coach Bryant, to be guest speaker at the banquet. Alabama had just won the national championship, but I'd first met Charlie as an assistant under Blanton Collier at Kentucky. Charlie played for Coach Bryant at Kentucky, and when the "Bear" took the Alabama job, Charlie joined him there. Charlie also traveled to Fort Thomas while recruiting, staying at our home and talking football with me late into the night. And now he was a candidate for the head job at Kentucky. I called Bernie Shively and recommended Charlie for the position. Whether I had any influence on the decision or not I can't say, but Charlie gained the nod. He invited me to join him as offensive coordinator, to my great pleasure.

I should mention that at Highlands High School, which I had the privilege to attend as a student-athlete and to return to as football coach, my good friend Owen Hauck assisted me in developing our successes. Owen was an outstanding coach in his own right. He replaced me at Highlands and later became a coaching legend at Boone County High School in Kentucky.

My four years at Kentucky saw some unusual occurrences. In

that first dismal season, we lost player after player. In the final game with traditional rival the University of Tennessee, we had plunged to only 17 active players. Quarterback Gary Woolum shifted the back-field into a single-wing type formation with Darrel Cox, a small left-handed running back from Miami sweeping left and right, with a run-pass option. Somehow we stayed in the game, behind only 9 to 10, with 12 seconds left to play. We lined up for a field goal attempt. With our regular place kicker out of the game, Clarkie Mayfield kicked a "knuckle ball" that barely scraped over the upright for a 12 – 10 victory.

Propelled by that victory into the coming seasons, our program vastly improved. We beat No. 1 Mississippi and No. 6 Auburn, back to back. The win over Mississippi in Lexington proved particularly memorable. Ahead by one point with two minutes to play, our All-American quarterback Rick Norton took huge losses to run out the clock. Ole Miss called time-out after each down, forcing us into a fourth-down punting situation. But our scouts had noticed that when Ole Miss put its punt return in place, only the defensive end remained to check the punter. At Highlands, I taught our quarter-back and punter, Roger Walz, to stutter-step when punting, to kick if the rush came, but to hold the ball longer before kicking if the return was on, in order to allow the coverage team to be there wait-ing on the safety man when the ball arrived. The final option was to run the ball for a first down if daylight appeared.

Kentucky's punter, Larry Sieple, knew the drill. He stood on our 10-yard line, fourth down and long yardage, waiting for the snap from the center. I called the offense from the press box. A light went on in my head. Larry wouldn't attempt to run the ball; after all, it was fourth and forty. But if he didn't find a way to get a first down, Ole Miss would line up, kick a field goal, and beat us 12 – 10. Ole Miss had perhaps the best field goal kicker in the nation playing in the game. I silently prayed that Ole Miss would put the rush on. But they didn't. Our opponent called a return scheme.

Larry took the snap, then stutter-stepped. The Ole Miss end crossed in front, and Larry began to run. It seemed like an eternity as he raced down the sideline, gaining the precious first down. Ole Miss never saw him. He continued down the field, gaining 90 yards for a touchdown, and sealing our victory 17 – 9. In his professional career, Larry punted for Don Shula with the Miami Dolphins, pulling out a victory over Pittsburgh with the same scenario, propelling Miami from the playoffs into the Super Bowl. Don later told me that Larry had pulled the trick on his own — but that he had learned it during his days at Kentucky.

Our offense at Kentucky led the SEC and won the national passing title. Several players from the offensive unit went on to the pros and did extremely well. Rick Norton became a first-round draft choice, going to Miami. Larry Sieple also made the trip to Miami. Tackles Sam Ball and Doug Davis went to Baltimore and Minneapolis, respectively. Wide receiver Rick Kessner traveled to Baltimore, outstanding running back Roger Bird to Oakland, and tight end Bob Windsor to the 49ers. After the fourth year at Kentucky, I was offered several head jobs. At Duke University, one of our great coaches, Bill Murray, was retiring, and I was considered there. A search team trying to fill the position at the Citadel expressed interest, too. But the job that really excited me was that of offensive coordinator at the University of Oklahoma.

Oklahoma was the top football program in the nation. Bud Wilkinson had retired from coaching, and Gomer Jones, his top aide, had become director of athletics. The former top assistant at Arkansas under Frank Broyles' highly successful program took the head coach position. Coach Jim McKenzie not only had worked in Arkansas, but he had played for Bear Bryant at Kentucky and was considered the best defensive coach in America. Jim called and asked me to join him in Norman as offensive coordinator. I had already taken myself out of consideration for the Citadel position. Despite the *esprit de corps* which made the president of the institution confident that the team could beat the very difficult opponents scheduled, I took one look at the upcoming games and had to disagree. I informed Jim McKenzie that I was still in the running for the Duke position.

Jim promised to keep in contact, and I went on to a second appearance to discuss the Duke position with Athletic Director Eddie Cameron and the university's committee. Mr. Cameron affirmed that I was indeed their choice, but President Knight was unavailable to confirm the selection. We would have to wait for official approval before an offer could be made. I returned to Lexington to await the decision.

The next evening, Eddie Cameron called and reluctantly explained that the president had hand-picked an Ivy League coach. Before I could feel the letdown — and not more than ten minutes later — Jim McKenzie had me on the phone. I let him know the situation. He asked me to come to Oklahoma, and the next morning I was on an airplane to accept his offer of a position as a top assistant at the University of Oklahoma.

So it was time to say good-bye to Lexington, where we had enjoyed not only our affiliation with the University of Kentucky but also our proximity to all the beautiful horse farms. Lexington, of course, is the horse racing capital of the world, with more than one hundred beautiful farms in and around the bluegrass area of Lexington. Naturally, we had to purchase a couple of horses for our daughters to ride. This was an exciting time for them. Among our many friends in Lexington were our minister, Don Herren, and his wife, Pat. Don built Southern Hills Methodist Church, where we became members, and when we left Kentucky for the move to Oklahoma, Phyllis and I were served the first communion by our dear friend before we departed.

At Oklahoma I joined a staff that Darrell Royal, head coach at the University of Texas, considered the strongest in major college football. Jim had put together a group including Pat James, another Bear Bryant protégé, who would head up the defense; Chuck Fairbanks, secondary coach, who later became head coach for Oklahoma as well as Colorado and the New England Patriots; and "Swede" Lee, a former linebacker coached by Darrell Royal. Offensive line coach Barry Switzer also later became head coach at Oklahoma before moving on to the Dallas Cowboys. The crew also included Galen Hall, receiver coach and later head coach at the University of Florida; freshmen coach Larry Lacewell, who now directs the scouting program for the Dallas Cowboys; and Billy Gray, who later joined Frank Broyles as top associate at Arkansas, handling their administrative matters. We had a staff with bright futures.

The first year at Oklahoma produced two big wins on national television. We defeated Darrell Royal's Texas Longhorns in the annual rivalry played out in the Cotton Bowl stadium. I always had a lot of respect for Darrell Royal. I shall never forget his saying, "If the game isn't important, why do we keep score?" We also beat Bob Devaney's Nebraska Cornhuskers on the traditional Thanksgiving Day game in a match-up that ABC called the Game of the Year. Bud Wilkinson provided color commentary. He was one of my idols in the coaching profession, and I spent several hours with him before the game, explaining our strategy for Nebraska. The game turned out to be very close.

Nebraska took the lead down the stretch, ahead 9 – 7 with only minutes to play. After receiving the kick off, we moved quickly into Nebraska's territory. With a third down and long yardage situation at the 35-yard line, we called a time-out. Out of field goal range for our kicker, we desperately needed a first down to give him the chance for a winning kick. In the press box, I'd been tracking Nebraska's long-yardage situations. They lined up into an even defense, with two defensive guards over our offensive guards. On the snap, they both rushed the passer outside our guards, leaving the lane open over the center. We hadn't called a draw play to the fullback the entire game, and they probably wouldn't expect that strategy. I called the play.

Coach Jim McKenzie grabbed the phones on the field, yelling, "Homer, are you crazy? We need a pass to get us a first down!" All I could reply was, "Coach, trust me." I knew at this point that if the play did not get us a first down, the game would be lost and my career would be abruptly curtailed. Nebraska again lined up in the pass rush. The ball was snapped. Our fullback took the hand off and not only picked up the first down but carried the ball all the way to the two-yard line. We quickly lined up and kicked the field goal, winning the game 10 – 9. I had kept my job at Oklahoma. After the game, I met Nebraska's young offensive coordinator, Tom Osborne, who congratulated me on the call. Tom later became Nebraska's head coach and won back-to-back national championships.

Oklahoma's quarterback, Bobby Warmack, played superbly during the season and later earned an All-American title. He wasn't the quarterback scheduled to start at the beginning of the season. In fact, he was No. 3 on the chart. In our first game against the University of Oregon, we failed the move the football. I asked Coach McKenzie if I could insert Bobby into the lineup, and I got the go ahead. Bobby led the team to a 35 – 0 victory. The next season after a victory over Tennessee in the Orange Bowl, Bobby Warmack would be selected as the outstanding player of the game. Bobby had worked around the clock all season long, polishing his skills. He hadn't been given much of a chance, but he proved himself a winner.

I'm fortunate to have coached four All-American quarterbacks in my career, finding one in each collegiate program where I accepted a job. Rick Norton stood out at Kentucky, and Bobby Warmack at Oklahoma. Greg Cook led Cincinnati, and Rice University's Tommy Kramer joined the others. All but Bobby Warmack would be picked in the first round of the NFL draft, and Bobby entered coaching and later became a successful banker in Dallas, Texas.

Our offense at Oklahoma led the Big Eight Conference. The calls for head coaching positions began coming through. Five of us top assistants were called frequently: John Ray of Notre Dame, Bill Pace of Arkansas, Bo Schembechler of Miami of Ohio, Johnny Majors of Arkansas, and myself. The situation reminded me of being recruited as a high school senior, because the five of us got to know each other and even passed in the hall going from one interview to the next. Coaching recruitment tended to be a tight circle anyway. On one visit to Kansas State, I met a young assistant basketball coach named Bill Guthridge. On a later visit to the University of North Carolina interviewing for the director of athletics position, I meat Dean Smith's top assistant: Bill Guthridge. He joked that we would have to stop meeting so often. Bill wound up as Dean Smith's replacement upon the coach's retirement from UNC.

After a tour of visits to several universities, I decided to remain at Oklahoma. Then one day I received a call from a close friend in Cincinnati. The University of Cincinnati's job was open. Would I consider it? The university's president and athletic director made call after call, and friends made their own contacts asking me to think about the position. The program was in a rut and needed a facelift. And it was near my home. Attending Highlands High School in nearby Fort Thomas had made me familiar with the greater Cincinnati area, and we had many friends from my days coaching my old high school team. Although we had turned down many job offers from top universities, the challenge of returning home and rebuilding a down-and-out program appealed to me. My wife, Phyllis, and three daughters always supported my career, despite the changes it entailed in their lives. We left for Cincinnati.

In my collegiate coaching years, the recruiting wars supplied many stories and lessons. One that stands out vividly in my mind was the time I took a young man and his parents to a restaurant in south Texas (back when such entertainment was permitted). The waiter led us to a table, but the father apparently did not like this particular table. He grabbed the waiter by his shirt and proceeded to belt him with blow after blow until several of us managed to pull the man off. With the waiter lying on the floor, the father declared that we would go to his club for dinner.

During the meal at the club, father and son talked animatedly about going downtown and beating up on some people. I realized I was dealing with rough characters. I didn't succeed in signing the young man to a grant-in-aid – fortunately, as it turns out. His problems continued, and he transferred from school to school.

I recall another incident where I took a recruit and his parents out to dinner in their hometown. We all ordered steaks. The mother asked for hers to be cooked medium well, but the father and son wanted theirs rare. When the waiter brought our meals to the table, the father and son looked at each other and shook their heads. Their steaks were not rare enough. The waiter blinked, but took the steaks back and quickly brought out two rarer steaks. Father and son again insisted that the steaks were not rare. This brought out the manager, who explained that if the steaks were any rarer, they would be raw. The two diners nodded and said that was what they wanted. I couldn't wait to get back to school to tell my fellow coaches I had found a young man who ate raw meat. He had to be tough! We did sign the young man to a letter of intent, but he never turned out to be as mean as I expected.

After I spent just two months on the job at Cincinnati, Oklahoma's Jim McKenzie died of a massive heart attack. He was only 37 years old. It was such a tragedy, this taking of a young, outstanding coach from his dear family and friends. The news shocked me when I heard it. Jim had just visited me in Cincinnati and had complained about pains in his arms and how tired he had become. This should have been a warning, but he didn't heed the signs which an older man might not have ignored. Upon Jim's death, Oklahoma's athletic director and president called to request that I return to replace Jim as head coach. I faced one of the toughest decisions I would ever consider. I had hired a staff in Cincinnati, each of whom later went on to gain more recognition. They included Leeman Bennett, later coach of the NFL Atlanta Falcons and Tampa Bay Buccaneers; Ray Callahan, later to become coach with the NFL New York Jets; Owen Hauck, my replacement at Highlands High School and now earning credentials as a successful coach in his own right; George Boutselis, later of the Baltimore Colts; Ralph Straub, who in the future went to Ohio State; and Jim Kelly, an outstanding receiver coach and one of Sid Gilman's greats.

I would have to leave them all. In taking the Oklahoma job, I would be required to keep the present staff through one season. I couldn't bring any members of my newly-formed Cincinnati staff. Unsure of what would happen, I turned down the Oklahoma position, even though it was thought one of the best coaching jobs in the nation. And I felt sorry for myself for a while. "Did I really pass on this great coaching career opportunity?" I asked myself.

I moved on with the Cincinnati staff, putting together a stellar program at UC. After our first season, Paul Brown and friends purchased the newly-acquired National Football League franchise for the Cincinnati Bengals. Paul came to Cincinnati, and we renewed our friendship. He invited me to join his inaugural staff as quarterback coach. I had to turn him down to continue my work in the collegiate ranks, and he turned to a young coach from San Jose, Calif., named Bill Walsh. Ironically, Blanton Collier was head coach at the Cleveland Browns, and eventually Blanton and Paul ended up as opponents. I admired both gentleman and learned so much football from these two super coaches that I felt torn by being caught in the middle of their rivalry.

The next season ended quite successfully. Before the University of Cincinnati's big game with Miami of Ohio, I received a call from the University of North Carolina. My lifelong goal had been to eventually become an athletic director at a top university, hoping to stay in the South. And UNC offered me just that post. Here was my dream — but 10 years too soon. I needed more experience in coaching, which I truly loved, and I had to turn down the job with regret. I forgot about North Carolina and becoming an athletic director at UNC or anywhere else, refocusing with my capable staff on our big game with Bo Schembechler's Miami team. Bo's team held a No. 1 national ranking for their defense, and we were ranked No. 1 in offense. We pulled out a big win, downing Miami 23 – 21.

After the victory, I received another call from North Carolina. The chairman of the search committee, Gerald Barrett, wanted to talk with me. Gerald A. Barrett was a member of the University of North Carolina Athletic Board and served as faculty representative to the board. He also represented UNC at the Atlantic Coast Conference and on the NCAA level. A professor in the school of business with a law degree, he led the search for the new athletic director for the Tar Heels.

Would I come to Chapel Hill to talk with the group, he asked?

Phyllis had attended the women's college of the University of North Carolina, and she encouraged me to listen. Reluctantly, I departed for an interview. After the meeting with UNC officials, I told Dr. Barrett on the way to the airport to catch my return flight to Cincinnati that I just wasn't ready to leave coaching. He then told me something that made me rethink my position. "We are not looking for someone ready to leave coaching," he said. "We want someone with the energy and expertise to take our program to the top. You are that person."

A few years earlier when I was top assistant at Oklahoma, UNC had been one of the schools I visited for a head coaching position. I had decided to remain at Oklahoma, but people remembered our conversation and were presenting me with the athletic director's position. Upon my return to Cincinnati, I discussed the UNC offer with Phyllis and my family. We came to the conclusion that while I was thinking about 10 more years as a collegiate coach, my long-term goal had come to me early. I needed to accept its arrival and move on. We left for Chapel Hill and enjoyed eight wonderful years there.

Bernie Shively, athletic director at Kentucky, gave me advice when I was a young football coach. He recognized my potential to one day become director at a major university, and he counseled me to remember three things. First, to always stay a little bit in debt, because any surplus encourages a school to take the extra money. Second, to always be building something, because people see that as progress. Third, he told me to never stay longer than seven years at any one place. He admitted that he had violated rule number three by staying at Kentucky a lifetime, but he told me that after seven years people were ready for a director to move on.

Subconsciously, I remembered his code. At UNC, except for Dean Smith's winning basketball team, the total program was down. In fact a few years before I arrived at North Carolina, students hung Dean Smith in effigy. Yet he went on to become the best coach in college basketball. In three years, we had taken UNC's sports program to the top nationally. Alumni and friends responded to our needs and supported us fantastically. It was a rewarding experience. And the predictable job offers were coming in to follow the program's success. During my tenure at UNC, I became interested in athletic administration and talked to the officials about beginning an academic program to train college students to become athletic administrators. Based on my own experience, I could see the need.

Only one school, Ohio University, offered such a program.

On my first day on the job at UNC I entered my office, closed the door, and waited for the telephone to ring. That was all I knew about athletic administration at that time! Later, as we started the Management Institute with National Association of Collegiate Directors of Athletics (NACDA), I got busy putting together "Leadership in Athletics," published by my friend Paul Myers of Success Motivation Institute. The program aimed to train young administrators for the position I held, preparing them in philosophies and organization techniques for the tasks before them.

With NACDA, I became close friends with Executive Director Mike Cleary and, during my own stint as president, worked with many outstanding leaders and directors of athletics across the country to build our intercollegiate programs with top administrators. They included Mike Lude, University of Washington; Jack Lengyel, Naval Academy; Bob Bronzan, San Jose State; Bill Flynn, Boston College; Fred Miller, Arizona State; Ben Carnevale, William and Mary; John Tower, University of Connecticut; George King, Purdue; John Clune, Air Force; Gary Cunningham, Fresno State; Frank Windegger, TCU; Bill Byrne, Nebraska; Jim Jones, Ohio State; Dick Schultz, Virginia; Don Canham, Michigan; Glenn Tucket, Brigham Young; Ced Dempsey, Arizona (who later became executive director of the NCAA); Carl James, Duke; and Bump Eliot, Iowa. Later on, this group encouraged me to accept the first presidency of the NCAA Division 1-A Directors of Athletics Association.

My eighth year at North Carolina brought a call from Henry Frnka of San Antonio, Texas. Henry and I had been friends for many years, and he had entered the petroleum business after a coaching career at Tulsa and Tulane University so successful that it gave rise to a running joke. At Tulsa during the 1940s, he competed against his good friend Bill Alexander, head coach at Georgia Tech. The two had winning seasons and met several times in post-season bowl games. The story finally arose that the two coaches got together each year to decide which bowl they would meet in after the regular season. According to the joke, Coach Alex would call Henry for a bowl suggestion. When Henry chose the Sugar Bowl, Bill would complain he was tired of playing in the Sugar Bowl and wanted to meet at the Orange Bowl for a change.

Henry Frnka retired from coaching and entered the oil business, but he stayed involved with football. He began a clinic in San

Antonio for high school coaches in Texas and surrounding states. I spoke to his clinic several times, and Henry asked me to use my coaching contacts to help him invite clinicians. The speakers headlining his clinic read like a Who's Who in collegiate football ranks: Bear Bryant, Darrell Royal, Frank Broyles, Hayden Fry, Tom Landry, Bill Walsh.

One particular coach was always an outstanding speaker — Grant Teaff of Baylor University. His message to the thousands of high school coaches who attended the clinic always inspired these young men to achieve their very best, but he spoke directly to a challenge of personal behavior. Grant took over a dormant Baylor football program in 1971. In three years he had taken his team to the 1974 Cotton Bowl as champions of the always tough Southwest Conference – Baylor's first championship in 50 years. His success as a coach and motivator of people at all levels made him a natural to become head of the American Football Coaches Association as Executive Director, an organization he has led to its highest level.

I first met Grant at Estes Park, Colorado, at a Fellowship of Christian Athletes conference (an organization now headed by another outstanding individual and leader – Dal Shealy). Grant was an assistant at Texas Tech at the time and went on to become the winningest coach in Baylor's history as well as the 1974 National Coach of the Year for his miracle season. Grant is a man of high principle and perhaps the most highly respected man in collegiate football history, and it was my pleasure, as his friend, to ask Grant to write the Foreword for this book.

To return to the story, Henry called to talk about the situation at Rice University. According to some of his close alumni friends, the school needed a leader in the sports program as well as a head football coach. At first Henry simply wanted me to talk with the Rice alumni to give them some direction to the program, but eventually he asked if I would be interested in the job. I didn't think so. I'd been offered the position before but rejected the job because the timing had been poor for me. And why would I leave North Carolina now? The program was in high esteem. Chancellor Sitterson had granted me a lifetime contract. UNC was a prestigious university.

But talks with Rice University continued, and ultimately their challenge to build up the program intrigued me. I told them I would be interested if I could develop an undergraduate degree program in athletic administration and chair the department in addition to being director of athletics and head football coach. My plan would be to coach for three years, then focus on the athletic administration programs. I had wanted to do that at UNC but had reached what seemed to be a dead-end in my efforts at that school. Progress was so slow as to be nonexistent. At long last, I accepted the position at Rice University. At the press conference, I remarked, "How could I turn the job down when they named the stadium 'Rice University Stadium'?"

The athletic administration school failed to take shape at Rice, however, creating another disappointment. In football we faced Southwest Conference opponents, playing the toughest teams at that time in the nation. A Rice alumnus even called me one time to advise me about a young man I should recruit. As the caller gave his credentials, I asked him if the young man he favored could play for Texas, Texas A & M, Texas Tech or another Southwest conference team. "Oh, no, he can't play for those teams," replied the earnest advisor. I politely asked the caller not to send the player my way because I had to play those teams.

Quarterback Tommy Kramer provided a highlight for my tenure at Rice University. We led the nation in offense, thanks to Tommy's quick throwing arm. He proved to be a consensus All-American quarterback, and Minnesota picked him in the first round of the NFL draft. He served as understudy to All-Pro quarterback Fran Tarkenton before taking over starting duties for the Vikings. The former Rice standout earned the nickname "Two-Minute Tommy" because he was the best of the best at taking a team on a scoring drive with two minutes remaining before the end of a half. He could lead a no-huddle, check-with-me scheme like no other quarterback.

After one season at Rice, I coached the Gray team in the annual Blue-Gray Game in Montgomery, Alabama, taking Tommy with me. We jumped out to a 34–0 lead by halftime. The bowl's representatives confronted me at the half, asking me to hold the score down to keep the TV audience with us.

The next year, I was invited to coach the West team in the East-West Game in Palo Alto, California, at Stanford Stadium. Working with Eddie Robinson, Grambling University's famous coach, brought back memories of his unforgettable talk at the Henry Frnka Clinic in San Antonio. "Give me your son on the goal line in the fourth quarter, and I will make a man out of him," said Robinson, later to become the winningest coach in collegiate history — 408 wins.

Inspiring in games as well as clinics, Robinson brought his quarter-back Doug Williams to the East-West match up. Doug later led the Washington Redskins to a Super Bowl championship and eventually replaced his old coach at Grambling when Coach Robinson stepped down. After 57 years coaching, he retired at age 78.

During the week we prepared for the big game, we stayed at the Ricky Hyatt in Palo Alto. Paul Brown would be staying at the same hotel. He had a winter home in La Hoya, California, and he came up for the practice to scout the college prospects for the upcoming NFL draft. Paul wanted to talk about the Bengals organization with me. Through the years, I had turned down offers to work with Blanton Collier at Cleveland, Tom Landry at Dallas, and others in the pro ranks. This was one area I wasn't sure about. Whether I lacked self-confidence (which was unlikely) or just wanted to stay in an educational institution I never figured out. I respected Blanton Collier, Tom Landry, and Paul Brown. Blanton Collier was probably the best technical teacher the game has ever known; Tom Landry, a real gentleman, and probably the best game-time, on-the-field coach ever; and Paul Brown, the leader who could have taken over General Motors or any other corporation and created success. They were some of the greatest coaches, not to mention people, ever to coach the game. This time Paul talked to me about becoming a general manager and even replacing him at Cincinnati. The talks continued for several weeks.

His son Mike Brown, the former bat boy who had first intro-duced me to his father at the Great Lakes Naval Base in 1944, was now his close associate and visited me in Houston. Finally I agreed to join the Cincinnati Bengals organization. Paul wanted me to coach the quarterbacks for a couple of seasons before moving into the administrative level. I'd be working with All-Pro quarterback Ken Anderson, who despite injury problems led his team in the Super Bowl under Coach Forest Greg four years later. A few games into the first season with the Bengals, Paul decided to alter the head coaching lineup and asked me to fill in for the remainder of the season. The Bengals organization was on a downswing, but we gener-ated a great attitude by closing out the year with consecutive wins. Our final game was a 49–16 victory over the Cleveland Browns under Art Modell.

After the season, Paul found himself pleased with the progress and asked me to remain the head coach. However, even though I preferred to organize my own group, Paul insisted I keep the same team of assistants. I respected each of the gentlemen and their coaching abilities, but bringing in my own people would have established my jurisdiction over the staff in ways that a leader needs. Paul would not be swayed, however.

Early in the year we were preparing for the big game with the Pittsburgh Steelers. Coach Chuck Noll had produced miracles in organizing the best football program in the NFL. They had won three Super Bowl championships with "Mean" Joe Green, quarterback Terry Bradshaw and the rest of the squad. This season would set up the chance for an NFL record fourth Super Bowl victory. The Steelers' Iron Curtain defense made it difficult to even pick up a first down, so we spent hours on end studying each of their 21 blitz patterns. Ken Anderson studied their defenses religiously and picked up six flaws, to which we responded with our designated offensive scheme. His use of these flaws led to six big plays for us, resulting in a 34–10 upset, the worst defeat the Steelers suffered in their four championship years. Isaac Curtis, Archie Griffin, and company performed like champions themselves that day.

But injuries took their toll on our team that season. We didn't have adequate replacements, and we found ourselves with a losing record despite finishing with another victory over the Cleveland Browns and owner Art Modell. Paul Brown took the Cleveland game seriously, and we all understood its importance. Art Modell had become majority owner of the Cleveland Browns, forcing Paul Brown out of his job there. Paul never forgot. After the season, Paul moved me into administration as an executive to train for the general manager position. My big job was now organizing for the draft. We had several young players, but the team needed another class or two to move into a competitive stage.

Before I could help Paul reshape the Bengals, however, I received a phone call from Dr. Joseph M. Pettit, president of Georgia Tech – a call that would ultimately give the final shape to my own long career.

CHAPTER TWO
WHAT WENT WRONG?

Did I really take this job? They told me it couldn't be done.

On April Fool's Day, 1980, I boarded an 8 a.m. Delta flight from Cincinnati bound for Atlanta and a 4 p.m. press conference. I planned to announce that I would take over as director of athletics of the Georgia Institute of Technology. Although such press conferences are common in sports, the incidents leading to this announcement were quite unusual.

As an executive with the Cincinnati Bengals in the National Football League, I hadn't entertained the thought of returning to the college ranks, where I spent many years of my coaching and administrative career. My own experience as director of athletics at the University of North Carolina in 1973, where I witnessed first hand a program "going broke" and developed pity for the person chosen to be the savior of that program, warned me away from programs that needed rebuilding. Last but not least, Georgia Tech faced the small matter of convincing me to accept a $62,000 drop in salary from my position with the Bengals organization. Other challenges I couldn't have predicted lurked over the horizon. So why did I accept this job?

In late January 1980, I received a telephone call from Georgia Tech's president, Dr. Joseph M. Pettit. I remember the call vividly. I was in a meeting with Paul Brown, majority owner and president of the Cincinnati Bengals, and his two sons, Mike and Pete, discussing the scouting system we were preparing for the upcoming draft. Paul's secretary interrupted: "The president of Georgia Tech is calling — an urgent request to speak with Homer." I looked at Paul. He nodded, "Go ahead, Homer, he may have a football player we want." Paul smiled, and I left for my office to take the call from President Pettit, who was no stranger. In 1973 when I was director of athletics at the University of North Carolina, he had asked me to join Dave Nelson of the University of Delaware and Ernie McCoy of Penn State in serving as consultants to the Georgia Tech athletic program. Over the years he sporadically called for additional advice. I hadn't heard from him in quite some time, however, and I wondered what had prompted the new contact.

Tech had hired Bill Curry, he explained, as head football coach. The program was adjusting to the departure of Athletic Director Doug Weaver, who was leaving for the athletic director's position at Michigan State. While we spoke I pondered possible recommendations I could make and threw out a few names for him to consider. And then he popped the question: "Would you be interested?" I thanked him for the flattery and politely answered that this was not a good time. Our conversation quickly came to an end, and we said our good-byes.

Ever persistent, President Pettit called again a week later, this time asking whether I would consult with Bill Sangster, the faculty chairman of athletics. We arranged a breakfast meeting in the Cincinnati Airport, and I prepared more recommendations for this position. I also put together a portfolio of my ideas for developing a model administrative program that I had begun shaping while I was director of athletics at the University of North Carolina. Talking through this document in the airport, we began discussing problems and opportunities in intercollegiate athletics, and my friendship with Bill Sangster took hold.

A former University of Iowa star athlete — and a coach's son — Bill grew up with a sports background. Not only was he was dean of the prestigious College of Engineering, but Bill was vice chairman of and faculty representative to the Georgia Tech Athletic Association

Board of Trustees. He understood the dilemma Georgia Tech faced. After meeting with him, I began to think about returning to college athletics with a flicker of excitement. For the immediate future, however, I returned to the Bengal's scouting board to prepare for the 1980 NFL draft. The draft picks that year cemented a strong squad, leading the Bengals to the Super Bowl two years later.

One short week after Sangster's visit, President Pettit called yet again, this time requesting that I meet with him and the Athletic Board. My wife Phyllis and I had planned to leave Cincinnati for a relaxing two-week vacation in Marco Island, Florida, but Pettit urged me to agree to a meeting as soon as possible. This time we arranged a meeting in the Miami airport. Phyllis and I drove across the Tamiami Trail (Highway 41) into Miami to meet with President Pettit and the Athletic Board's search committee of Kim King, W.J. Blane, Tom Coleman, and student-athlete Tom Daniel. Miami's airport lived up to its reputation, leaving Joe Pettit to open the meeting with no wallet, identification, or money, victim of a trained pickpocket — but with a perfect analogy to the Georgia Tech athletic program. "The Athletic Association doesn't have any money either," he said to me. "Can you help us?"

I couldn't believe this beginning . . . was he kidding? We made small talk for a while until the conversation evolved into more serious discussions of the state of affairs of intercollegiate athletics. Finally I started to explain the student-athlete total person concept I had been developing, and the idea struck a chord of interest among the search committee members. They enthusiastically noted that the program's concepts matched the value Georgia Tech placed on integrity.

Driving back to Marco Island, Phyllis and I considered the possibilities of working with the Atlanta institution. Just before we left to return home to Cincinnati a few days later, another important call came through with the caller asking to speak with me. It was the legendary football coach Bobby Dodd, perhaps the most respected coach of our time.

In the fall of 1944, as a young 17-year-old senior at Highlands High School in Fort Thomas, Kentucky, I had received an exciting phone call from Bobby Dodd. Acting coach for the retiring Bill Alexander, Dodd was slated to take over head coach duties going into the 1945 season. He apprised me of the situation and asked me to meet with Ray Ellis, a Kentucky high school coach. Ray had agreed to join Coach Dodd's first staff and install the "T" formation.

A meeting in Louisville went smoothly; Ray explained that I fit the kind of quarterback he wanted to take to Georgia Tech. Like other young athletes at the time, I was highly recruited, with Kentucky, Tennessee, Cincinnati, Miami of Ohio, and Indiana Universities paying calls. But Ray inspired me with his confidence in my ability to contribute to his planned offensive strategy. And he clinched the deal by sparking my enthusiasm with a recording of the school's "Ramblin' Wreck" fight song. I signed a letter of intent to attend Georgia Tech and rode the Greyhound Bus back home to Fort Thomas, elated about the opportunity I'd been given and the future that awaited me.

World War II and the United States Navy had different plans for me, however. I got off that bus to find official papers calling me to report immediately to the Great Lakes Naval Station. My stint in the navy delayed my date with Georgia Tech for more than three decades.

When Coach Dodd called me in 1980, again asking me to come to Georgia Tech, I remembered my excitement — and disappointment — from years past. His call was encouraging. And it was probably the single reason Phyllis and I even seriously contemplated a return to the collegiate ranks.

President Pettit followed up with a call to our home in Cincinnati, and I promised to have an answer ready in three days. Pettit faced stiff opposition from the venerable Paul Brown, who strongly favored my staying with the Bengal organization. When I met with Brown the next morning, he argued against my even considering the possibility of leaving. With such a strong reaction from Brown, I prepared to turn down Georgia Tech for the third time.

In the midst of scouting program details, I decided to save time the next day to call the university president to explain my decision. The call never got made, though. In the meantime, Paul Brown approached me again, concerned that he may have been a little hard on me the previous day. If collegiate sports drew me so strongly, he would give his blessing to my decision.

I was back to square one, with a very big decision to make. At age 53, I knew this would be my last career change. Phyllis and I pondered the decision that evening, batting around the huge challenges that a return to collegiate athletics entailed. The challenges included one that enticed me irresistibly: the opportunity and responsibility for building another program with the student-athlete total person program as a cornerstone. I called President Pettit the next day. I chatted with his administrative assistant, Janice Gosdin, who had been keeping me informed of Georgia Tech's activities. When President Pettit came on the line, I accepted the position.

Details remained to be worked out. We had never discussed terms or the contract. To my surprise, he said my salary would be $53,000 on a year-to-year contract. He reiterated that the program had no money. I began to have second thoughts. He was proposing to give me less than half of my $115,000 salary with the Bengals. But he offered the opportunity to have a radio and TV show, and to run camps — the same privileges afforded the head football coach. I'd have to undertake these ventures myself, but again the words "opportunity" and "challenge" intertwined in an exciting way. The position would be more difficult than any I'd ever held.

Contracts had never concerned me before because I had always believed a firm handshake was a binding agreement. I accepted the position despite my second thoughts about this difficult yet attractive return to the collegiate ranks, agreeing to hold positions as both director of athletics and assistant to the president of the Georgia Institute of Technology, starting April 1, 1980.

And so it was I found myself at that press conference in the old Hotel Castlegate. President Pettit introduced me as only the fifth director of athletics in the school's history, following Heisman, Alexander, Dodd, and Weaver. Bob James, commissioner of the Atlantic Coast Conference, which Georgia Tech had joined just one year before my arrival, was present. One of the great leaders in intercollegiate athletics, he was someone I had met long before.

During my tenure as director of athletics at the University of North Carolina from 1968 to 1976, I served one year on a committee to select a commissioner for the Atlantic Coast Conference. After the sudden death of Big Jim Weaver, the first commissioner, the conference faced a leadership crisis. Jim had put the conference on the map, and each of the member schools had gained prestige. To find a replacement, our three-person committee began a strategic search. Bob James emerged as a frontrunner, and when the vote came he was the unanimous choice. That selection turned out to be valuable in several ways. Bob was a master in bringing people together, and he increased the income from TV, post-season games, and the ACC basketball tournament. Under his guidance, the ACC became a leader in fundraising and in finding creative ways to add much-needed dollars to each school's budget.

At the press conference in Atlanta, I spoke briefly to the gathered listeners and reporters, emphasizing my belief that Georgia Tech was a "sleeping giant" that would soon be competitive once more. After I finished speaking, the media pounced. David Davidson, a writer with the *Atlanta Journal-Constitution*, asked, "How do you plan to make Georgia Tech competitive without adequate funding?"

There was that word again. The issue of financing kept popping up. Was there something more than what I'd been told? I left the press conference and headed to the campus Athletic Association to meet the staff and coaches. Entering the small, cramped quarters I looked around me and realized that the program had declined considerably since I had served on the consulting team seven years before. I silently wondered to myself, "Why did I take this job?"

I began realizing that I truly had my work cut out for me. Restoring the program and making it move forward would be the biggest challenge I'd ever accepted.

Returning to a hotel room where I would stay until Phyllis and I could find a home, I sat down to decide the first order of business. Without a doubt, I knew I had to find out how the program had bottomed out. The first step in making it come alive again and to be successful was to account for its decline.

The school had a great worldwide reputation. Georgia Tech was an outstanding technical institution, and academics combined with the football traditions of triple legends Heisman, Alexander, and Dodd. The "Ramblin' Wreck" fight song summed up the confident strength of the university. I began researching the problems.

My homework began by checking past budgets and reading board meeting minutes for details and specific facts. I continued the task by discussing areas of concern with past and present Georgia Tech coaches, interested alumni, and media representatives. A single, central problem began to unfold. After a few days of studying the past, I got to work on the future. On the flight back to Cincinnati, I scribbled out a plan of action, listing six key points.

1. Install the student-athlete total person program.
2. Develop a competitive total sports program within the Atlantic Coast Conference.
3. Develop a sound financial base.
4. Bring facilities up to a competitive level.
5. Hire competent and quality coaches and staff to implement the plan.
6. Design the program to benefit the entire institution.

Phyllis went to work on selling our home near Cincinnati while commuting to Atlanta to search for a new one, and I rolled up my sleeves for the task of rebuilding the program at Georgia Tech. I knew I'd be putting in long, hard, and mentally intensive hours to bring the program back. Unloading my gear in the office that would be almost a home-away-from-home in the coming weeks, I met the director's secretary for the first time. Ann Harrell had served Bobby Dodd and Doug Weaver, my two immediate predecessors. She was a lovely lady unafraid of facing the past. "At one time your office was a broom closet," she remarked to me upon our meeting. I liked her attitude, and to my good fortune the grand lady stayed with me for eighteen years, during which time we developed a partnership that carried into our retirement years.

Ann Harrell looked with an experienced eye at the job I faced, and my wife Phyllis quickly understood both the size of the task and what my arrival meant to those in my new office. When Phyllis toured the facilities and examined the situation, she made two observations. "Homer is out of his mind," she first pronounced. Her second comment came after she saw staff sitting around, reading paperback books. "They are in for a huge awakening," she noted.

My research quickly uncovered the reason that Georgia Tech had fallen to such a low level: lack of funds. Georgia Tech left the Southeastern Conference in 1964 to become an independent, with the main bone of contention being the so-called "140 Rule." The SEC permitted member schools to have enrolled at any one time a maximum of 140 student-athletes awarded grants-in-aid for football and/or basketball. Tech believed the "140 Rule" to be grossly unfair.

SEC schools normally awarded about 20 grants for basketball, dropping the football ceiling slightly but leaving 120. The particulars of the rule were most important, however. SEC regulations stated as late as the fall of 1963 that each school could bring in or certify 55 new football grants-in-aid annually. At the end of the year, the limit dropped to 45. At the beginning of the 1964 recruiting season, the limit fell even lower to 40. By the time the limit of 40 was voted in, Tech had already left the conference.

Georgia Tech's problem with the "140 Rule" was that the SEC regulation favored schools with higher dropout rates of student athletes. With a cap of about 120 grants for football, any school that carefully screened recruits and assisted student-athletes in completing their degrees faced a limit on the number of new recruits it could field. This limit on the number of fresh players hampered a coach's ability to reshape teams for greatest competitiveness. In short, success in keeping students in school limited a program's chance for success on the playing field.

Tech left the SEC when the limit of recruits per year was 45. Suppose that a school brought in that number of men each year for four years, for a total of 180 student-athletes. With an attrition rate of 10 per year because students failed in their work or for other common reasons, the total limit of an estimated 120 football players would be affected — not the number that could be immediately recruited from the freshman class to take those players' places. Assuming an attrition rate of 10 per year, each school would have 150 players on campus receiving grants for football when only 120 were allowed. Schools with lower attrition rates, like Tech, would have 30 players more than the limit, not even counting the five to 20 men "red-shirted" and allowed to stay for a fifth year, still on scholarship.

Coach Bobby Dodd explained it at the time quite simply.

"Careful surveying of prospective student-athletes (which must be done to get them in school), and a well-planned program of tutoring all signers that needed it after they became students, cut our losses of grant-in-aid students to a figure below that of any other conference schools. . . . Much below that of the majority of the SEC schools (by actual count taken from a study made by the SEC commissioner's office). This resulted in limiting our recruiting program to the extent that we realized we could not comply with the rule and continue to field a representative team," he said.

"This was not fair to our school, our alumni, our players or anyone connected with our program. We did not want to leave the southeastern conference. It was not a 'spur of the moment' decision to do so. We had given the matter long and careful study and sincerely regretted that for the good of Georgia Tech there was no alternative," Dodd concluded.

Tech officials made it clear they would go along with any limit from 30 to 50 new men being permitted to come in each year. Georgia Tech simply proposed that the limiting should be done at the freshman or first-year level. That way a school would not be penalized for carefully screening student-athletes and then ensuring that they stayed in school until graduation.

This principled stand led to hardship for the school. A public state institution without membership in a prominent conference will find that funding passes it by. The school and athletic department had excellent leaders, but without an adequate financial base it was not possible to compete. The golden years of Bobby Dodd from 1950 to the mid-1960s could no longer carry the program. Fifteen years without growth, from 1965 to 1980, had stymied the operation. At the same time, other programs within major conferences like the SEC, ACC, Big Ten, Pacific Coast, Southwest, or Big Eight entered a new era of intercollegiate varsity sports and dynamic growth. Only Notre Dame and Penn State managed to stay at the top while keeping independent status. The gap between conference and non-conference schools became wider and wider during that period.

I learned a startling fact that made the situation even more grave when I met with John O'Neill, business manager of the Georgia Tech Athletic Association. The institution was forbidden from helping the athletic program financially by any means. Georgia state legislators had set a policy in the 1940s that tax dollars could not be used for athletics. Not one cent would be coming from the "Hill" to assist the program. The program had to be resurrected by its own resources, and it had to be self-sustaining.

An immediate problem loomed, however, focusing my attention on the program's very life. The 1980-1981 budget of $2.1 million included a fiscal year running from July to the next June. By September of 1980, the audit report showed a negative fund balance of $354,000. Growth would have to be put on the back burner. We had to make sure the program survived that year. And the possibilities for finding funds looked slim.

Football ticket sales for the 1980 season reached an all-time low. The program had no marketing leader or plan in place. Only 40 people bought season tickets to the basketball games, and no student fees supported the athletic offerings. Tech's radio contract of $25,000 per year beat out all major colleges for lowest fees. Finally, the Alexander-Tharpe Fund, which raised private money for scholarships, brought in just over $600,000 — the lowest amount in the ACC. As I added up the revenues and deducted the expenses, the fact that we were terribly short became clear. Football, the only revenue sport, could not carry the load. With overwhelming negatives, finding positive aspects to the situation seemed impossible. We were going broke, and it was as simple as that.

Finding help proved difficult. The city's crime rate made recruiting student-athletes tougher, as did the university's academic standards. We had last-place finishes for all our athletic teams in the ACC, and our sports facilities were considered the worst of any school in the United States. But I had to find something positive about the program. It was up to me to find some pluses to start a "building" program.

The biggest plus came quickly to mind: Tech's people. Georgia Tech people are smart, loyal, hard working, and successful. With their involvement, the program could be put together. My job was to provide the direction, leadership, and motivation to make the plan work. We needed to "sell" the Tech people.

Just as I realized this answer, I got word of two meetings that dampened my excitement.

President Pettit attended one group meeting on campus that debated whether Tech should drop football or move to a lower level of competition with a non-scholarship program. Across town, Bobby Dodd met with another group and commented that "Georgia Tech athletics is at its lowest mark in history." With such high-profile questioning of the school's athletic programs, I had to wonder if I was being fully informed.

When I made the trip back to my small office, my secretary

informed me that Tom Landry of the Dallas Cowboys had called. Returning the call, I chatted with Tom. I respected him tremendously both as a person and as a very successful NFL football coach. We had been on several Fellowship of Christian Athlete programs together, and his greatness as a leader came through clearly. As we talked, Tom explained that Dan Reeves, his offensive quarterback coach, was leaving to take over the head reins of the Denver Broncos. Would I be interested in joining his staff, he asked? For a moment, my thoughts flashed onto a screen showing the difficult job I had taken over at Georgia Tech — and here was an offer to leave it all behind. The fantasy left as quickly as it came, and I regained my senses. I had made a pact with Georgia Tech and believed strongly in fulfilling that commitment. Saying goodbye, I went back to the drawing board for turning around the program and saving it from bottoming out.

Each segment of operation needed an overhaul, with a trial-and-error process to go forward. Meeting with the coaches to get their input, I found the majority highly negative — and with good reason. They had very little to work with because of the lack of funds. If funding was the impossible answer, I had to look for a variety of ways to initiate change in other directions until I could get a handle on the situation.

First, I would have to set the example, with a positiveness that convinced the staff, coaches, supporters, and institution that we would succeed. I began organizing a five-year plan, knowing that we not only could but would achieve our goals in those five years. At the time I was uncertain about how to accomplish the plan, but I was confident we would be successful. But I could not do it alone. The staff, coaches, alumni, and friends would have to join in and believe Georgia Tech would be great again in five short years. Always keeping that time frame in mind, I bought time until we could come up with strategies to accomplish this unbelievable task.

I had to teach the staff and coaches my philosophy — the Attitude Technique Philosophy (see Appendix B). This would be the catalyst for achieving success. In the beginning I wasn't sure how many were buying the concept. But I knew the approach would work. I had succeeded in the past, and I turned again to it with confidence in facing the future. In time, this would be passed on to our players as the Total Person Concept. I set up workshops and required perfect attendance. I even put on seminars for interested alumni and friends of Georgia Tech, creating more opportunities for building the support necessary to solidly implement the program.

Change came to one person at a time. Business manager John O'Neill was from the "old school." John, who later became one of my close friends, understood my methods of success and brought a strength to his own work that made him dependable. He was a former football player for Coach Dodd and a true Georgia Tech man. I could depend on him to keep plugging away until some miracle occurred.

Without a staff or other support, Jack Thompson led the fundraising efforts through the Alexander-Tharpe Fund. He needed help. One person could not generate enough income to provide adequate scholarship funding. Especially when we had very little to sell.

Jack had a varied background in collegiate sports — he was an outstanding swimmer at the University of Kentucky, swimming coach at the University of South Carolina, and came to Georgia Tech as a football recruiter for Coach Bud Carson, and later for Coach Bill Fulcher and Coach Pepper Rodgers. Jack was also responsible for the televised coaches' shows. He got this assignment from Coach Dodd, who, though he did not personally benefit from the income generated by the shows, knew it was a "must" in the modern world.

Jack knew many of the Georgia Tech people and was anxious to jump-start the football program. I asked about Georgia Tech clubs but found that only one existed. That lone club charged only a $15 annual membership fee and was not set up for fundraising. So the question remained: how could we get the program back to respectability — and could it be done at all?

Before I could move forward, another stone was thrown at me. I was informed that Georgia Tech might be in violation of the National Collegiate Athletic Association rules. I knew that Georgia Tech had an unblemished record because of men like Coach Alexander and Coach Dodd and that Tech had never faced a major violation that resulted in placing the program on probation status. I wanted this problem cleared up. It had to be taken care of immediately. I assembled the entire staff and the coaches and made it clear: we would do it right! If *anyone* broke a rule, he could pack up and leave. This would be a clean program. I felt it was extremely important to protect Georgia Tech's heritage and values, and of course, our new program. Ethical violations would not be tolerated on my watch!

The next looming problem to solve was that of facilities. This was a huge endeavor. During those first five years, I kept a personal journal that included the obstacles we had to overcome and how we managed to surmount each difficulty. I felt sure there was a solution — we just needed to find it. Some of my entries about the state of our athletic facilities reveal the problems we faced.

Wow! Of my many challenges, this may be my biggest! I just cannot believe the state of conditions — we rank at the bottom of all major universities. The stadium at Grant Field is in extremely poor condition. It has not been maintained. South stands deplorable. The engineering report states "unsafe, condemned — must be repaired or destroyed." East stands will follow. Press box not far behind. The maintenance budget is peanuts — like applying band-aids to gunshot wounds. The locker rooms have not changed significantly for thirty years or longer. The cinder track takes me back many years. The coliseum for basketball is in sad shape. Both teams and officials shower together in the same shower room. This is unbelievable. Baseball, tennis — not up to standards. Football practice fields need to be overhauled.

The antiquated facilities make recruiting quality athletes extremely difficult. We will have to bring them in late at night and get them out early in the morning. The less they see the better our chances. I discovered the "lost key" policy. During recruiting visits the locker rooms are locked. A graduate assistant has the key, but he can't be located!

Athletic facilities had taken on heightened importance between 1965 and 1980. The recruiting wars for top athletes instigated a race to build better facilities rivaling those of competing schools. Without adequate funds, Georgia Tech was losing ground fast. Interest in even trying to build competitive facilities was waning. The message was loud and clear: "It can't be done!"

Chapter Three

THE FIRST FIVE-YEAR PLAN (1981-1985): PURSUIT OF (ACC) RESPECT!

The good news was that before my arrival, plans were already on the drawing board to build a football complex. The cost was estimated at $3-4 million. Georgia Tech would not, and most probably could not, survive without a new facility that would allow us to compete for the top athletes. Roberts and Company, solicited to design the building, had been founded by L. W. "Chip" Robert Jr., who had served as captain of John Heisman's football team in 1908. Now his grandson, Lawrence W. "Chip" Robert IV, was in charge of the company and became instrumental in the completion of the new facility.

Also, a fundraising consultant group was brought in to provide the expertise in conducting a feasibility study and raising private funds to cover the cost. It would not be possible to borrow funds when the program was already in financial trouble. There was no other way but to raise money to pay for the total cost.

An outstanding football player from the late 1940s, Ewell Pope became one of Atlanta's successful developers and proved a good choice to serve as general chairman of the steering committee. He worked with Kim King, who was responsible for organizing the committee and for the conception of the new facilities. George Mathews, W.J. Blane, Deen Day Smith, and others also became involved in the initial effort.

Kim King and his group approached Coach Bobby Dodd, asking him to serve as honorary chairman of the fundraising campaign group. Coach Dodd declined, stating that he could not lead an effort when he personally believed there wasn't any way the projected amount of money for a new facility could be raised. He promised to visit with prospective donors to do his part in coming as close as possible to the goal, however, and King's group had to settle for that reduced commitment. Ewell and Kim arranged for Dodd to meet with President Jimmy Carter at the White House in 1979. Hugh Carter, the president's nephew and a Tech alum, organized the meeting in hopes that the president could enlist the State of Georgia's help in financing the new building. Carter's enthusiasm outflanked Dodd's reticence. Upon being introduced to Dodd, President Carter congratulated the coach on accepting the responsibility of chairing such an important committee and providing an invaluable service to the Georgia Tech community. Not one to contradict the president of the United States, Coach Dodd accepted the compliment and resigned himself to accepting the commitment made on his behalf by the world's most powerful leader.

It was true. Never in Georgia Tech's history had a fundraising campaign been attempted to raise any amount like two or three million dollars. Soon after my arrival, a meeting was held to discuss the campaign. It was exciting that this endeavor could illicit so much interest. There was a sense of urgency and the feeling that things were going to happen. Support was on its way. Leaving the meeting, my positive spirit started up the scale. Warren Heeman, vice president for development, and his staff were brought in to lead the campaign. Their experience in handling such matters was a real plus. With the appointment of Heeman, the plan was a "go."

Kim King continued to play a key role. Kim, a successful developer in the area, had been an outstanding quarterback for Coach Dodd's last football team. He provided the color analysis for Georgia Tech's football radio broadcasts with the famous Al Ciraldo ("Toe Meets Leather") and supplied the positive spirit we needed. He had also been a member of the Georgia Tech Athletic Association's selection committee that brought me to Georgia Tech.

We needed a major gift to get the ball rolling. Fuller E. Callaway

Jr., of the Callaway Foundation, was approached. Coach Dodd and I drove down to LaGrange, Georgia, to meet with Mr. Callaway. He said he would help if others would match his gift and if the new facility would bear the name of his close friend, Arthur B. Edge, Jr. Mr. Edge was a classmate and a 1926 graduate of Georgia Tech's textile engineering program. He later served as president of the Callaway Foundation but regrettably passed away in 1979. After our meeting, Fuller invited Coach Dodd and me to fish in his lake, and Coach Dodd, an avid fisherman, accepted his kindness. After our more casual visit with Mr. Callaway, President Pettit and Warren Heeman made several official visits, and the $1.5 million matching gift was secured. Many gifts followed. The building was coming closer to being a reality.

Fuller Callaway's formal education included LaGrange (Georgia) High School, the Georgia Institute of Technology, and the Eastman School of Business in Poughkeepsie, New York. In 1935 Fuller became president of Callaway Mills in LaGrange, heading the company which he and his brother Cason had created in 1932. He founded several textile research institutes that gave new dimensions to the methods of production and the quality of products in his industry. Callaway towels and carpets became the standards by which excellence was measured in their product lines. The success of the Callaway mills helped produce a foundation that made significant gifts to churches, educational institutions, hospitals, art centers, and many other worthy causes. Fuller passed away in 1992, leaving a mark as an industrialist and as a philanthropist.

While we were in the midst of soliciting funds, it hit me — a football-only building would be a huge mistake! We needed a complex that would house the entire sports program. The present athletic department was antiquated. This was our big opportunity to build the entire department. I was sure I could read the minds of the board members just by seeing how they looked at each other with unspoken disbelief as I told of this grand plan. I could just hear them saying to themselves, "How can we build a building twice the size of the one that we're struggling to find the money to build now?" Then, as if a spirit moved through the entire room, one by one each member exclaimed, "Why not? Let's do it!" Then the entire group looked towards me. "You do it!" It was my idea, and it was my job to accomplish it.

Expanding the project required widening the number of contributors. I was sold on the idea of a facility to host all sports, and soon a host of benefactors, from major corporations to individuals, got on board the project. Southwire, the Bryan family, Tom Bridges, Sid Goldin, Alvin Ferst, the Day family, the Hightower family, the Daughtrys, Drew Hearn, Peachtree Doors, Fred Holloway, W.B. Adams, Frank Whitley, Ziegler Tools, Dan Shepherd, Mundy, Buck Mickel, Bud Parker, Dan McKeever, George Mathews, Henry Maddox III, Erskine Love, and many others joined the effort.

The dedication and groundbreaking ceremony for the new complex took place with a large steel ball swinging toward the old naval armory building on the northeast corner of the stadium property to make room for the Future of Georgia Tech Athletics. Jerry McDonald of the Class of 1936 oversaw the construction to ensure that the Georgia Tech Athletic Association wasn't shortchanged in any way on the project. I could also depend on my good friend Forest Fowler to keep me advised. I believe he voluntarily supervised every component of the building's construction. When I didn't hear from Forest, I knew things were going smoothly! The facility was completed three years later in 1983 at the cost of $8 million. We remained short of funds, though, and huge debt-servicing costs would hang over our heads unless we could find a way to raise additional money. We came up with a slogan, "We must burn the mortgage."

I received a call from Paul Duke, Bobby Dodd's first football captain in 1945, an All-American center and a successful developer of a technology park in Atlanta. Paul asked what we need to burn the mortgage. After hearing the amount, he responded, "A check is on the way!" We celebrated in the new lobby of the Arthur B. Edge Jr. Intercollegiate Athletic Center by symbolically burning the mortgage. It was a gala affair despite the fact that we celebrated while the Edge Center was still under construction.

But the event did give us another opportunity to explore the possibilities for parking, which was practically unavailable on game days. If we were going to bring people to the campus for athletic events, we certainly needed some place for fans to park. We negotiated with the university to construct a parking deck on the Peters Park property adjacent to the new center and the north end of the stadium, working the cost into the financing with help from parking fees. The Athletic Association would use the parking facility on football game days, and the decks would be open for university use at all other times. This plan was an important step in building the relationship between the Athletic Association and the Georgia Tech administration.

The Arthur B. Edge Jr. Intercollegiate Athletic Center had everything necessary for a complete program. The Alexander-Tharpe Fund, Inc. (our fundraising operation); sports information (the media-communications operation); ticket office; administrative offices; meeting rooms; and coaches' offices for all sports in one place instead of scattered as in most other collegiate programs. We were all together, helping to cement a family concept and loyalty among people throughout the program. I wanted each sport to be the same as far as recognition was concerned. Those that excelled would get more attention, but in our "home" atmosphere, we were all equal. When student-athletes came to the center for meetings and food service, they would get to know the other athletes and coaches. This brought about a good feeling.

But one thing was missing. We needed a place where individual players, coaches, or groups of players could meet in a quiet place according to their own spiritual needs. We formed a group of interested people, and the idea of a chapel began to flourish. Deen Day Smith, Polly Poole, Bert Stumberg, Paul Duke, and Guy Rutland formed the chapel committee, and the plan unfolded. The space on the second floor was visible from the lobby atrium. Deen Day Smith commissioned a renowned New York artist to create a work in glass just over 23 feet by 9 feet, artistically depicting athletes of various sports kneeling in moments of reflection before participating in events. Across the bottom of the huge glass structure was etched the passage from Hebrew scripture selected for the movie *Chariots of Fire*, which had inspired countless young athletes around the country: "Now the Lord sayeth, them that know me, I will honor" (Samuel 1, 2:30).

Although the chapel was designed specifically for nondenominational spiritual use by athletes or athletic groups, a few complications remained. As a state-assisted school, Georgia Tech needed to keep state and religious matters separate. This issue was brought to the attention of President Pettit and the board of trustees of the Georgia Tech Athletic Association. Even though the athletic program did not receive any aid from the school, state, or government, it was still considered to be public property. Several campus meetings addressed the problem, and those meetings confirmed the desirability of providing a physical space for spiritual contemplation, open to the entire athletic community. Eventually the chapel's success at achieving that goal satisfied critics, and the chapel stayed its course.

During the early days of the Edge Center Construction, it was evident that I still had to face the ordeal of coming up with a plan to get us out of debt in order to keep the program alive. As we entered the first football season in the fall of 1980, Bill Curry and his staff worked hard to put a competitive team on the field, but the overall talent did not match the schedule. We brought a 1-8-1 record into our season closer with the University of Georgia, which was led by the highly successful head coach, Vince Dooley. Undefeated Georgia, led by Hershel Walker, was headed for the Sugar Bowl and a meeting with Notre Dame for the national championship. The game was a mismatch. (Ironically, Notre Dame's only blemish was a tie with Georgia Tech 3–3 when Coach Curry moved tight end Ken Whisenhunt to quarterback for the game.)

Two weeks prior to the game a creative thought bounced out of my subconscious. What if ABC would televise the game? UGA would have to agree to the terms. Because we were not yet a football-playing member of the Atlantic Coast Conference (and wouldn't be for three years because of a scheduling problem) we could make our own deals. I put in a call to Roone Arledge at ABC. During my tenure at the University of North Carolina I had served on the National Collegiate Athletic Association TV Committee and had chaired a negotiating subcommittee that met with the three major networks at that time — ABC, CBS, and NBC — to negotiate television rights for collegiate football. ABC was awarded the "rights" to televise games. Boldly, I asked Roone for a big favor, to televise our game with UGA. Roone replied, "You have got to be kidding — this game is a mismatch. Our ratings will suffer considerably. There are other big games that are on our list." He kept repeating all the negatives, then told me he'd get back to me. To say the least, my hopes were not high. A few days later he called to ask how much we were asking. We need $354,000 to get us out of the red. Roone heard the amount and replied, "I can't change our schedule for this year, but will put the UGA game on next year at Georgia Tech." Next season, Don Bernstein of ABC called to confirm the agreement. The money from the broadcast took care of our financial woes and "saved" the program. However, I would soon be facing other difficulties.

Along with the title director of athletics, President Pettit added the title of assistant to the president to my duties. He felt it was necessary that I had a role as either vice president or assistant to the president for athletic and recreational affairs on campus. This meant that I would be a member of his cabinet and would meet weekly with representatives from all areas of the campus administration. This was helpful because it gave me insight into all that was going on in the world of academia. In time, it would become extremely important in structuring our entire program and working with the rest of the university. (President Pettit also noted that it was unusual to have a Ph.D. in an athletic department and felt it would be appropriate for me to be referred to as "Dr. Rice," rather than "Coach Rice," as I had been called throughout my entire career.)

My next order of business was to evaluate each sport and the coaches. Bill Curry, a former Georgia Tech All-American center and an NFL player for twelve years, was highly respected. Bill had been coaching with Bart Starr, head coach of the Green Bay Packers, when Georgia Tech called him back home to take over the sagging football program. Bill replaced Pepper Rodgers, another Bobby Dodd product. President Pettit explained to me that Pepper's departure had been unpleasant, in that he had sued the department for damages. Since this had occurred before I came aboard, I was told that it was not necessary for me to be involved. However, I also realized that this disagreement was going to affect not only Georgia Tech, but many good people on both sides. John Hunsinger, a friend of Pepper's, arranged for us to meet. I had known Coach Rodgers for many years as a colleague in the coaching fraternity. He was considered one of our best. Unfortunately, an unbelievably tough schedule, terrible facilities, and a lack of funds had made it impossible for Pepper to be successful at Tech. Fortunately, we were able to resolve the dispute without court action. It would have been a shame for Pepper not to be asked to return to his former school on special occasions and to continue friendships that developed over the years.

Although Coach Curry suffered in the win/loss column during the first years, his presence was key to developing the "start." Bill never hedged when asked to help with any part of our rebuilding program. He was a master of seeking needed funds, and much of our early progress was due to his efforts. He became a strong advocate of the Student-Athlete Total Person Program. It would take time to build a competitive football program, but Bill was on target and laid out plans to reach the winner's circle.

Basketball, under Head Coach Dwane Morrison, would require a "real fix." Just as the stadium needed a facelift, so did Alexander Memorial Coliseum. There was very little interest in basketball at Georgia Tech, and becoming a member of the Atlantic Coast Conference, the most successful league in the country, was a huge challenge. One of the best teachers in the game, Coach Morrison kept the program competitive as an independent team in the Metro Conference. However, jumping to the ACC with virtually no budget would make Georgia Tech easy prey for teams like North Carolina, Duke and Virginia. Coach Morrison never had a chance.

As for the other sports — baseball under Coach Jim Luck, track under Buddy Fowlkes, golf headed by Tommy Plaxico, tennis under Walter Johnson, swimming coached by Herb McCauley, wrestling under Coach Lowell Lange, and gymnastics coached by Bill Beavers – all were on the brink of disaster. Although we were out of debt, the only way to fulfill the upcoming 1981-82 budget would be to drop these secondary sports. Georgia Tech would have ended up the big loser in that scenario because ACC membership is contingent upon sponsorship of football, basketball, baseball, track, golf, and tennis. We had to meet this next financial challenge or lose our standing in the athletic community.

This situation reminded me of the circumstances that led to the admission of Georgia Tech into the ACC. I was serving as athletic director at the University of North Carolina when South Carolina withdrew from the ACC because of issues surrounding the ACC policy requiring entering freshmen to score 800 on the Scholastic Aptitude Test and because other conferences only required a 1.6 grade point average. South Carolina felt that the ACC faced a major competitive disadvantage. The ACC decided to replace South Carolina with another university to bring the membership back to eight.

Willis Casey, athletic director at North Carolina State University, and I met with John McKenna, associate athletic director at Georgia Tech, regarding the North/South basketball double header held in Charlotte, North Carolina, each year. The original teams were North Carolina and North Carolina State vs. Clemson and South Carolina — the North Carolina state schools against the South

Carolina state schools. McKenna, a respected administrator from Georgia Tech and a former successful coach at Virginia Military Institute, was invited to bring Georgia Tech into the double header to replace South Carolina. At the same time, we discussed the possibility of Georgia Tech becoming the eighth member of the ACC. The Atlanta market could become a TV bonanza. Admission to the ACC was finalized under the management of Doug Weaver and President Pettit in 1979. Coach Whack Hyder of Georgia Tech brought his teams to the North/South double header and beat both UNC and NC State.

Knocking off the top ACC school made the other members of the ACC sit up and take notice. Coach Hyder had coached Rick Yunkus, one of the best players in the nation, and before that Roger Kaiser, All-American and later a very successful coach in his own right. Coach Hyder was famous for beating Adolph Rupp's teams from the University of Kentucky. I remember those defeats well, as I was an assistant football coach at the University of Kentucky at the time and my office was next to Coach Rupp's. He would come back to Lexington talking to himself after each one.

It was time to concentrate on the sports required by the ACC — football, basketball, baseball, track, golf, and tennis. The others would have to be put on hold until I could find the funds to keep these sports afloat. We knew by the 1970s that a four-dollar football ticket would no longer pay for the entire program, and this led to the establishment of foundations like the Alexander-Tharpe Fund at Georgia Tech. A student fee helped defray the costs of the so-called "minor" sports. I remember selling the students at UNC on the importance of a competitive total program. If the football team is successful, it reflects well on the entire university. A successful athletic team gives everybody a good feeling about the school and name recognition for the university, which helps all students in the job market. Wouldn't they go along with the student fee plan to help less recognized sports programs that cannot make up income in ticket sales? The UNC student body supported the fee structure. I hoped Georgia Tech students would do the same.

Football was the only sport that produced significant income, but even that was not enough to carry the other sports. I believed that in time we could make basketball profitable. That left baseball, track, golf, and tennis. It would be up to the Alexander-Tharpe Fund to raise the money needed for scholarships, if indeed football and basketball could carry their own weight. A student fee was the answer. After several meetings with President Pettit, we finally gained his approval but still needed to attract student support. We had to convince the students that the additional fee had merit before Pettit would approach the Georgia Board of Regents to request official approval.

Dick Fuller, vice president for administration and finance, helped tremendously by arranging a forum for various groups on campus to discuss the issue. A host of people pitched in to the effort, including football coach Bill Curry. Student groups, fraternities, and sororities across campus attended meeting after meeting. The students asked for a referendum and by a narrow margin approved the fee increase. In turn, the student government and its president, Jack Markwalter, voted to approve the plan. The injection of one million dollars into the budget saved the program for the time being.

Our elation couldn't last long considering the ongoing crisis, and it didn't. We soon found yet another shocker in store for us. As I noted in my journal at the time:

Received another "blow" today — a complaint from the United States Civil Service Office of the Justice Department (Title IX Issue) that we did not support a women's program (gender equity). We are twelve years behind on this — with our financial situation, adding a women's program, raising private funds for the new intercollegiate center and parking deck and losing in all sports, makes this an interesting situation. I will have to dig in. To add to our concerns a Charlotte, N.C. newspaper reports our low academic graduation rates in the Atlantic Coast Conference — 38%. In addition a Raleigh, N.C. newspaper reported — The ACC has made a huge mistake by bringing Georgia Tech into the conference. Our image needs a "blood transfusion."

The complaint from the Civil Service outlined a clear threat: Develop a women's sports program, or lose federal funding and grants for the institution. The Athletic Association supported women's club sports but no official university teams. Hardly any income was available to address this serious deficiency. And the Title IX requirements stipulated that women's sports must be varsity and equal to the men's offerings.

During the first month of 1981, the NCAA convention passed

new rules for Division I-A schools, requiring seven sports to be sponsored for both men and women. Although we had made a big step forward in keeping athletics alive, we were two steps behind in making sports equally accessible to all students. With just enough progress for ensuring survival of the program, this was no time to give in.

We needed a miracle — and we got one. The ACC put its men's basketball TV package out to bid, and Commissioner Bob James met with the eight athletic directors to work out the strategy. C.D. Chesley had held the rights for the conference since its beginning in 1954, but Commissioner James believed we could triple our income.

Fortunately, I had a good knowledge of the facts of this venture, thanks to what I'd learned about the TV industry while serving on the NCAA TV Committee as the UNC athletic director. I met privately with Jim Keyo, athletic director at Maryland, and we agreed to push for the maximum revenue. Willis Casey, athletic director at NC State, had the math down cold and spoke for our group. Thanks to the solidarity and skills of our group, Lenny Klompus won the rights for $3 million. A year later, Rick and Dee Ray bid for the rights, pledging the fee of $18 million over three years to the ACC — a fee which would continue to grow significantly in future years. Broadcast rights for the ACC basketball schedule developed into the largest payout to any conference in the country.

Georgia Tech reaped huge benefits from this achievement. From a $2.5 million budget with a $354,000 shortfall in 1980, our budget grew in two years to more than $5 million. We could meet the requirements for offering seven women's sports! Our core sports of basketball, volleyball, and three-season track — featuring cross-country, indoor track, and track and field in the fall, winter, and spring seasons — counted for five of the required number. By adding tennis and fast-pitch softball, we continued diversifying women's sports while meeting the federal regulations.

In my early years, I met periodically with President Pettit to keep him informed for his monthly meetings with the full Athletic Association Board of Trustees. President Pettit need to be aware of and understand all of my plans because he served as chairman of the board of the association, which was incorporated as its own entity just like a private business. He confided to me that he actually knew very little about how an athletic program operated, asking what seemed to be elementary questions. I began convincing him how important a successful sports program could be in benefiting the university as a whole. We would also develop young people in the Student-Athlete Total Person Program who would become an asset to society after leaving with their degrees. In time, President Pettit became a strong advocate.

The complex tasks of simultaneously building men's and women's sports programs while assembling a competitive administrative staff monopolized much of my attention. The staff was beginning to take shape with Business Manager John O'Neill, Development Director Jack Thompson with the A-T Fund, Jim Luck overseeing facilities, George Slayton in academics, Bill McDonald in sports medicine, Jim Schultz in sports information, and Lawton Hydrick as strength coach. But with even this emerging organization, could I provide the leadership and motivation for us to develop a successful program in five years? I didn't have time to speculate, however. All my efforts had to be spent in moving forward.

* * *

I would have to apply the Attitude Technique philosophy to move the program ahead. It had worked before. Would it work again in this different situation?

To lead a successful program on any level, it is imperative that one be trained to undertake the task. I gained my own training through a philosophy developed early in my life, learned from many people. It began when I was 12 and my father presented me with a book by William Danforth titled *I Dare You*. The philosophy I put together came to be called the "Attitude Technique."

Just as football has various physical techniques that must be taught, mental techniques have to be learned because the mental directs the physical. With the Attitude Technique, you control your thoughts and ultimately your destiny. The first step is changing negative thoughts to positive ones. When a negative thought enters your mind, stop for a full minute, then change it from negative to positive. Over time your whole attitude will change, and a leader with a positive approach remains in high gear and passes this attitude on to his or her subordinates. The Attitude Technique philosophy governs success in all areas of life, including achieving a positive self-image, optimal health, a successful career, and financial independence.

Principles of Motivation

Everything begins with an idea. If you control your mind, you can control your future. To be completely successful we must base everything on *truth*. If we are not truthful, we will fail. A lie cannot withstand the test of time. Motivation is a spark that ignites us to do great things. We plan it. We write it out. We may even record it on tape. We begin acting out the role we must play to accomplish our goals. Consistency and repetition pay off. The role becomes a ladder to climb. The higher we climb, the more aware we become of our potential.

Motivation involves seven principles. Each principle represents a step up the ladder.

Desire

The first principle is that *you must desire to accomplish something.* Whatever you want, fix it in your mind in exact detail then write it down so it will become absolutely clear. This is the commitment, the beginning. Whatever the need, you must understand that you never receive anything without first giving. It may be your time or your efforts. Whatever it is, give before you expect to receive.

Faith

The second principle is that *we must have faith in the outcome.* This is a state of mind that may be created by affirmation or repeated instructions to the subconscious mind. A mental image of yourself already accomplishing what you want, seen over and over again, will project the faith you need to achieve your desire. Faith in yourself and faith in your destiny is an essential and important step in your climb up the ladder. "All things are possible to him that believes" is one way of expressing this principle.

Imagination

The third principle is that *we must have imagination.* Man can create anything he can imagine. Whatever we can visualize and have faith in, we can achieve. The power to create new ideas comes from combining previous experiences. When you creatively imagine something, you are actually causing it to come into being. The process by which it comes to pass is a mystery, but the method for making it happen is this: picture the things you want to do; hold them in consciousness; try to pattern your actions in such a way that you are constantly working toward the fulfillment of the desires you hold in your imagination. That is affirmative use of your imagination.

Planning

The fourth principle is that *we must have organized planning.* Whatever you desire in life, cannot be done alone. Select one or more individuals to work with you in developing your plan. The more minds you can get together working for a common purpose, the more related information will be available. Great ideas are a combination of related ideas. Pick the individual or group with care. They must be hard-working, conscientious people you respect. Arrange to meet with your group at least once a week. Make your plans faultless. Each morning you must know exactly what you are going to do and why. You must be a leader to direct your plan.

Organized planning will take you a step closer to your desire. By arranging daily work so that we can succeed in little things, we can build an atmosphere of success that will carry over into larger and more important undertakings. I organize each day – when to get up, when to sleep, when to work, relax, and plan. By planning each moment, I am able to do three times as much as when I do not plan. This is written motivation.

Decision-Making

The fifth principle is that *we must be able to make a decision.* Lack of decisiveness is the major cause of failure. Successful people reach decisions promptly and change them slowly, if there is ever a need for change. Failures reach decisions very slowly and change them rapidly. Never make an important decision without getting all the facts. It is better to pause or hold until the facts are in and then make a decision and stay with it. Learn to make decisions because in not deciding, you fail to act; and in failing to act, you invite complete failure. All great men are men of quick decision. Quick decision flows from initiative, accumulated knowledge, and experience.

Persistence

The sixth principle is that *we must have persistence.* When everything indicates it is all over, go that extra mile and succeed. This is the difference between success and failure. This is the separation of men from boys. Persistence is a state of mind. It can, therefore, be cultivated.

All successful coaches are persistent. They keep coming back against great odds and succeeding. Paul Brown, Vince Lombardi, John Wooden, Paul Bryant, Bobby Dodd, and many others experienced defeat but would not give in. Their willpower took them to the top.

The Subconscious Mind – Our Human Computer

The seventh principle and the ultimate key to success is that *we must understand and use the subconscious mind*. It is the magic of success. This is the most important principle of the entire system. Once you understand this element and put it into positive use, your life, your success, everything can be and will be whatever you want it to be. In fact there is no way it can be any other way.

Our mind, our thoughts control our destiny. The scientific explanation of this is simple, and it is my strong desire that through this writing God will supply me with the ability to explain it to you. Not only to explain it, but to present it in such a way that you will make a firm commitment to utilize this powerful force in your everyday life. If you will do this, then my contribution to mankind will be fulfilled. This is my high purpose. The technique of attitude is wrapped up completely in this one principle.

From a very early age everything you heard, saw, or felt was stored in your subconscious. Your conscious mind collects and your subconscious performs. This is the exact process of a computer. Your subconscious does not care what you give it. It will perform with whatever material it has. If you have given it negative thoughts all these years, then you must and will perform as a negative person. When you do something you are sorry for later, it cannot be helped because this is your subconscious performing as you planned it.

The subconscious mind, or our human computer, has three basic functions. First, with its understanding of physical needs it maintains the well-being of the body – your very life. Second, in times of great emergency it springs into action and takes supreme command. Third, it works in mysterious ways when called upon for help and can be trained and utilized by the conscious mind. It can be used to solve a problem or achieve anything you desire strongly enough.

How can you use it for your benefit? First, be sure that you are asking for something that is rightfully yours to have and is within your ability to handle, for the subconscious manifests itself only according to the capabilities of the person. Second, you must have patience and absolute faith. The subconscious will not work for you unless you believe it can.

How can you believe? Start saying, " I believe, I believe." Say it 20, 50, 100 times. When you verbalize "I believe," your subconscious will respond to this and begin recording. Then you really start believing. This is the power of suggestion. This is the technique of training yourself toward success. You control your thoughts; therefore, you begin controlling your performance.

Conveying your need to the subconscious must be done in the spirit that the work has already been accomplished. Many times something has happened that you felt had happened before. Often it has, but only in your subconscious. While it is necessary for you to feel and to think yourself successful, it is important for you to go one step further and actually see yourself as already successful. The final step is to wait patiently while the subconscious is assimilating the elements of your problem and then goes about its own way to work it out for you.

The solution will be revealed to you, the correct course of action indicated, and you must follow immediately and unquestioningly. There must be no hesitation on your part, no mental reservation, no deliberation. Take the course of action. One day you will find yourself, through the aid of the subconscious, in the position you sought.

The subconscious mind always brings to reality what it is led to believe. Human imagination and concentration are the chief factors in developing the forces of the subconscious mind. In athletics, the mental picture determines the muscular reaction. If there is no mental picture, what happens is a mere guess. This means there must be almost endless concentration of thought in order to succeed.

Repetition is the fundamental process. In football, the repetition of a particular play brings about successful execution. Successful execution results in players believing in the play. A play that is practiced sparingly and used sparingly is a hit-or-miss proposition.

The Attitude Technique is not a ticket to fame and success overnight. It is intended only as a key to unlock the door that opens on the path that leads to the goal of your desire.

Your subconscious operates in terms of goals and end results. Once you give it a definite goal to achieve, you can depend upon its guidance system to take you to that end. You supply the desire by thinking in terms of the finished product. Your subconscious then supplies the means. The reason is simple: when you feel successful and self-confident, you will act successfully. When the feeling is strong enough, you can literally do no wrong. In time you will not only feel successful but you will expect to be successful.

The Attitude Technique still enables me to approach my life with the proper mental framework every single day. However, my biggest enjoyment is passing this technique on to others. Hearing remarkable success stories from others always kindles my enthusiasm to continue my own work. This has become my high purpose in life. (Note: to read further about how I originally developed the Attitude Technique philosophy, see Appendix B.)

* * *

Now it was vitally important to get out and share our vision with the people of Georgia Tech. Meetings were scheduled throughout the state of Georgia, surrounding states, and key cities in the country — not to mention a few international locations. (I must mention that with all of my automobile travel around the state, I was ever thankful that my good friend Billy Bridges, owner of Capital Cadillac, furnished me with a sparkling new automobile each year. I was particularly thankful on the day I was rammed in the side by a truck and escaped possible death because of the protection of the car's center-structure steel bar. The automobile was destroyed; I was knocked unconscious, but quickly recovered – thanks to the makers of Billy's Cadillacs.)

My message was the story of the future with hope. We would succeed and bring back to Georgia Tech the respect it deserved. We would do this with integrity. In addition, the Student-Athlete Total Person Program needed to be sold, and I was the salesman. The program was no mere lip service to the ideals of developing student athletes, as the media and some critics charged. The program actually made student athletes successes in the real world after graduation. And as a further bonus for Georgia Tech, it provided the impetus for major gifts later.

During the first three years I traveled and spoke to alumni groups in 61 different places. I came back a second or even third time for most of those groups. Bob Rice, the executive director of the Georgia Tech Alumni Association, met with me about setting up Yellow Jacket committees in each of those locations. While invigorating on one level, this massive project tremendously taxed my energy. Despite the exhaustion of intense travel, I gained motivation through meeting some of the finest people I'd ever come across. With their involvement, we could build the program to a high level.

John Carter replaced Bob Rice upon Bob's retirement, carrying forward the good relationship we had developed. In most schools, the athletic department and the alumni association don't usually work together in harmony, but Georgia Tech proved to be an exception. John Carter, vice president and executive director, led the Georgia Tech Alumni Association to several national honors and always showed his support by cheering on the Yellow Jackets. Working with John and the alumni presidents made Georgia Tech a stronger university.

It was rewarding for me, as well. Each president brought a special style and type of support for athletic programs, and our goal of developing student-athletes of strong character who would be a credit to our school after graduation. Starting with Frank Smith in 1980, the lineup included Richard Bell (1981), Tal Dryman (1982), Don Chapman (1983), Lamar Oglesby (1984), Rem DuBose (1985), Geoffrey Gill (1986), Ben Dyer (1987), Lawton "Mac" Nease (1988), Bobby Joe Anderson (1989), Oliver Sale (1990), Shirley Mewborn (1991), John Staton (1992), Hammond "Buck" Stith (1993), William Knight (1994), Frank Maier (1995), Milton Stewart (1996), Hubert Harris (1997), and Frank Spears (1998). In the beginning of the relationship, several alumni came forward with the energy to offer help whenever needed. Support by people such as Jim and Nona Bell led the group to step forward.

So many people supported the program that their names would fill a book: Cary Brown, Turner Warmack, Jim Terry, Louis Jordan, Roy Burnett, Bob Bush, Pete George, Dwane Hoover, Aaron King, Charles Jones, Carl Reit, Dr. Sid Williams, Robert Worley – and so many others that I could go on and on. The point is, Georgia Tech people are proud of their school, they believed in its integrity, and, as long as that symbol was maintained, their loyalty was sustaining.

The members and elected officers of each committee played key roles in our development. Beginning with $100 membership dues, the Alexander-Tharpe Fund soon reached the $1 million mark. At the same time, a new leader emerged in the person of the bright young man from Augusta who had served as student body president, supporting the campus vote for raising student athletic fees. After his graduation, Jack Markwalter, who had also acted as student representative to the Board of Trustees of the Georgia Tech Athletic Association, accepted the position of assisting Jack Thompson with soliciting contributions. He had no prior experience in funds development, but he had a positive attitude. As a former board member he understood the situation quite well, and he believed in the purpose of building the program in five years. Jack connected with Georgia Tech people exceptionally and became a big hit.

With the administrative staff in place, the revenue base was solidified. The coaching situation remained a challenge. Most of the head coaches in men's sports were stepping down.

Bill Curry had been hired in January of 1980 as head football coach, just prior to my arrival in April. Bill went through two tough years before winning began. He patiently built his staff and recruited players equal to our competition, forming a solid program at last.

Of course I wanted football to win big. Football was my own sport, and I selfishly provided the "means" to that program first. With its long history at Georgia Tech, football had a special place in the university's identity. The sport had put Georgia Tech on the map. From the first season in 1904 under John Heisman, then through Bill Alexander and his successor, Bobby Dodd, no other school in America had produced three such legends. And each won a national championship: Heisman in 1917, Alexander in 1928, and Dodd in 1952.

Although Georgia Institute of Technology was a premier academic institution with a prestigious engineering college, football had been the vehicle that brought attention to the campus. On the practical level, football had to succeed to finance the total athletic program. Bill Curry engaged in making the pieces of this puzzle come together, making success attainable.

Men's basketball followed in the order of priorities. In March of 1981, I set out to find Georgia Tech a basketball coach, searching nationally to find the ideal leader. My experience from more than seven years at UNC had taught me that basketball could develop into a huge profit center if the right coach could be brought on board. In the highly competitive ACC, such a person was crucial.

Dean Smith, head basketball coach at UNC in Chapel Hill, advised my efforts. One of the most successful coaches in the history of the game, Coach Smith was magically adept at winning close games. With his deep knowledge, he helped me put together a list of candidates, avoiding those who might bend the rules in order to win.

We separated the names into three categories, noting established coaches, top assistants at successful programs, and young coaches on the way up. After the ACC Basketball Tournament at Capitol Center near Washington, D.C., I stayed in the area in Baltimore to begin the search.

Before a candidate could be brought to Atlanta to be interviewed by the Athletic Association Board of Trustees' Search Committee, I had to do the preliminary work. I extended invitations to interested coaches to meet me in Baltimore or to allow me to visit them in their own towns, with my goal being to find three candidates for each experience category.

The interest candidates showed surprised me. In spite of our poor record, antiquated facilities, and the school's difficult academic standards, the position attracted people more than I expected. Perhaps the chance to compete in the ACC, or my association with Dean Smith, or the idea of living in the city of Atlanta – or all three factors – created interest. Outside of its own state, Georgia Tech continued to be held in high esteem.

Inside the state, the school was the butt of jokes, however. I cringed to hear people laughing about the school, and my competitive nature motivated me to do something to stifle the snickering as quickly as possible.

Basketball offered a unique opportunity to stop the embarrassment. A successful basketball program could be built and become powerful much more quickly than football. The NCAA limit of 20 to 25 scholarships per year made recovery much slower in football. The right basketball coach with just a few blue-chippers could jumpstart the program, using the smaller numbers to advantage.

The coach search required my complete concentration, and I got very little sleep in two weeks at Baltimore. After compiling my list and getting ready for the interview process, I invited candidates one by one to Atlanta. One coach brought his lawyer "agent" with him, producing a list of 33 demands on a long legal pad. After realizing I would be working for the new coach full-time, I politely escorted the two back to the airport. But one coach quickly gained my attention, even though he was in the third category. He was a young coach on the way up.

As director of athletics at UNC I watched the arch rival match up of UNC and the University of South Carolina in the semi-finals of

*the ACC Basketball Tournament in Greensboro, N.C. The tourna-
ment pitted the two teams against each other in the only qualifying
opportunity for the NCAA tournament. Frank McGuire coached
South Carolina that year, but he had won a national championship
for North Carolina in 1957, with young Dean Smith of the Air
Force Academy joining him on the North Carolina coaching staff
the following year. Coach McGuire left to join the professional
ranks before returning to South Carolina at the collegiate level,
bringing with him a formidable experience in the sport.*

*The lead in the UNC-USC game switched back and forth, pro-
ducing a close game that kept fans off their seats, if not biting their
fingernails. In the last two minutes, South Carolina regained the
lead, and the team's captain began dribbling and evading North
Carolina players to run off the clock. In the days before the NCAA's
40-second clock rule, the only way for UNC to stop the clock was
to foul the dribbling point guard. Awarded shot after shot from
UNC fouls, the captain connected on nine straight free throws,
cementing South Carolina's lead and berth in the finals. The game
was memorable. So was the South Carolina player. That player was
Bobby Cremins.*

Bobby Cremins fit exactly what I thought we needed. After a stint
in the professional leagues, Bobby returned to South Carolina to
serve as assistant under his former coach, Frank McGuire. From
there he took the head job at Appalachian State in Boone, North
Carolina, taking over a program that finished 4-24 the previous
year. In six years, Bobby had won the Southern Conference
Championship three times, been named coach of the year three
times, and made three trips to the NCAA playoffs. He understood
the ACC, and he knew how to recruit the northeast and eastern
seaboard for prospects. Bobby and his wife, Carolyn, made the trip
to Atlanta to meet with the search committee.

Most of the committee members favored an older, more experienced coach, though. And Appalachian State didn't have the ring of
familiarity that major universities carried. Bobby Cremins was going
to be a tough sell, despite his talents.

Established coaches wanted an elaborate package. But could
they handle the difficulty of losing at the beginning? Would they be
willing to do the hard work necessary for establishing another program? I'd seen many coaches make a lateral move from a successful

program and then become a failure in a new location.

Bobby Cremins didn't want a fancy, cushy contract. He was will-ing to put in the hours to make the program successful. He could handle the price of coming to Tech for the chance to create a win-ning program that bore his mark.

Jim Carlen, a former assistant football coach to Bobby Dodd and a successful coach at schools including West Virginia, Texas Tech, and later South Carolina, seconded my opinion about Bobby Cremins. Jim called me about Bobby, high on the young coach's promise, and confirmed my instincts.

After spending several more weeks on the search process, I meet with President Pettit. He still believed in bringing in a coach from the first category, but he would support my decision to recruit Bobby Cremins. In the end, the board agreed. We hired Bobby Cremins, making a decision that would turn out to be the most spec-tacular choice possible. Bobby became the most successful basket-ball coach in Georgia Tech's history, driving the university's program to ACC championships, NCAA appearances, national recognition, and — above all else in our desperate bid to keep the sports pro-grams alive — a handsome profit that helped save athletics.

As Jim Luck moved into the position of assistant athletic direc-tor for facilities, we faced the time to hire a head baseball coach. The constitution and by-laws of the Athletic Association Board of Trustees allowed that body to hire and fire the head football coach; at my request, we added similar oversight of the basketball coach, as well. All other coaching positions circumvented this restriction, but I kept the president and board members informed of my deci-sions. In turning to the baseball coach search, I recognized that the ACC regularly sent teams to the NCAA College World Series in Omaha, Nebraska, for the national championship, and the confer-ence was known for its strength as a baseball league.

A successful young coach quickly surfaced. Jim Morris, top assistant at perennial powerhouse Florida State, lead the group of candidates. As head coach at Dekalb Junior College, Jim had taken his team to the national championships for several years. Our pro-gram ranked at the bottom of the league with poor facilities, but Jim Morris believed he could turn the program around to become a national contender. He was our man. Jim quickly backed up his words with action after being hired, and Georgia Tech became a nationally ranked program.

The track program at Georgia Tech lay under the direction of Buddy Fowlkes, one of the school's best sprint champions. As an athlete in the 1950s, Buddy was a three-time total point champion in the Southeastern Conference. When he was 34 years old, he set a world record in the 100-yard dash at 9.5 seconds and became known as the "fastest old man alive." In discussing the program with Buddy, I found him to be a coach with a positive attitude. This seemed strange, considering the fact that Georgia Tech still had a cinder track — and even that was in poor condition. How could he possibly expect to recruit an athlete? Other programs offered state-of-the-art running surfaces and full scholarships. But Buddy told me he could be successful. And he proved himself correct, finding athletes and inspiring them to attain several individual national championships and high team finishes in the NCAA.

Could golf follow these successes? The Georgia Tech golf program had not won a tournament in 27 years. The minuscule funds available to this sport covered the purchase shirts for the team. With limited scholarship aid and a restricted travel budget, the sport was on a fast road to nowhere — except to a last-place finish. Although the program developed Larry Mize into the Masters champion in Augusta in 1987, the sport needed much help. Most perplexing of all, how could the program have fallen away from the traditions of Bobby Jones and Charlie Yates?

Graduating from Tech in mechanical engineering in 1922, Bobby Jones became the greatest amateur golfer of all time and the 1930 Grand Slam winner. Charlie Yates earned the title of NCAA Champion in 1934, and as an All-American went undefeated in the 1936 and 1938 Walker Cup competition. Given this exciting history, the program should have been well supported. I began the search for a head coach, trying not to match the current program but to find someone who could instill the strengths of the past into the sport's future at Georgia Tech.

Puggy Blackmon, an excellent teacher of the game and head of the national Junior Golf Program, had no collegiate coaching experience. Yet everyone I called in the collegiate world to gather names of potential candidates seemed to mention Puggy. "Call Puggy — he knows all the college coaches," everybody told me. Then a light came on in my head. As head of the junior golfers, Puggy would also know all of the collegiate golf prospects. Puggy also was involved with the American Junior Golf Association when he had contact with the top high school players. Puggy worked with Charlie Brown, general chairman of the Junior World Cup, and Charlie gave me information regarding Puggy that proved instrumental in the hiring process.

When Puggy and I discussed the possibilities of his becoming Georgia Tech's head men's golf coach, he seemed extremely interested. After one more meeting, he agreed to accept the job, and even remarked, "I will deliver to you a national championship." (In 1993, Georgia Tech finished one stroke behind the University of Florida to earn a close second for that NCAA title.) The golf program flourished. And my instincts in the hiring process were being labeled by my peers as lucky. If that were true, I must have been carrying a horseshoe in my back pocket and a rabbit foot on a chain around my neck!

Tennis remained. It was the last of the seven required ACC sports that we needed to address. Would the lucky horse shoe and rabbit's foot prevail in this last search? Ironically, a person just like Puggy Blackmon surfaced in tennis. Gary Groslimond headed the World Tennis organization in Atlanta. He knew all the young tennis players from coast to coast, presenting Georgia Tech with a recruiting bonanza. Gary had some coaching experience as an assistant at Stanford University, which he had also attended as an outstanding tennis player. As head of World Tennis, he had also gained experience in marketing, which proved valuable in building a successful collegiate program. When approached with a job offer, Gary accepted — to our good fortune. He quickly put the program in place, eventually leading Georgia Tech to the championship circle.

The head coaches of men's sports in football, basketball, track (including cross country, indoor track, and outdoor track and field), golf, and tennis were now in place. Every sport required for membership in the ACC now had a leader with talent, connections, and a vision. My job then was to provide the means for each coach to succeed. This meant funds for recruiting, operation, and facilities that matched the competition. Before I could spend the time to address these needs, I first had to turn to the needs of the women's programs.

Federal laws had instructed civil service units to enforce Title IX, requiring women to be given similar athletic programs to those for men. Not meeting this goal would mean losing all federal grants — which for Georgia Tech represented millions of dollars. To make the situation more pressing, Georgia Tech lagged behind other schools in developing an equitable women's sports program.

I had been through the process of building a women's program before at North Carolina, where in 1970 we had awarded to Cammy Timberlake the first grant-in-aid to a female athlete in the ACC. Although Georgia Tech was about twelve years behind, I had an idea of how to get started. To meet this huge challenge, I turned for help to North Carolina. One of the prize performers at UNC was a young lady from Gloucester, New Jersey, named Bernadette McGlade. She had become assistant women's basketball coach at her alma mater. I called Francis Hogan, head of the women's program and with whom I worked in the 1970s, receiving her recommendation that Bernadette be tapped to begin a program at Georgia Tech.

Bernadette had been a star player on the women's basketball team and easy to remember. An unselfish player and a team leader, she holds the rebounding record for both men and women at UNC even until today. If she accepted the challenge, Bernadette would become the first female coach in Georgia Tech's history. I offered her the position, and she accepted the job. Another top pick without any experience in such a huge undertaking, Bernadette soon performed so well that I named her assistant athletic director for women's sports. She turned her talents toward building all seven women's sports and complying with the federal statutes and NCAA rules.

With a handle on the sports programs, we reached the time for shifting into high gear and creating the funds to build facilities to a level competitive with opposing teams. My plan called for a working committee for each sport, with each head coach playing a prominent role. Not many coaches under ordinary conditions would have accepted this responsibility, but integrating head coaches into the plan was totally necessary — and every coach at Georgia Tech cooperated. As we entered the campaign, I was amazed at how the coaches took charge, using the marketing expertise each possessed to promote programs.

Every committee needed a key alumnus to serve as chairman. They began to step forward. Football gained Kim King; basketball, Taz Anderson; baseball, Randy Carroll; tennis, Bud Parker; golf, Charlie Brown; and track, Morris Bryan. With the Arthur B. Edge Jr. Athletic Center in place, football had acquired a state-of-the-art facility, including offices, meeting rooms, and locker rooms. The stadium and Rose Bowl practice fields needed a great deal of attention,

however. Practice fields failed to drain properly when deluged with
seasonal rain, leaving the fields bare of grass by early fall. Ewell
Pope made a direct gift to resod and rework the fields to meet the
standards of a competitive practice field. Charlie Smithgall III later
provided funding for lights. With these improvements, the Rose
Bowl fields immediately took on an upgraded appearance.

Grant Field and the stadium property represented a bigger challenge. As gifts became available, we added a new scoreboard.
Aluminum seats replaced the word out wooden bleachers. A fence
built around the field added security. General maintenance
improved tremendously, but Grant Field needed more than a touch
up here and there. The oldest collegiate stadium in NCAA Division
I-A, Grant Field needed a major overhaul.

Although gifts were beginning to arrive, we needed major funding in the millions of dollars to make the necessary improvements.
The South Stands obviously would have to go. They had been condemned years ago. Not knowing how to accomplish this end, I knew
that the first step to take would be to confer with President Pettit
about this undertaking.

Meeting with him, I explained in detail the facilities dilemma. A
stadium marked an investment in sports program and in the university's image. Stadium renovation was crucial to both. Dr. Pettit
took it all in, stood up, walked over to the window of his office,
and looked out the window for several moments. I sat waiting,
wondering what was going through his mind. He turned and
offered a solution.

Georgia Tech was planning a centennial campaign to raise needed funds for the institution, he explained. The campaign would
focus on private gifts, not state tax dollars. President Pettit offered
to recommend that the Athletic Association receive five percent of
the total amount raised.

A committee met to lay out plans for the centennial campaign,
setting the goal at $100 million. After that meeting, Paul Duke, Polly
Poole, and Russ Chandler each called me. The three phone calls
informed me that the Athletic Association would indeed receive five
percent of the goal, totaling $5 million, for the stadium renovation.
I was ecstatic. I called the president and thanked him. His solution
provided the break we needed to fix the stadium, making a major
commitment to the football program and contribution to the university's public image.

Within three years, President Pettit became ill, dying just months later of cancer. Losing him was a deeply sad event to me. He was a creative, strong, and determined president of Georgia Tech, and I personally felt indebted to him for hiring me to come to the university. Henry Bourne became acting president, continuing the centennial campaign and bringing President Pettit's vision to double its original goal. The campaign raised more than $200 million dollars, providing five percent — which could mean $10 million — for the stadium renovation.

Exploring the possibilities with Dr. Bourne, we discovered that no literature specifically spelled out this promise. Even though the first brochure alluded to funds for the building program, no other information could verify the arrangement. The three friends who had called me — Paul, Polly, and Russ — all remembered. But the five percent, whether $10 million or $5 million, never came. The Athletic Association did not receive one cent from the successful campaign.

The stadium renovation had to be put on hold.

In the meantime, Warren Heemann, vice president for development, sold Mrs. Edna Wardlaw, widow of William A. Wardlaw, Jr., on making a gift to build a facility replacing the South Stands. I'd often suggested to the Athletic Board members and the president's cabinet that adjoining academic and athletic structures be built at a future date, encircling the stadium. It seemed that my vision had never been understood. But the Wardlaw gift provided the opportunity to bring this to fruition.

Oddly enough, the Athletic Association was not brought into the discussions about constructing the new building, even though doing so would involve demolition of the South Stands. When design started, we were finally brought into the crew. Named the William Wardlaw Building, the five-story structure was to cost $3-5 million. The field level housed a much needed strength center, supplementing the small cramped quarters of the other weight-lifting area under the North Stands. Two levels provided parking for the urban campus. One level hosted the Georgia Tech Foundation and a Gordy Entertainment Dining Room, named in honor of Frank Gordy, owner of the famous Varsity Restaurant across the interstate from Georgia Tech. The Georgia Tech Development Group would use the top level for its operations.

The university asked the Athletic Association to bear 40 percent of the facility's cost, which might be up to $2 million at the higher estimated cost. I met with the Athletic Association facility committee to discuss our obligation. Members questioned whether the Athletic Association should carry two-fifths of the cost. The strength center occupied only 10,000 square feet of the ground floor and didn't even require furnishings. An adjacent room could be used as a fitness room during football season and visitor's locker room. Previously I had observed the teams leaving the field at half time, crisscrossing to reach their locker rooms. From the west benches Georgia Tech players walked to the northeast corner of the stadium, and visitors on the east side to the northwest corner lockers. By using the Wardlaw Building, which would be located on the south end, a potential free-for-all could be eliminated.

After negotiations continued, we were allowed to use the parking level and the Gordy Dining Room on football days. But the facility committee still felt that 40 percent was too steep a portion for the Athletic Association to take responsibility for. The building was not yet built, however. As I pondered ways of splitting up the building's cost and space, another vision hit me: What if we designed the facility with skyboxes and executive suites on a higher, sixth level? Could that produce income to break the impasse?

Just visualize driving on game day into an indoor, reserved parking space. Taking an elevator to the top floor of a personalized suite for a bird's eye view of the game. That would be easy to sell! But would people pay for end zone skyboxes? Studying skyboxes around the country, we put together a plan.

As a former football coach, I had always believed that the endzone, high over the gridiron, gave the best place to watch a football game. You could see the entire field and the game as it was being played. My teams always shot game films from the endzone. Once people experienced skybox luxury and the dramatic game view from the endzone, the boxes would sell. We constructed 12 suites, developing a pay-out plan over six years. After that period, the boxes would become profitable and contribute to the income of the program. Beers Construction Company, with CEO Larry Gellerstedt, began building the Wardlaw Building.

Yet financing again reared its ugly head. Plans called for the Georgia Tech Foundation to pay 60 percent and the Athletic Association the remainder. Our legal advisor cautioned us that the percentage formula did not represent the same sum we had discussed earlier. Arthur Howell, attorney with Alston and Bird, joined me in attending a meeting to discuss the agreement, but Howell rejected the papers on behalf of the Athletic Association because the building's cost had soared. The estimated price tag for the Wardlaw Building now would be approximately $9 million — almost doubling the higher estimate of the earlier facility.

The Athletic Association's finance and facilities committee met in a special session. Members were extremely upset and agreed with Mr. Howell that a joint contract should not be signed. At the time, President Pettit was ill, and it was difficult to discuss the stalemate with him. I didn't know where to turn. But I knew that the skyboxes would not provide enough income to pay the Athletic Association's share, whatever the final agreements were.

At the same time, we couldn't enter into another campaign. The timing was wrong, because it was too close to our previous campaign to raise funds for the Edge Center. In addition, the institution was involved in its own campaign. Georgia Tech's centennial gave the university a unique opportunity for raising money in 1985. I would have to seek out several major gifts from sources that would not compete with either our earlier efforts or the centennial campaign.

Paul Duke rose to the occasion, making another gift. Another former player and successful entrepreneur, George Mathews Jr. offered his assistance. His major gift encouraged our program immeasurably.

George Mathews, a 1948 Georgia Tech graduate, played under both Bill Alexander and Bobby Dodd. After earning an advanced degree from Harvard University, George founded the Intermet Corporation, a $500-million company and the largest independent foundry in North America. In football, he will be most remembered for his fumble recovery during a game with Navy. When a Navy halfback fumbled on the one-yard line, George caught the ball in mid-air, raced 99 yards for a touchdown, and helped his team defeat the high-ranking Naval Academy.

Hugh Spruill stepped forward next. He offered an arrangement to sell land, but the property would not be available for several years as Hugh waited for the real estate market to rebound. These three proposed gifts, along with income from the skyboxes, would cover the Athletic Association's obligations.

The final cost for the facility came through: more than $14 million. The Georgia Tech Foundation and the Athletic Board never actually met together, so information was never clear during the entire process. The lack of communication caused misunderstandings and hard feelings between the two groups. Nevertheless, the building turned out to be a tremendous asset for Georgia Tech. It added significantly to the football stadium, although many more meetings and difficult feelings had to be overcome before the issue of the facility's cost could be settled.

In the meantime, we were involved with upgrading or building adequate facilities for other sports. The Alexander Memorial Coliseum, used for basketball, was in critical condition. I'll always remember going to a game my first year at Georgia Tech. The crowd was sparse. A few students wore sacks over their heads in protest. As rain fell on the arena's roof, it dropped from the ceiling onto fan seating. With so many seats available, though, patrons simply moved to a dryer section in the coliseum.

The locker room was in disrepair, and the facility's general appearance was sub-standard. When ACC teams appeared in our arena, I invariably took heat from the other school over the facilities for visitors. Finally I took several board members on a personal tour to see the terrible conditions. George Brodnax had a singularly strong reaction. A former All-American end for Coach Dodd, George remarked that the situation was a disgrace for Georgia Tech.

Taz Anderson, another product of Coach Dodd's golden years and a former professional football player, took a strong interest in the program. He stepped forward, showing a keen willingness to get involved. He introduced me to Bill Reynolds, of the architectural firm of Smallwood, Reynolds, Stewart and Stewart. He also brought me to meet Earl Shell Jr. of Hardin Construction Company. Both had graduated from Georgia Tech. Taz solicited their advice on how we could renovate the coliseum and make the facility presentable. Another former Georgia Tech football player, Morris Harrison, helped to add the electrical engineer for the coliseum.

The Alexander Memorial Coliseum needed to serve three sports: men's basketball, women's basketball, and women's volleyball. The question was how to improve a 6,900-seat arena with a leaky roof and out-of-date locker rooms. Could it be done? Clyde Robbins, vice president for facilities on campus, entered the discussions. Each year the coliseum also served four times as the site for commencement and housed other campus activities.

The team of experts provided miracles. The coliseum gained a new roof, and seating was expanded for a capacity of 10,000. Courtside box seats were added. A new floor and goals turned the arena into an attractive gymnasium. And to top off the renovation, a new locker room building housed a pressroom and VIP room named in honor of Coach Whack Hyder. The building was named in memory of Jim Luck, who along with Sgt. Gary Beringause was one of two campus police officers killed in a terrible automobile accident prior to the Georgia Tech-UGA football game in Athens in 1986.

Basketball in the refurbished arena turned out to be a huge success, not only in terms of championships but at the gate. From 1983 on, the coliseum sold out before the season opened. Renovation costs ran into the millions, but the program became solvent and made the payments.

Baseball, with Jim Morris at the helm, got off to a fast start. Randy Carroll, who made the All-American team while playing under Jim Luck and later toured the professional ranks, turned out to be a key person in organizing the Grand Slam Club. Coach Morris was his own entrepreneur of sorts. He handily marketed his program. But as with other sports, the baseball stadium lay beyond repair.

Into the picture stepped a young alumnus, Russ Chandler. Russ achieved success in a variety of ventures and had expressed an interest in making a gift to his alma mater. A portion could be earmarked for athletics. As we discussed the possibilities, baseball seemed the right program for making the most of his generosity. The new stadium featured a press and VIP box, attractive locker room, field improvements, and lights for night games, putting our baseball team in a competitive mode instantly. Jim Morris eagerly sought a national championship. With the program in place, a first-class stadium, and fence signs that even made the field look like an attractive minor league ballpark, he gained momentum toward that goal.

Dean George Griffin came to visit during the initial years of my tenure in the early 1980s. A treasure trove of stories, Dean Griffin also aided more Georgia Tech students, past and present, than any single person or group I knew. He was an institution. In fact, he was Mr. Georgia Tech. A third-teamer on John Heisman's football squad and assistant under Coach Bill Alexander, he also served as dean of students for 22 years until he retired. He never left Georgia Tech until his final days at the age of 92.

George Griffin had also been track coach at Georgia Tech, and track always remained his favorite sport. As he left my office, he always suggested, "Please build us a track." He even picked out the site for a new track – a piece of land between the football practice field and the tennis courts that belonged to the Athletic Association. He explained that in 1928 when Georgia Tech, under Coach Alexander, returned victorious over the University of California in the Rose Bowl (the game of the famous wrong-way Riegels), Coach Alexander bought the land with the profits to build the baseball field, football practice field, and the tennis courts.

At the time he spoke to me, the vacant land was being used for student intramural fields. We measured the area for an NCAA qualification track and field, but had to find a way to make sure the plan benefited the students on campus and not just athletes. I met with Dr. James Reedy, head of the health and performance science department. His program included intramurals and club sports. He suggested installing artificial turf on the student activities center fields on campus. By adding lights and avoiding natural turf which was difficult to maintain, the fields would be available for students at all times.

A group from England was eager to install their version of artificial grass. They even offered that if we would accept their product, they would install the fields for a lower cost so they could gain a model for their plans to sell their product in the United States. After a trip to London to view a field with their grass in place, we made a deal for the installation. With a fence, new lights, and a financial plan for the project completed and in place, the students gained access to a class facility supplementing the Callaway Activities Center.

In turn, we got the go-ahead to build the track. With the space provided, the arrow turned back to me to locate funding for the venture. The Class of 1933 stepped forward to offer help. Representing the alums, Fred Storey met with me and confirmed that the Class of 1933 would contribute the necessary funds for a track to be named in honor of George Griffin. Track Coach Buddy Fowlkes supplied the expertise and selected the proper company for the project, which turned out to be another friend of the track world: Morris Bryan.

Morris had been instrumental in the early success of the State of Georgia Hall of Fame. We visited often about details concerning the track. We wanted to secure a state-of-the-art facility. Morris planned to apply the funds to add a stadium for track events. Sadly, Morris died before we began construction. His wife, Rebecca Alexander Bryan (stepdaughter of Coach Bill Alexander), and family contributed the financial resources. Upon completion, the George Griffin Track and Morris Bryan Stadium were ready to host the ACC Track and Field Meet.

The track program for the conference meet consisted of men's and women's cross country, indoor track, and outdoor track and field. In one swoop, the facility became available for training and competition supporting six sports.

Puggy Blackmon continued elevating the golf program. Charlie Yates and Charlie Brown, leaders of the newly-formed Tee Club, aided in providing extra funds to make golf a revenue sponsoring sport. Jim Dellinger, another strong supporter, provided funding for the Dellinger Golf Center, a meeting and relaxing area for the golf team located under the East Stands of the stadium at Grant Field. Puggy, another entrepreneur, had been highly successful in locating several golf courses around the metro area. East Lake was considered home base, but the golf team enjoyed playing on many of the elite Atlanta-area courses. As director of athletics at UNC, I had the responsibility of a campus golf course where the UNC team practiced. This was a plus — and a minus. Having a facility close by was helpful, but being limited to one course was a negative. Competitive tournaments required practice on a variety of courses, and having the opportunity to practice on several types gave a team an advantage. At the time, this philosophy was winning the recruiting wars in golf.

We were making headway with our facilities. Football was much improved but would need major renovations in the future. Alexander Memorial Coliseum, the basketball arena, had also improved. Baseball now had a class facility, and our track was state of the art. As we added women's fast pitch softball, it would be necessary to shift around campus because of the lack of space. Eventually, we secured a place near the Atlantic Steel property off Fourteenth Street for a new facility.

Tennis presented a next step for both men and women. In my first year, six courts joined the corner of Tenth and Fowler streets across from the coliseum. An attractive small stadium built at one end memorialized Earl Bortell, former Georgia Tech professor and tennis coach from 1934 to 1962. As I explored a potential sponsor's interest in building a tennis center, I met Albert "Bud" Parker, former tennis team captain in 1958. He and his brother William Parker, an Emory alumnus and chairman of the Campbell Foundation, provided funding for the director of athletics office in the new Arthur

B. Edge Jr. Intercollegiate Athletic Center, in memory of their late father, William A. Parker.

The tennis committee, nicknamed the "Racket Club," was no sooner assembled than funds started arriving at a rapid pace. Coach Gary Groslimond busily worked at putting together a staff and recruiting on a national level. In each sport, we developed a committee by contacting former letterman. While this strategy worked well for men's sports, it did not succeed for women's because Georgia Tech's varsity women's program had barely been started. The women's committees successfully "piggy-backed" on sports also offered for men's teams, including basketball, track, and tennis.

Our former tennis lettermen included two giants in the business world. Nelson Abell, founder and CEO of Abell Corporation in Monroe, Louisiana, and William "Bill" Moore of San Francisco, California. Little did we know at the time that these two gentlemen would make a huge impact on Georgia Institute of Technology's future success. Later, Nelson Abell made several significant gifts to the institute as a whole instead of just the tennis team and the sport facility.

The plans that developed specified resurfacing and building twelve high-tech tennis courts, a stadium for the upper six (which were reserved for tournament play), an adjacent indoor facility, tennis shop, and a locker room to bring our tennis program up to collegiate competition for nationally ranked positioning. The financial aspect, as usual, remained to be solved. Bud Parker visited with Bill Moore in California. I quickly realized that Bill was perhaps the institution's most successful alumnus. His story of founding and becoming chairman of the board of Kelly-Moore Paint Company in San Carlos, California, inspires any audience.

Captain of the Georgia Tech 1938 SEC championship tennis team, Bill Moore never lost a match and was an All-Southeastern Conference pick. During that period, NCAA tennis did not recognize an All-American team, but he was a true All-American in any collegiate circle. Mr. Moore agreed to provide the funding to build the indoor tennis center, making possible a class facility. He not only financed the facility but set up a matching gift program to endow the men's's tennis scholarship program in honor of Albert "Bud" Parker for his work in leading this group. With the completion of the Bill Moore Tennis Center and progress being made to make all varsity sports competitive, I faced the time for addressing remaining critical areas.

Other sports lacked the potential donors who could be drawn to official teams, leaving men's swimming, wrestling, and gymnastics without sponsors to provide funding. ACC rules setting football, basketball, baseball, track, golf, and tennis as the criteria for conference membership forced Georgia Tech to emphasize fundraising to develop those seven men's sports above all others, and Title IX and women's NCAA sports also limited what could be done for club players. Amazing progress had been made in supporting core sports, but less for the others. The looming issue ahead, however, involved finding ways to meet Georgia Tech's rigorous academic standards.

MIT, Carnegie Melon, and Cal Tech were all academic counterparts of Georgia Tech, but those schools conspicuously stayed out of the sporting arena that the Yellow Jackets dared to enter. Georgia Tech represented the only technological school attempting to compete in NCAA Division 1-A sports. With the university's long and famous athletic tradition, alumni eagerly followed their home team's progress and strongly supported playing at the NCAA Division I-A level. It also was completely clear to us that the faculty and alumni would never consider lowering academic standards on the way to recruiting competitive players. Proud that they had survived the academic regimen of their own programs to earn a Georgia Tech degree, alumni insisted that the standards they had met remain high.

Each year freshmen entering Tech are instructed during orientation meetings to look to the person on their right, then the one on their left. "Only one will make it," advised group leaders, emphasizing the academic discipline necessary for earning the right to wear a Georgia Tech class ring. When I arrived to become athletic director, the student body graduation rate was 33 percent — exactly what orientation leaders warned.

And yet the limited curriculum of the university pared down the types of courses and majors that athletes could select. Engineering, science, management, and architecture formed the heart of the course offerings. All students needed at least five units of science and math, including calculus, as a minimum for graduating, even with the least technical major possible. Without "Mickey Mouse" courses to make up hours or provide relief from the grinding course work, athletes with demanding practice and game schedules faced a true test of mind and body.

The Scholastic Aptitude Test scores of entering freshmen continued to rise, pushing the admission bar higher for athlete and non-athlete alike. Yet it was my job to make sure athletes got in and

stayed for this excellent education. When it became common knowledge that a new admission requirement would be put into place, I
began hearing naysayers once again urging, "It can't be done at
Georgia Tech." Somehow we had to turn that negative belief into a
positive approach, finding an opportunity in the situation.

Georgia Tech undoubtedly boasted the toughest academic program of any major Division I-A school in the country. In meetings
with coaches, various groups, faculty members, President Pettit, and
particularly with Frank Roper, admissions officer and registrar, it
became clear that we had to develop a plan of action. First, we needed to raise our recruiting sights to the national level. The state of
Georgia ranked forty-seventh in the nation in SAT scores. We had to
be willing to travel distances and widen our pool to acquire recruits
to meet the standards. This would cost more, soaking up the existing recruiting budgets and forcing them to grow. Second, we had to
keep to a minimum the number of risky athletes we pursued.

This formula proved successful — and not following it meant
disaster, with big problems and losing seasons. Interestingly enough,
we found that our recruiting goals correlated directly with a student
athlete's character. Athletes with higher academic backgrounds
adjusted better, became more skilled athletes, and proved to be winners. Academically risky students, who perhaps had more talent,
also had more trouble adjusting to the discipline of college sports
and academics.

We added a third emphasis to cement the first two goals: an
aggressive tutorial program to give students the best opportunity for
reinforcing their class learning and encouraging academic success.
We knew this would be expensive and require space for creating an
academic center in the athletic department. George Slayton, the lone
academic supervisor, occupied a small office in the old Heisman
gym. He scarcely had any equipment or space, but he had a vision
and a plan, which was much more important.

George hired tutors from young faculty and graduate students to
help the athletes retain and reinforce what they learned by attending
classes. Athletes had to meet tutors on the university campus to use
these services. The problems of matching tutors, athletes, and subjects
presented one difficulty, and when athletes did not keep their appoint-
ments that created another. George suggested another plan to me.

The new Arthur B. Edge Jr. Intercollegiate Center stood completed,
with several levels containing athletic facilities. A football locker room,

sports medicine area, and rooms for equipment, laundry, and rehab were tucked into the ground floor, and the first floor housed the Alexander-Tharpe Fund, sports information, a ticket office, accounting operations, administrative offices, and meeting rooms. The second floor's space included the dining room, football offices, and meeting rooms, while the last level contained coaches' offices for basketball, track, baseball, golf, tennis, volleyball, and softball as well as a chapel. A large unfinished section had been reserved for future expansion. George had his eye on claiming the remaining portion.

An academic center built in that area would provide a place for a study program, tutorial sessions, and a computer room, all in a central location. If well supervised, the center could be a productive component of the academic program as well as a positive recruiting tool, explained George.

He was right, of course. The unfinished space would be perfect for the academic center. The only problem was simple: how to pay for it.

Jack Thompson's A-T Fund, that was how. With 61 Yellow Jacket Clubs, the interest in his venture grew rapidly. Membership fees advanced from a $100 minimum to $500. They doubled to $1,000, jumped to $5,000, and then reached $10,000. Interest in his program soared, with a plan organized to offer life memberships for $100,000. The last goal found many skeptics who could not believe we would ever get the highest level off the ground.

Drew Hearn, an avid Georgia Tech supporter for many years from Charlotte, North Carolina, took up the challenge, becoming the first life member. Fees for the life category could be used for special projects because they did not go into the annual scholarship budget. After consulting with Drew, we agreed that his gift would initiate funding for the new academic center, to be named in memory of his father. The Andrew Hearn Sr. Academic Center comprised an attractive complex and a showplace in one, catching the attention of those of us who used it every day as well as those just visiting. Prospective student-athletes and their parents especially came away from a tour of the center impressed by the university's commitment to academic excellence.

Even better, our athletes' grade point averages improved considerably, just as George Slayton had predicted. Within a few years, we raised the graduation rate of athletes from 38 percent to over 70 percent — much higher than that of the student body. Making the

NCAA Honor Roll, having coaches in place, bringing the facilities to a competitive level, and with an administrative staff functioning very effectively, we found national recruiting easier and paying off more often.

Ticket sales improved tremendously. Basketball season sell-outs became common. And our student-athletes were taking a Georgia Tech degree with them when they entered the world after college sports. We had turned negatives into positives.

Although academic standards were tough, the pay-off was graduation day. Our graduates received top job offers. Georgia Tech ranked among the best schools in Division I-A, and our graduates were wanted on the job market. They knew how to work. They were smart. They became successful in the "real" world.

We followed up on graduates with surveys that showed athletic experiences at Georgia Tech had produced many pluses. Student athletes learned the transferable life lessons of self-confidence, persistence, and a winning spirit through sports and by working toward their Georgia Tech degrees. Even above those two programs, another course of learning set Georgia Tech athletes apart from those of other institutions, providing a base for building success in all areas of life. That third course was the Student-Athlete Total Person Program.

The first female coach in Georgia Tech's history and a woman who rose to be senior associate athletic director at the university before being drawn away to become associate commissioner of the ACC, Bernadette McGlade knows more about the Student-Athlete Total Person Program than any other person. In Appendix B, Bernadette outlines the concept in detail, sharing her knowledge and insight about this important program.

The five-year plan was an overwhelming success. Coming from the bottom of the league to reach the top in such a short time required — and produced — startling accomplishments. And it had been completed in 1985, exactly 100 years after Georgia Tech's founding, adding cheers to the centennial celebrations. The football team had defeated arch rival University of Georgia for two straight years, the team scored a victory over Michigan State in the All-American Bowl in Birmingham, Alabama, and Bill Curry was Coach of the Year. Basketball won its first ACC championship with Mark Price and John Salley, and moved on to the NCAA Final Eight. Bobby Cremins was Coach of the Year. Baseball won its first ACC championship and entered the NCAA playoffs. Jim Morris was Coach of the Year. Golf won the ACC championship with Puggy Blackmon being Coach of the Year. Track produced several ACC and NCAA individual champions, with Buddy Fowlkes Coach of the Year. In tennis, Brian Shelton and Kenny Thorne won individual ACC championships, and Gary Goslimond was Coach of the Year. As it turned out, 1985 was recognized as the best total sports year in Georgia Tech's 100-year history. The six sports required by the ACC had followed the plan to the top of the ladder — a wonderful tribute to those who had paid the price to make this leap of success possible. Players, coaches, staff, and faithful alumni and friends had brought Georgia Tech back to respectability. Erskine Love, chair of the centennial campaign to raise more than $200 million for the school, told me that our success contributed to that of the campaign.

The jokes and sneering had subsided. Georgia Tech fans were coming out of the woodwork. The city of Atlanta was bubbling over with pride in our success. Georgia Tech felt good about its new life. Funding was flowing into the institution. Our graduation rates came to pass even 80 percent. The Alexander-Tharpe Fund approached $4 million, and the Athletic Association budget had reached $10 million with a $2 million reserve. With facilities competitive with our opponents and championship trophies lining up inside the athletic center, it was time to plan the next five years. Could we stay on top? Could I provide the leadership? Were we ready to move into the second phase of the 1980s? While the word "I" surfaces inevitably in telling a story from one person's point of view, the real story involves more people than can be counted. I can't take credit for this success story; it was a team effort. Everyone who played a part in the program made a difference, making the vision we shared a reality.

CHAPTER FOUR

THE SECOND FIVE-YEAR PLAN (1986-1990): SEEKING NATIONAL RECOGNITION!

Ending the first five years as the best sports year in Georgia Tech's history was exhilarating. The feeling wouldn't last forever without hard work, though, so it was time to plan the next five years and begin driving toward making that project just as successful.

In seeking national recognition, it was important that I again turn to the Attitude Technique Philosophy. First and foremost, there must be a dream. Dreams crystallize into reality when you apply the "Attitude Technique" formula. The overpowering idea or ideas you hold in your mind about the type of program you want to lead is the dream that will shape the future of your program. We knew what kind of program we wanted. Our goal was clear.

Keep in mind that I classify goals into four categories: ultimate, long-range, intermediate and immediate. The ultimate goal is the highest of all. This is probably an intangible but nevertheless a professional goal for an organization. The long-range goal represents several years and can be either tangible or intangible. Clearly, our goal of national recognition, with a five-year plan to reach it, is a good example of a long-range goal. The intermediate goal is probably a tangible attainment that can be accomplished in less than one year. Immediate goals are generally tangible accomplishments

reflecting something needed or wanted now, today, next month, or
before the year is up.

For goals in each category there must be a plan of action con-
sisting of seven steps to follow: 1) commitment, 2) deadline, 3)
ingredients, 4) giving something in return, 5) visualization, 6) belief,
and 7) expectancy.

Goal-achieving breeds confidence within the organization.
Confidence is built upon an experience of success. It is literally true
that success breeds success. Even a small success can be used as a
stepping stone to a greater one.

One thing is certain: leadership qualities necessary to achieve set
goals are in great demand. You will be in demand if you can bring
people together for a common purpose. You can do that if you follow the goals program.

The successful manager has the ability to control action, reaction, and inaction. A leader acts instead of reacting. This is a vital
personality trait in becoming a good manager. How fast can you
analyze a situation, make a decision and correct it, and then look to
the future without continuing to dwell on the past problem? What
is your recovery time?

A leader must get the job done through people. Therefore, I
believe that the greatest managerial skill attainable is that of being
able to gather good people. This means that you should not be looking for credit for getting the job done. Give the credit to those who
work for you. There will be enough for you and for them. And
remember one other thing, ethics and progress are entirely compatible. Organizations have succeeded with no regard for ethics or personal values, but that is the exception, not the rule. Never break a
rule, no matter how small. Then, when the victory comes, it will be
totally satisfying. This is the only true success we enjoy. Hiring quality personnel in the beginning can lead to this positive result. The
highlights of Georgia Tech history have been a matter of quality
people with absolute integrity.

When making decisions, be sure to get all the facts. Remember,
however, that the leader must make the ultimate decision. The person who has the responsibility for the consequences should make the
decision. Group decisions have many pitfalls. Decisions can be
spread too thin. Who "faces the music" if things go wrong?
Remember, you can delegate authority, but you cannot delegate
responsibility.

Whether in terms of goal-setting or any other part of an operation, you must realize one thing. You will always have problems. If you run out of problems, you have set your goals too low. It gets back to our attitude. Is yours positive or negative? I encourage my staff members to change the word "problem" to "opportunity." As one of my assistants said recently, "Coach, I had a lot of opportunities today." That brought some laughter, which made me realize that the change of semantics, from problem to opportunity, generated a positive reaction.

Performance is knowledge: knowing what to do and how to do it. Performance requires action: taking the first step and doing it enthusiastically as if it were impossible to fail. You must expect your staff members to make a contribution to their duties and assignments. You must expect ideas to turn into action.

Any important ideas concerning the operation should be implemented in three simple steps. First, write out the procedure. Second, think of ways things can be done, instead of ways they cannot be done. Third, be positive about your work. A positive attitude leads to success. Negative thoughts, conversations, or attitudes lead directly to failure.

* * * *

I would need to bear these "Attitude Technique" lessons in mind as we worked to bring our second five-year plan to successful fruition. The dramatic 9-2-1 season and All-American Bowl victory over Michigan State in 1985 signaled a curious plateau in the path toward our vision of national rankings.

Our first bowl win since 1972, the victory brought back to mind Doug Weaver. He was the man I had replaced in 1980; in 1985, he served as athletic director for our bowl opponent. A former football coach and outstanding athlete from Michigan State University, Doug had returned to his alma mater to direct the sports program. He also served on the NCAA Football Playing Rules Committee, of which I was chair. Doug brought a legal background to the committee's work that we called upon repeatedly in supplying the language for the new rules the committee enacted. Doug had hired Bill Curry before he departed for Michigan State.

In 1986, as we headed into our final regular season game with Wake Forest, we anticipated signing a contract with the Blue Bonnet Bowl in Houston, Texas. Coach Al Groh of Wake Forest, former assistant coach at University of North Carolina under Bill Dooley during my directorship, had disciplined nine of his starters for the game. They would not play. Georgia Tech was highly favored, but lady luck was not on our side that day. A close loss to Wake Forest knocked us out of the bowl picture. We had lost a number of seniors from the 1985 squad, and 1986 was a rebuilding year. Nevertheless, the future looked bright.

As Bobby Cremins was gearing the basketball team to repeat as Atlantic Coast Conference champions, Phyllis and I were headed for a vacation on Marco Island, Florida. We had stopped over in Gainesville, Florida, for the night, and early in the morning before we departed for the last leg of our trip to Marco Island, I received a telephone call from Bill Curry. His message came through clear and concise. "I have accepted the head job at Alabama," he said. The University of Alabama was a football mecca. Paul "Bear" Bryant, the winningest football coach in NCAA Division I-A history, had retired and been replaced by one of his former players, Ray Perkins. After a four-year stint, Ray was moving to Tampa, back to the NFL. Ray and Bill were teammates with the Super Bowl champion Baltimore Colts.

Fulfilling a request to speak to a Fellowship of Christian Athletes conference in Miami prior to the Super Bowl game to be played at the Orange Bowl the next day, I contemplated whether to stay over for the game. The match-up between the Baltimore Colts and the Dallas Cowboys had been hyped, but my own interest was already high. Jim O'Brien, rookie wide receiver and placekicker for the Colts, sent me tickets. Jim had played for me at the University of Cincinnati. Leading the nation in scoring with his touchdown pass receptions from quarterback Greg Cook and his placekicking chores piling up extra digits from points after or field goals, he was an exciting player to watch. On the FCA program was Bill Glass, a former great for Paul Brown's and Blanton Collier's world champion Cleveland Browns. Bill and I discussed the possibility of taking in the game and decided to sit together in the stadium the next day.

It was a close game, and Tom Landry's Cowboys led late in the fourth quarter. Baltimore moved the ball into field goal range, however, and called a time out with six seconds to play. Jim O'Brien trotted on the field. As he lined up for the kick, Dallas called two consecutive time outs. During the break, I related to Bill Glass how just a year ago I was coaching the University of Cincinnati in a similar situation in our final game of the season against Miami of Ohio. With three seconds left to play, Jim O'Brien kicked the winning field goal to defeat Miami. Now he was put into a parallel situation, but this time for the championship of the world. Jim made the field goal, giving the Colts the Super Bowl victory. Bill Curry, quarterback Johnny Unitas, and wide received Ray Perkins shared the victory handshake with us after the game.

With Ray returning to the NFL, Bill Curry seemed a great choice for the Tide. He represented all that is good in intercollegiate athletics. He would not bend a rule, no matter how small. He stepped into one of the premier coaching jobs in the profession. Bear Bryant put Alabama on the map with his national championships and numerous consecutive bowl appearances.

I first met Coach Bear Bryant in 1959 at the Southeastern Football Clinic in Hollywood, Florida. Tony Leone, a promoter from Miami, was putting on one of the largest football clinics ever staged. Top collegiate and professional coaches headed a list that also included two high school coaches: Dave Hart Sr. from Johnstown, Pennsylvania, and myself from Highlands High School in Fort Thomas, Kentucky. I was scheduled to lecture just prior to Coach Bryant. As I was leaving the stage, Coach Bryant stopped me. "Homer, wait until I finish. I want to talk to you." To say I was nervous would be an understatement.

Why did Coach Bryant want to see me? After his lecture, we met in his room at the Diplomat Hotel, where he asked if I would be interested in a job at Alabama. Before I could respond, he invited me to stop on my way back to Kentucky to spend a few days at his summer home on Lake Marion in Alabama. The prospect made me, a young high school coach, ecstatic.

I accepted his hospitality and stopped by his lake home. On his screened-in porch he had installed a large chalkboard where he conducted his own clinic with two assistants, Howard Schnellenberger and Charlie Bradshaw. He showed me the chalk and instructed me to diagram my offensive thinking about the triple option using the formation I called the short "T." I illustrated the short "T" by moving a blocking back in the "T" formation into the space between the offensive guard and tackle, just a yard off the line of scrimmage. This offensive pattern produced national scoring records on the high school level.

After a few relaxing days as Coach Bryant's guest, we drove into Tuscaloosa to his office at the university where he introduced

*me to members of his staff. As we talked, I mentioned a manuscript
about the short "T" concept that I was writing. To my surprise he
invited me to stay at his lake home that summer to work on the
book. This was too much for me to believe! I was awed to even be
in his presence, much less to spend leisure time, days on end, with
him. It was almost overpowering, and I forced myself to get away
to clear my thoughts.*

*Returning home, I wrote Coach Bryant a letter thanking him for
his many kindnesses but letting him know that I didn't feel I could
leave my high school team just then. Each year until his death,
Coach Bryant called to continue our relationship. In 1974, he
arranged to fly me to Tuscaloosa in a private jet to lecture to his
entire staff about the triple option. When I got home from the clinic, I found a truck pulling up in our driveway with an extravagant
gift from the coach: boxes of steak, sausage, bacon, and other vari-
eties of meat, which he extended as his own thank you.*

Bill Curry departed immediately for Alabama. We had to move
just as quickly to find a new football coach, so Phyllis and I loaded
up our automobile after Bill's call, preparing for the four-hour drive
to Marco Island. I asked Phyllis to drive while I took a legal pad out
of my briefcase to jot down potential prospects. My Boy Scout training came in handy: I always kept a short list of coaches to consider
in the event such an emergency occurred. As I scribbled names into
separate categories, I thought of a coach I had always admired:
Bobby Ross at the University of Maryland.

Bobby had produced three ACC championships in five years, taking his team to bowl after bowl. He had just left Maryland for a job
with the Buffalo Bills of the National Football League. Was I too late?
Where was Bobby Ross now? We had to stop to find a telephone.

Phyllis pulled off I-75, and I dialed Greensboro, North
Carolina, to talk with ACC Commissioner Bob James. Would he
be there to answer the phone? Commissioners travel frequently to
national meetings, so I held my breath, waiting to see if he would
be home. Luckily, he answered.

"Bob, Bill Curry is on his way to Alabama. Where is Bobby
Ross?" I asked. Bob replied that the coach would report to Buffalo
on Monday. Our phone call was on Saturday. I had to work fast.

But first I had to be sure of Bobby Ross. I liked him as a coach,
a person, and a friend. Were there any skeletons in his closet,
though? Absolutely not, Bob James assured me, calling Bobby as

clean as Mr. Clean himself. "He has absolute integrity — the best coach I have ever worked with," he added.

What concerned me was that Bobby had chased an official after his game with North Carolina that year, earning a penalty his team had to face the next game. Bobby had been restricted to the press box and not allowed to coach his team from the sidelines. Bob James explained that the situation was more complex than it seemed. The scoreboard indicated that North Carolina had used all of its timeouts when the team actually had one remaining. The referee failed to notify Coach Ross, and as the game clock wound down North Carolina called its final time out, lined up, and kicked the winning field goal. All Bobby had wanted was an explanation, but because the dispute had been shown on national television, the conference decided to take swift action. As commissioner of the ACC, Bob James had to support the punishment despite his personal respect for Bobby. The coach was one of the nation's finest at the college level, and James hated losing him from the conference to the NFL.

Trucks roared by as we conversed by phone next to the interstate, making the conversation difficult but necessary business. I thanked Bob and dialed Bobby Ross' home in College Park, Maryland. Over the sound of traffic, I explained to his wife, Alice, why I was calling. She encouraged me to call back that evening. I sensed that perhaps Alice was not excited about moving to Buffalo.

After the call, Phyllis drove us on to Marco Island where people had left messages already about the vacancy. David Davidson, a writer for the *Atlanta Journal-Constitution*, always had a knack for tracking me down. This was big news . . . Bill Curry in Alabama. It had already leaked, and now sportswriters and newscasters were trying every angle for getting more of the story. Before I could put a call in to Bobby Ross, the phone rang, and fortunately, I heard the voice of John McKenna, retired associate athletic director at Georgia Tech.

I'd asked John to serve as a personal consultant to me at Georgia Tech because he possessed a wealth of knowledge about intercollegiate athletics and was a good source of intelligent information. He had also helped work our football schedule into the Atlantic Coast Conference.

Coach McKenna asked me if I'd thought about Bobby Ross. It was remarkable that Bobby was on his mind, too. I learned that the coincidence wasn't so surprising, though. Bobby had been John's quarterback at Virginia Military Institute in the 1960s and returned to coach the freshman team. John had directly influenced Bobby's career, and now John recommended his protégé as the right man for the position at Georgia Tech.

At last I reached Bobby. We discussed the possibilities of his interest in Georgia Tech, but he explained the complications. He had already signed a contract with Buffalo and was scheduled to report by Monday at noon for the last month of 1986. We had fewer than 30 hours to figure out a solution. Bobby asked me to call Marv Levy, Buffalo's head coach.

Marv Levy was in California, and I would have to track him down. While coaching at Cincinnati for the Bengals, my team had played Kansas City, coached at the time by Marv Levy and his assistant, Bobby Ross. Bobby left Kansas City for the head job at the University of Maryland, replacing Jerry Claiborne, who wanted to return to his alma mater, the University of Kentucky. He had played at Kentucky under Coach Paul "Bear" Bryant in the late 1940s. Coaching circles were just that — interwoven patterns where former players and present coaches came around to old places, filling new positions.

Reaching Coach Levy, I explained the situation with Bobby Ross and asked permission to talk to Bobby about the position at Georgia Tech. Always the gentleman, Marv gave permission immediately. Relieved, I called Bobby back, and we discussed the particulars surrounding the job and its future. Bobby had turned down head coaching positions at Purdue and the University of California at Berkeley after leaving Maryland, accepting a job working with his former Kansas City coach. We discussed details thoroughly and agreed to talk again on Sunday.

What if Bobby Ross didn't work out? I had to consider others for the job. My short list included three others I was prepared to pursue. Replacing the head coach was just the first part of my task, and I had to move quickly on another. Bill Curry was taking his entire staff to Alabama, including our head trainer, Bill McDonald. Bill was one of the finest trainers any college might hope to find, and he served all of Georgia Tech's sports programs. Losing him affected athletes across the board. We had to find another trainer, and fast. Losing a head coach sets off a chain reaction, with whole circles of people moving from one school to another. Like when Ray Perkins went to Tampa to replace Leeman Bennett. . . .

Leeman Bennett, former coach of the Atlanta Falcons in the NFL, had coordinated offense at the University of Cincinnati for me in the late 1960s. Ray Perkins replaced Leeman at Tampa Bay, bringing his own trainer and putting out of a job the earlier trainer, Jay Shoop . . . who was now available! I put a call in to Warren Morris, trainer at the University of Georgia who also served as chairman of the Trainer's Association of the United States of America. As chair of the NCAA Rules Committee, I received Morris's report every year about the injury situation in collegiate sports. He advised national organizations about his profession. But who could he recommend to replace someone with Bill McDonald's skill and knowledge?

Jay Shoop, it turned out. Without hesitating, he named the suddenly unemployed and eminently hireable Jay Shoop. I put in a call to Leeman Bennett, asking my good friend about the trainer. Leeman strongly endorsed the selection. Jay had a good background and had gained experience working with the Falcons, which was why Leeman had taken him to Tampa Bay. I called Jay in Tampa Bay, which was only a short distance from Marco Island. He agreed to drive over to meet me, and he impressed me immediately. I hired him on the spot.

Jay turned out to be one of the top prizes for Georgia Tech, once again confirming those instinctive decisions. He eventually became associate athletic director for sports medicine and played an important role in shaping the medical team during the 1996 Summer Olympics, which were held in Atlanta at Georgia Tech's Olympic Village.

During the busy Centennial Capital Campaign, the less noticed exchange of trainers accompanied the much publicized change of head football coaches. Another major passage loomed on the horizon for Georgia Tech. With President Pettit's death, the university faced a transition. In 1986 Henry Bourne served as interim president until the Board of Regents selected a new head for the institution.

Dr. Bourne and the Athletic Board of Trustees were faced with hiring the new coach in the midst of a critical fundraising effort and personnel search. I'd kept President Bourne informed, along with my reports to Bill Sangster, faculty chairman of the Athletic Board. Before Bobby and I could talk the next day, I received a call from Marv Levy telling me apologetically that I would have to talk with the Bills' general manager and president, George Wilson, about my negotiations with Bobby. That conversation with Wilson carried a direct threat to Bobby Ross: if Bobby talked to me, he could forget the Buffalo Bills.

Bobby and I made contact, talking off and on during the day in between the inquiries of sportswriters doing their best to untangle the secrecy. As far as I know today, only those in the innermost circle knew I continued talking to Bobby after the ultimatum. By late Sunday evening, Bobby agreed to come to Georgia Tech if I could assure him he had the job.

Of course, responsibility for hiring the next coach lay with the Georgia Tech Athletic Association Board of Trustees. I couldn't guarantee anything until their vote. I assured Bobby that I would recommend him to the board, and that I was sure that they would go along with my recommendation. But Bobby wasn't as sure. If something went wrong, he would be out of a job in Buffalo, too. I finally told him that if the board turned down my recommendation we would both be looking for a job. He seemed unappreciative of the humor, but agreed to meet me the next morning in Atlanta.

Calling Dr. Bourne, I asked for a special session on Monday, December 8, at 4 p.m. My next call went to Bill Sangster, requesting that he talk with other members of the board. Bill realized what a treasure Bobby Ross represented and supported my decision to present him to the board. Two more calls followed: Bobby Dodd and Bobby Cremins. Both men enthusiastically approved of the choice.

Early Monday morning, our potential head coach boarded a flight from Washington, D.C., to Atlanta. Phyllis drove me to Ft. Myers, Fla., so I could catch a flight home. It was a short vacation. Bobby Ross and I met at the Atlanta airport and drove together to the president's home on Tenth Street, where he could hide out until we could move the board forward.

Word leaked out of Buffalo that Bobby was going to Georgia Tech, producing a media onslaught. I hurriedly got ready for the board meeting and set up a press conference for 7 p.m. in case our project proceeded as planned. The board met that afternoon in the downstairs of the president's home for one hour, ending with a unanimous vote to offer Bobby Ross the head football position at Georgia Tech.

The eighth football coach in Georgia Tech's history was escorted into the conference room and introduced to the board that had approved his selection. After cordial formalities, we whisked him away to the press conference to meet the media and Georgia Tech faithful on hand. Famed *Atlanta Journal* sports editor Furman Bisher noted the resemblance between Bobby Ross and Knute Rockne. Both had one thing in common, wrote the editor. They both knew how to win. Today Furman remains one of the top sports-writers of our time – a highly respected columnist and leader of many activities in and around Atlanta. I enjoy reading Furman's columns filed from different parts of the world. He must be the most traveled sports columnist ever!

As athletic director, I could turn the football program over to Bobby with confidence. Finding Bobby signaled the time for me to address other areas of concern for the Athletic Association.

I always kept with me a long list of items that fell under my purview – from individual sports programs, to facilities, to depart-ments and programs, even to off-campus duties like NCAA-wide organizations to which I belonged. Of course, unlooked-for items surfaced regularly, needing immediate attention.

The state of intercollegiate athletics has been, and will always be, concerned with making certain we are doing the right things. Are we recruiting fairly? Are we making sure these young people are stu-dents as well as athletes? Are we in control of our programs? So many avenues present themselves, leading away from those right decisions — professional sports agents, gambling possibilities, or other distractions that a young amateur athlete faces almost daily. Over and above the academic load, the time spent in practice, train-ing, contests, and travel stretches a student. I always believed the Total Person Program was the answer to these questions. It turned out to be a positive approach.

We were governed by the Atlantic Coast Conference and National Collegiate Athletic Association. These bodies were com-prised of the member schools within them. The NCAA, like any large organization, had what seemed like endless pages of legislation and interpretations to help staff implement its regulations. At times, the federal government became involved.

During President Ford's term, the gender equity issue was before Congress. While I was director at the University of North Carolina, I was called as a consultant to Congress. It was an interesting expe-rience, and one that created other opportunities through the years.

During the 1983 ACC basketball tournament in Greensboro, North Carolina, I sat in a hotel room and visited with Chuck Neinas, executive director of the College Football Association. The CFA included about 60 of the top universities engaged in NCAA Division I-A football. The Big Ten and the Pacific Eight were not members of the group. We discussed the state of affairs of intercol-legiate athletics, particularly the academic side. The graduation rate was abnormally low for most of the institutions in NCAA Division I-A. I related my experience in the NFL — so many players were entering professional sports after four years in college without degrees and, more important, also lacking evidence of having received a quality education. Only a few of those athletes ever made the professional teams. The majority failed to make the grade and ended up without a professional contract or a decent education.

Chuck Neinas took action after our discussion. Dr. Fred Davidson, president of the University of Georgia, was president of the CFA at the time. He put together a group of presidents, coaches, and athletic directors, and we met at Sapelo Island, Georgia, to lay out a plan of action. In order to qualify to enroll at an institution, we recommended that incoming student-athletes have a minimum score on the Scholastic Aptitude Test (SAT) and a minimum 2.0 grade point average in college preparatory course core subjects. This standard changed the thinking of all colleges in recruiting and graduating their student-athletes.

At one point later on, Congress investigated suggestions from the Internal Revenue Service regarding the charitable status of athletic programs. Gene Corrigan of Notre Dame, Frank Broyles of Arkansas, Joe Paterno of Penn State, and I made the trip to Washington, D.C., to confer with congressmen about the potential bill that could send all schools scrambling for funds. Our meeting was effective, and fortunately the bill never materialized.

As we entered the fall of 1987, the Georgia Board of Regents finalized the search for the institute's new president. John Patrick Crecine accepted the post, making him the ninth president of the Georgia Institute of Technology. In our first meeting he showed a clear interest in athletics.

Before he arrived, I received a long, detailed letter from a former University of Georgia football star. By that time working as a successful young lawyer in Atlanta, Billy Payne described his vision of bringing to Atlanta the world's largest sports event — the Summer Olympics. He wanted to confer with me, and Kim King arranged the introduction. Billy wanted not only to bring the Olympics to Atlanta but to use Georgia Tech for the Olympic Village. Like most things Billy Payne does, his proposal showed planning, vision, and promise. And he was personally convincing.

President Crecine walked into his new office on September 1, 1987. For his first day on the job, I had scheduled a meeting with President Crecine and Billy to discuss Georgia Tech's Olympic future. Billy brought several charts to display the project in the president's office on campus, and the concept of Atlanta serving as host city for the Olympics was electrifying. As he moved on to present the village plan with Georgia Tech as the proposed site, Pat Crecine became engaged with the idea. An Olympic enthusiast and fellow visionary, President Crecine joined the growing network of support for an Atlanta bid. His decision to allow the campus to play a central role in Olympic life placed Georgia Tech on center stage for the world from that day until the games ended July 19, 1996.

If I'd ever asked what could top the success of rising from the bottom of the ACC to the top in the first five-year plan, I had my answer now. With the long-range goal of preparing Georgia Tech to host the Olympics, our next plan would be national recognition.

This would require, first, upgrading our Student-Athlete Total Person Program. We had made this our mission. To make the program completely prosperous, we had to convince everyone in the Georgia Tech community to believe in the program. We personally had to commit to emphasizing how important it was to develop young graduates who had just earned their degrees to thrive in the real world. The program taught life skills as a vital companion to sports participation. The ability of student athletes to flourish after leaving Georgia Tech was the yardstick that showed our program's true success.

Moving up into the national rankings could only happen with excellent coaching and successful recruiting. Added to that second task, a third of establishing and nurturing a support staff and administration dedicated to these purposes tied all three elements together. As always, adequate funding had to be found to provide the means for our goal to be reached.

Selecting Bobby Ross as head football coach elevated enthusiasm to a high level. Since 1980, we had doubled season ticket sales, and students had again begun filling the stadium. Our marketing approach had begun paying dividends. And the Alexander-Tharpe Fund made more financial support available each year.

The new coach's first game renewed fervor for the sport with a 51-12 win over the Citadel. The nationally-ranked North Carolina Tar Heels journeyed to Atlanta the next week, and having the league leader for competition brought out the Georgia Tech students for a showdown. In the fourth quarter with a 23-7 advantage, we were ready to score from one foot from the end zone. Instead of plunging into scoring territory, Georgia Tech fumbled, opening the way for

North Carolina to make a dramatic comeback and narrowly win the game. I often thought back to that moment and wondered what a victory would have meant to the rest of Georgia Tech's season. Instead of gaining momentum as might have happened, Georgia Tech's team stalled that season and the next, garnering only one Division I-A victory in the two seasons.

The stock market's "Black Monday" on October 19, 1987, triggered fears that the economy might not just idle but plunge. From Friday, October 16, the stock market fell 628 points. Some financial experts recalled the market crash of 1929 and warned investors to beware of their financial futures. Our own university's supporters expressed concerns over their ability to weather a financial disaster. Losing football seasons and cautious donor support would take a toll on the program.

To those of us old enough to remember the 1930s, Black Monday was a reminder of how much we take for granted these days, and of how quickly the many benefits we enjoy can be taken away. The Georgia Tech Athletic Association experienced two consecutive deficit years. Although Bobby Cremins was winning big time and the other sports took their share of victories, football and the down market knocked the athletic program to its knees. We could not lose sight of our mission, however. Developing young student-athletes for the future had to be our overriding concern. But without a winning football program, outside interest would wane and the financial means for the Total Person Program would dwindle.

Going into Bobby Ross's third season, we lost our first three games. I believed in Bobby. He and his capable staff were doing the right things. Only time would prove our faith in him right, but did we have enough time?

Ironically, Georgia Tech faced the coach's former university in the fourth game. Bobby Ross had taken the University of Maryland to many Atlanta Coast Conference championships and bowl victories. But for Georgia Tech, the game was a must win. The players met before the game, hit Maryland hard during the match, and scored a victory. The Georgia Tech squad grew up that season by taking charge. Using what they had learned from Coach Ross, the team reversed its momentum and finished the season 7-4, setting the stage for bigger things.

Now that each of our sports programs had come on line and begun achieving national ranking, I realized we had to form a solid marketing and promotional package for our program. Marketing represented a new challenge for the athletic programs. In the early years when I was director of athletics at UNC in the 1970s, we knew that revenue sources had to be created if the athletic programs were to survive. I sent my associate Bill Cobey on many fact-finding missions, including to the NFL. Through my personal contacts with the league, Bill visited and taped conversations of the NFL promotion departments. The NFL and other professional sports developed several revenue pockets to promote their sports, but colleges — required to carry multiple sports for conference membership — had no such institutional help. We needed our own methods of fundraising.

Jim Kehoe, athletic director at the University of Maryland, met with me several times to look into this issue. We both realized a person needed to be hired to direct such a program. Jim retained Russ Potts (later athletic director at Southern Methodist University), and at Georgia Tech I worked with Craig Stewart, who came to Atlanta from being assistant to UNC's Bob Savan. At Georgia Tech, we experimented with many marketing plans, knowing that finding a profitable program had to be found to ensure the success and survival of athletics.

Each of the 61 Yellow Jackets Clubs took on the responsibility to aid a local radio station and sponsor broadcasts of football, basketball, and baseball games. Charlie Smithgall III, president of WNCC, won the rights to broadcast our games, and we all pitched in to build a network of 60 to 80 stations across the state and surrounding areas. Kim King had a vested interest in the radio station. He continued as color analyst with Al Ciraldo announcing play-by-play for football. Coaches Bobby Ross, Bobby Cremins, and Jim Morris each produced segments featuring football, basketball, and baseball for the program.

Given my own involvement with radio shows through the years, I eventually settled on a pregame show with Kim King called "Quarterback's Corner." The network predicted good ratings with excellent revenue, but a problem with the station arose and its owners decided to put the station up for sale. With a long-term contract for the show signed, this placed the Athletic Association in a bind. The station would not sell without Georgia Tech property, so the Athletic Association voted to stick with WCNN. After the sale, the network deteriorated to the point that the Athletic Association tested legal remedies but eventually just had to wait until the contract expired in 1998 for the contract to be resolved.

Marketing is a tricky business, particularly in a community with professional sports. Promotions had to be initiated so we could compete against the draw of professional play. I hired Norman Arey to help organize the marketing program because he understood the media. As a feature writer for the *Atlanta Journal-Constitution* and national sports news writer, he combined newsroom experience with the business acumen gained from having his own marketing firm. He quickly organized our sports information department with Mike Finn at the head. Frank Beall brought in the advertisers, and Norman negotiated a huge sum for our radio rights. His contacts with the coaches' TV shows and "Sideline Sports" prospered. As Norman moved on to focus on his own company, another bright star developed. Kevin Bryant learned under Jack Thompson's tutelage, moving our marketing department into the corporate world. Good things were about to happen.

As the income situation began to stabilize, another long-settled predicament came back to life: payment for the Wardlaw Building. I met with President Crecine to work out a solution. We would give up two major gifts, a potentially lucrative land sale, and revenue from the Wardlaw executive suites to cover the Athletic Association's 40 percent. The only clinker was that the Georgia Tech Foundation Board requested up-front funds — before the land would be sold. Again, the Athletic Association's Financial Committee balked. Polly Poole, mediator for the negotiations, masterfully brought the two sides together in an eventful agreement that finally closed the deal. The Athletic Association signed on reluctantly, still not convinced the agreement represented its interests sufficiently. Regardless of the precise split in the final arrangements, approval provided closure and allowed the two groups to turn to other projects. In my opinion, neither side had a complete understanding of the other's perspective. The Wardlaw agreement was a hard lesson in cooperation, laying groundwork for the Athletic Association and the Georgia Tech Foundation to form a coalition to work more closely from the start in the next project that brought them together. Although there were misunderstandings between the Georgia Tech Foundation and the Georgia Tech Athletic Board in the early years, we ultimately became close partners in projects that benefited Georgia Tech and the campus in later years. I deeply appreciated the Foundation Board's extraordinary leadership: John Staton, Charlie Brown, Julian LeCraw, Buck Stith, John Weitnauer, Pete Cross, and many others.

As I look back to those years of the 1980s, the number of events astounds me. The program gained so much, and constant change characterized the period. Putting together the right coaches and proper staff always topped my list. My interest in student athletes was clear. They deserved nothing but the best possible education from Georgia Tech, benefiting from the top-rate academics. Sports would teach them many life lessons, but the specific life skills practiced in the Total Person Program would help them cope with the real world. And I insisted on that paramount goal. I wanted student athletes to hear people who were out in the professions and making strides in their careers. Seminars each Thursday were mandatory, bringing together for an all-too-brief 20 minutes student athletes, coaches, and staff. We listened to top statesmen, television personalities, enterprising entrepreneurs, presidents of companies, and leaders in the surrounding community tell their fascinating stories of challenges met and surpassed. These energizing sessions gave student athletes insights into setting their future goals.

We developed a student athlete advisory board where representatives from each of our 17 sports conferred. This group helped plan the sessions and brought to my attention the specific concerns of our athletes. At each sports year's end, we held a Yellow Jacket Annual Banquet. This family affair honored our student athletes, the top Yellow Jacket Clubs of the Alexander-Tharpe Fund, and others who excelled in their contributions to the program. Attendance grew from the sparse first year until with more than a thousand in attendance we had to find larger and larger spaces for the event. Eventually only the World Congress Center could accommodate the number who attended.

Despite this success, another sad event occurred during the second five years when our dear friend, Coach Bobby Dodd, passed away. Fortunately, before Coach Dodd's death Pat Crecine gained assistance from Chancellor Dean Propst and the Board of Regents to enable us to name the stadium at Grant Field after Georgia Tech's number-one legend. Bobby Dodd Jr. brought his father to my office where President Crecine and I had the privilege of informing him that the stadium in which he had coached — and won — so many games would be known as the Bobby Dodd Stadium at Historic Grant Field.

Like any athletic director, I had two jobs. With a full-time schedule on campus, I juggled my off-campus job of speaking to various groups and working with multiple conferences as best I could.

Alumni and Yellow Jacket clubs called for presentations and speeches, and being involved in national committees of the NCAA, ACC, and NACDA took up more time. Chairing several of those committees required advance preparation and constant traveling, taking me away from campus. On top of that, the NCAA Division I-A directors of athletics began a separate association. Serving as president of that group presented a special challenge. The operational funding necessary for an increasing number of sports, particularly in the wake of Title IX and the development of women's programs, required business skills and decisions beyond most directors' experience. In response, NACDA began a management institute to train people for the new problems of athletic administration.

The first management institute proved memorable. We invited four professors from a large Midwestern university to teach us how to be managers. Because of my background with Paul Meyer and the Success Motivation Institute, I had already attended several leader and management programs. The four professors talked to us in a language none of the directors completely understood, so I interpreted by putting their words into sports language. For the next management training, I was asked to lead the event, adding to my off-campus chores.

I needed to spend as much time on campus as possible, however. So much change was happening. We had to add more people to administer the programs because of our growth and to keep a close eye on each of the sports. Jim Murphy, an accountant with Peat, Marwick & Mitchell, came to us as chief financial officer, as well as treasurer of both the Athletic Association Board of Trustees and the Alexander-Tharpe Fund Board of Trustees. A graduate of Davidson College, Jim had also played football and baseball for his alma mater. He earned his masters degree in economics at Georgia Tech, then gained credentials as a certified public accountant. Lawton Hydrick, the young man who moved from graduate assistant coach to strength coach on his way to taking charge of all our facilities, had weathered the responsibilities thrust on him so early and done quite well.

Unfortunately, a situation in our men's tennis program in 1988 placed Georgia Tech in a very difficult situation. Honest mistakes made the program appear to have run aground in its management, making it necessary for Georgia Tech to change the program's leadership and place sanctions on its own program. Had we not taken swift action, the program may have been charged with a major violation that could have resulted in NCAA probational status. Georgia Tech had never been sanctioned by the NCAA in the university's long history, and I certainly didn't want the first time to be on my watch.

Jean Desdunes, an All-American tennis player from Clemson, took over the head men's tennis coaching position. We cut back all scholarships and began the program all over again, rejecting any right to recruit off campus for three years. The NCAA accepted our self-imposed penalties, keeping Georgia Tech's record clean. The program had finally earned a national ranking and an ACC championship, but the voluntary restrictions dashed hopes of immediately following up on those achievements. Brian Shelton and Kenny Thorne, two of the finest players in the country while playing for Georgia Tech, had begun preparing for their careers. I asked them to stay as student assistants to aid in the transitional period, and both agreed to serve in that capacity while finishing their degree work. The two went on tour later, with Brian playing at Wimbledon several times and winning key national championships. Kenny Thorne's consistent ability to win on tour propelled his own playing career, and Kenny eventually returned to Georgia Tech, later becoming director of the tennis program under Dave Braine.

We gradually moved toward our second five-year goal of national recognition. Baseball coach Jim Morris produced four ACC titles and took the team to seven straight NCAA playoffs. After consistently keeping his team in the top of the polls, he eventually led them to the number-one rank in the country. Jim achieved another honor with his selection as coach of the United States All-America team. He produced several All-Americans, including Kevin Brown.

Kevin Brown came to Georgia Tech on his own with the intention of being a student only. A baseball scout informed Coach Morris that he had seen this youngster in high school and that he deserved some attention. Jim invited Kevin to come by the baseball field and pitch batting practices. He accepted and after the student struck out a battery of hitters, Coach Morris realized he had a winner. And win he did — big time! Kevin went on to pitch for the Florida Marlins, taking the professional team to a World Series championship, and earning for himself one of the highest salaries paid to a major league baseball player.

Bobby Cremins' basketball program – with All-Americans Mark Price, John Salley, Dennis Scott, Kenny Anderson, and Brian Oliver – marched to six straight NCAA playoffs and at one point received a number-one ranking under Bobby's coaching.

Bernadette McGlade took over as coach of a women's basketball program at least 12 years behind those of other schools. Once she had solidified the program, I convinced her to move to the administrative side of athletics. In making the transition, she turned the reins over to her sister, Agnus Berenato, who had been assistant coach under Bernadette. Ida Neal, our first All-ACC player at Georgia Tech, became administrative assistant to Bernadette, who was placed in charge of our compliance program.

Our golf program achieved its own number-one ranking with four-year All-American David Duval leading the way to four ACC championships and seven consecutive NCAA playoffs. Women's fast-pitch softball joined the sports offerings, with Regina Tomasila as first coach. Herb McAuley oversaw changing swimming to a club sport because of safety problems with the Old Heisman Gym which made the pool unavailable. One of the great swimmers at Georgia Tech, Herb provided a reminder of better days for swimming, before the program dropped to a lower level. President Pat Crecine's enthusiasm for swimming eventually brought the sport back to varsity level, with Brad Leeman coaching.

Women's tennis under Julie Wrege was always competitive. The program made an astounding jump from AIAW Division III to NCAA Division I-A, despite its meager background for the move. Julie Wrege always came to my aid when I needed help with the program, proving herself one of the great troopers in our plan to build women's sports. Rick Davidson eventually became the women's tennis coach, and he led the team to a winning record against ACC opponents. When Rick left tennis for business opportunities, Sue Hutchinson from Miami University (Ohio) took over.

Buddy Fowlkes' track program made its own rise into national rankings, with Antonio McKay as NCAA indoor and Outdoor 400-meter champion. He also raced in the 1600 relay in the 1984 Summer Olympics in Los Angeles, winning a gold medal passing the baton. James Purvis, NCAA indoor and outdoor 110-meter high hurdles champion, passed through along with Derick Atkins and other outstanding sprinters. In women's track, Dee Todd from Northwestern joined our staff as head coach of the program. She brought the added bonus of being niece of Leroy Walker, a long-time close friend of mine. Leroy coached the United States Olympic Track Team for years. I knew him from my UNC days when he was director at North Carolina Central in Durham, a mere eight miles away. Later he became chancellor of that institution, served on worldwide

Olympic committees, and became president of the USOC as the committee moved toward the Summer Olympics in Atlanta. We gained the opportunity to renew our friendship when he made trips to the city.

Shelton Collier, volleyball head coach, brought with him experience from coaching the United States volleyball team and as head of the sport at the University of Pittsburgh. He was a welcome addition, whipping the program into shape to gather national attention. Two sports dropped into club status during this time, making for disappointment along with the more positive achievements. Despite Coach Lange's tremendous background in wrestling, we couldn't carry additional men's sports while trying to provide even the minimum of women's programs. Bill Beavers' gymnastics team lost out because it lacked competition. Although Bill was one of the best in the business, the ACC didn't sponsor a gymnastic program, cutting out a significant source of support for building programs in the region.

On the administrative side, our academic center became the focal point of our entire program. The rigorous academic programs at Tech made it necessary to have top people in charge. Scott Zolke, a lawyer from Chicago who played football at Tech and maintained a high grade point average allowing him to graduate with honors, headed up the program. Another bright star, Bernie McGregor, graduated from Harvard and proved instrumental in developing diverse tutorial programs for our student athletes. Todd Stansbury, another football player at Tech, developed tremendous relationships with the campus. He headed our academic center for many years, along with Joan McCarty-Roper.

Joan and the staff were always contacting former athletes who had left without completing their degrees. Through a national program called Degree Completion, an extension of the Total Person Program, the Athletic Association was allowed to pay the tuition cost for ex-players to return to campus to finish their course work and finally graduate. This not only elevated our percentage of graduates but gave those former players a boost in the job market.

We would hire other young men and women to the athletic department's academic staff because of our need to help athletes conquer the institution's rugged academic program. One of our former student-athletes, Thomas Covington, a tight end on the 1990 national champion squad, joined the ranks after a stint with the San Francisco 49ers.

When you hire good people and they succeed, your staff will get offers from other institutions, though. Constantly we received requests for permission to talk with our people. Larry Travis was one such case. An All-American football player at the University of Florida, Larry had tremendous administrative talents. He became one of my right hands when he shifted into administration, making it really hard to see him move first to Kansas State as director of athletics and then to Western Carolina in the same position. Susan Phinney, who worked with Larry in football recruiting, later replaced Jack Markwalter (when Jack left for Harvard Business School and a career in finance) to become vice president of the Alexander-Tharpe Fund, working alongside Jack Thompson, the senior vice president. Jack and Susan were responsible for the huge increase in fundraising for scholarships that benefited our entire sports program. They also were called upon to speak at various national forums. Jack became president of the Athletic Development national organization.

Assistant coaches on Bobby Cremins's staff always were wanted. Perry Clark left for a head job at Tulane University. George Felton accepted a position as head coach at the University of South Carolina. Ben Jobe traveled to the University of Alabama at Huntsville to become head coach there before moving on to Alabama A & M. This constant change reflected our ability to strengthen the coaching and administrative staff, paying an inconvenient but sincere compliment to Georgia Tech's programs.

The staff was in place, superb coaches in command, and highly recruited athletes signing letters-of-intent. Even financial concerns found a remedy through the Income Plus Program, which brought in marketing dollars from the corporate world, ACC TV revenues, which were at an all-time high, radio rights, and high ticket sales. It was time to begin the final year of the second five-year plan. Would we be able to clinch our goal of national recognition?

In January 1990, Coach Bobby Cremins and his team began competition against ACC foes, the toughest in the country. Dennis Scott, Brian Oliver and freshman Kenny Anderson lead a well balanced team to a second ACC championship and seventh consecutive NCAA playoff trip for the Yellow Jackets. Dramatic wins over LSU, Michigan State, and Minnesota in the NCAA regionals propelled the team into the Final Four. Georgia Tech's appearance in the championships, hosted that year in Denver, was the first in the team's history. Despite losing by a narrow margin in the semi-finals to eventual champion University of Nevada at Las Vegas, the trip to the Final

Four provided a tremendous highlight in our overall program. Bobby Cremins earned honors as National Coach of the Year for his efforts.

In the spring, Coach Puggy Blackmon's golf team finished first in the ACC and within the top six nationally. Baseball under Coach Morris continued its four-time ACC championship with its seventh trip in a row to the NACC tournament. And the 1990 football season certainly was one to remember! After an unbeaten season, an Atlantic Coast Conference championship, and a 40–23 win over arch rival University of Georgia, Georgia Tech went on to defeat the University of Nebraska in the Florida Citrus Bowl to claim the national championship. The highlight of the season, however, happened November 3, 1990, in Charlottesville, when the University of Virginia, ranked No. 1 in the nation, fell to the Yellow Jackets. Georgia Tech came from behind to tie the game 38–38. Then with just six seconds remaining, Scott Sisson kicked a perfect field goal to win the game 41–38.

Led by captains Daryl Jenkins and Jeremiah McClary, along with Joe Siffri, Marco Coleman, All-American safety Ken Swilling, and quarterback Shawn Jones, the team recorded a fourth national championship for Georgia Tech, following in the tradition of coaches Heisman (1917), Alexander (1928), and Dodd (1952). The Jackets were No. 1 in the nation once again, thanks to Coach Ross, who was named National Coach of the Year. When we added up all the points for our total sports program that year, 1990 had to be the best sports year in Georgia Tech's history, surpassing even 1985. We had achieved our goal of national recognition. Despite being a technological institution with high academic standards, having a small alumni base, and competing with local professional sports community for fan support, Georgia Tech had become a major player in athletics. And we'd regained respect for the institution.

Our overall plan proved successful, featuring the Student-Athlete Total Person Program, allowing us to graduate 87 percent of our student-athletes, and providing improved and competitive facilities while retaining outstanding coaches and excellent support staff. It was time to add up the assets and compare them to our liabilities to set goals for the next five years. We had to maintain the program, but could we improve? Could we continue increasing our revenue to offset the higher costs of making the program better? And when should I retire?

Retirement was something I had carefully planned since the mid-

1950s, a forethought after two things happened to make me think early about my life after a career. One of my former professional baseball managers, Eddie Cassada, became so successful in his later occupation in California that others referred to him as an insurance guru. He invited me to join him. My heart was in coaching, though, so I declined. He offered a part-time position through an agency in Cincinnati to help me during my high school coaching years from 1950 to 1961. He knew I always worked off season to supplement my family's income. His second invitation fell on readier ears.

The training program for selling life insurance not only taught me how to sell but was at the same time a motivation to plan my financial and estate future. In six months, I led the company in sales. At the Million Dollar Round Table meeting in Chicago, I met Paul Meyer, who was an insurance agent from Columbus, Georgia. He had an idea — one that later produced a multi-million dollar business.

A young entrepreneur at age twenty-one, Paul started as a life insurance agent in Columbus, Georgia, becoming the leading salesman in his area and the youngest member of the Million Dollar Round Table. In the 1960s, he founded Success Motivation Institute, Inc. He put out his first product: A 33-rpm record of the book, Think and Grow Rich by Napoleon Hill. Later he added others to develop many motivation and goal-setting programs. His products were the first on the market to provide a format for developing a complete, written goals plan. He expanded his program around the world. One of his favorite quotes —"The most successful leaders are those who recognize the creative potential of everyone of their team and make productive use of it"— summed up his own success and the advice he shared with others. Paul Meyer is a true giver, both in personal relationships and monetarily.

As the first to begin motivational programs, he distributed The Strangest Secret by Earl Nightingale first on records and then on tape cassettes. We kept in contact, and he sent me each program he produced. I studied his material almost religiously until I understood how to apply the principles to my life and family, and then to the teams that I coached. Paul's programs provided me with the Total Person-Total Success concept. I learned that we need to strive to be successful in all areas of our life: spiritual, family relationships, health, career, and financial. Through the insurance training and Paul's messages, I learned how to plan for my future. In 1955 my plan was to retire at age 65. That date would be February 20, 1992, barely into our next five-year plan.

On my sixty-fourth birthday in 1991, just two months into the new year, I pondered my earlier decision. By February 20 we were just barely past reaching our second set of major goals, becoming the best program in Georgia Tech's history and returning to national status. And I was one year away from the age at which I had decided to retire.

Georgia Tech and the city of Atlanta had begun gearing up for an official Olympic bid, with Billy Payne, A.D. Frazier and Company leading the way. To host the sporting event, Atlanta first had to win the right to represent the United States in the bidding competition. President Crecine invited me to accompany him to Washington, D.C., to meet the U.S. Olympic Committee. To this day, I strongly believe that Dr. Crecine's influence played a major role in the crucial goal of earning for Atlanta the right to serve as the country's entry into the host city competition for the 1996 Summer Games. His genius in combining electronic and computer-based technologies for monitoring athletes in the Olympic Village at Georgia Tech won over the U.S. Olympic Committee.

Billy Payne then took the group to Toyko for the final bid submitted by cities around the world eager to host the Olympics. Former Mayor Andrew Young, a key member of the Atlanta Committee for the Olympic Games (ACOG), proved instrumental in collecting early votes. Georgia Tech's metric computerized display of the entire Olympic Village structure garnered more votes. Atlanta was in the running.

I did not make the trip to Tokyo, so like millions of Atlantans I watched the TV intensely as committee members prepared to award the host delegation its prize. We were stunned and thrilled when the committee announced the 1996 Summer Olympics host city: Atlanta.

Atlanta had won! The Summer Games would begin in July 1996, leaving us five years to plan and construct the Olympic Village. President Crecine soon made two important moves. First, he named Russ Chandler mayor of the Olympic Village. In that position, Russ would negotiate between the campus and ACOG, volunteering his time to smooth the way for meeting the needs of the two groups as best as possible. Second, President Crecine hired General Bill Ray to build the Olympic Village.

With Georgia Tech so deeply involved in a world-class event, I found myself rethinking the next five-year goals of Georgia Tech athletics — and reconsidering my retirement plans. I sat down in my home office to look at the suddenly more complex situation. Before I got up from my desk, I received a phone call inviting me to a meeting with President Pat Crecine. A contract was presented to me through 1997. President Crecine and the Georgia Tech Athletic Association Board of Trustees asked me to stay on, taking us through the 1996 Summer Olympic Games and into the post-Olympic era. The Board of Trustees had always been a pleasure to work with during my years of service. I have mentioned several of these members during this writing, but several others contributed much to our success – including Bill Schaffer, Jim Stevenson, Bob Tharpe, Dan McKeever, Gerald Thuesen, and Bob McMath. Many others also helped me tremendously in shaping the program.

My personal plan to retire at age 65 would have to be adjusted to age 70. Phyllis and I agreed we should do this. The historic venture of the Olympic Village coming to Georgia Tech was in itself extremely appealing. I signed the contract. And then it hit me. The Athletic Association would take on a double whammie. Continuing the growth of the Athletic Association's sports programs and planning the Olympic Village would require twice as much effort.

Fifteen-year-old Homer with his parents, Grace and Dr. Sam Rice.
(inset): Homer's brother, Robert Cecil Rice.

Playing football at Highlands High School, Ft. Thomas, Kentucky, and as an All-American quarterback at Centre College.

On duty in the U.S. Navy at the liberation of the Philippines.

As head coach, University of Cincinnati.

As head coach, Rice University.

With Paul Brown, founder and president of the Cincinnati Bengals.

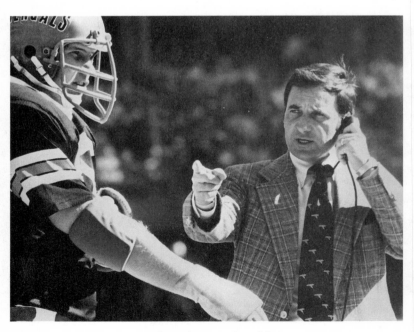

At work on the Bengals' sideline.

In his office at Georgia Tech, shortly before retirement.

Accompanied by his wife, Phyllis, and daughters (l-r) Nancy Hetherington, Phyllis Ingle, and Angela Miller, as he receives the Corbett Award.

With Georgia Tech Athletic Director Dave Braine in front of Homer's plaque on Tech's Wall of Legends.

Enjoying the good life on Marco Island, Florida, with Phyllis.

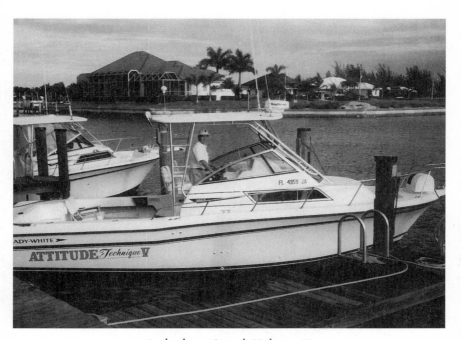

On his boat, *Attitude Technique V*.

With friends Bill Moore and Bud Parker on the Broken O Ranch in Montana.

Fishing for trout on the Sun River.

CHAPTER FIVE

THE THIRD FIVE-YEAR PLAN (1991-1996): WORLD ATTENTION!

It was time to plan the next five years. Calling this period the third five-year plan would be just a convenience. Actually, the time would stretch into seven years because of the Olympics, the post-Olympic period, and my eventual retirement. Which wouldn't come just yet. I would continue as director of athletics and, in President Crecine's altered organizational structure, my new role of executive assistant to the president. This challenge topped all others. I had to oversee and encourage even more growth in the athletic programs and also find time to assist with the Olympic Village arrangements. The latter task increased the duties of everyone on our staff, in some cases by doubling responsibilities.

To achieve success in both the Olympic Village and in the department of athletics, it would require total discipline of time. Again I turned to the Attitude Technique Philosophy, which involves time management.

Proper use of time is an important key toward leading a successful and happy life. The harder we work, the luckier we get. Bob Richards, the former Olympic pole vault champion, starting at age 13, spent over 10,000 hours in preparation for his event and became a world champion. Put 10,000 hours wisely into any work, and you will become the champion of your desires.

I am a strong advocate of what I call the "Test of Time." Once you have made a list of everything you think you are involved in, break your day into three parts—morning, afternoon, and evening—and divide your tasks among these sections. This is the basic document. Experiment with this test for one full week.

Start each day when you awaken and record the minutes you are actually engaged in some activity (no matter what it is) under the hour it occurs. When the day is over, total up the number of minutes. In this way, you will discover how much time you are spending on each item. No matter how thorough you believe your list to be, it is likely that other responsibilities, activities, and surprises will occur that you did not anticipate. Be sure to list telephone calls and interruptions on your task list and on your time test. They consume an inordinate amount of time. When I first used the "Test of Time," I found that I was allowing the telephone and other interruptions to rule my day.

Once you find out where your time is going, you can begin to work out plans to utilize the minutes in a productive manner. At first you will forget to record certain items. Stay with it one full week to get a good test.

A friend once told me that the verse in Proverbs 20:13 is interpreted, "If you love sleep you will end in poverty." Stay awake, work hard, and there will be plenty to eat. Many great men throughout the world's history had one thing in common – each was an early riser.

Prepare each day, and you will become highly organized and very efficient in your work and personal life. Always allow for surprises. They are bound to occur, so be flexible and learn to adjust. By writing out your daily plan, you will be able to make adjustments and get back on schedule. Plan, then relax. You will accomplish three times as much as you have previously. The greatest asset of such a plan is that it promotes living by action, which requires less effort than living by reaction. It is amazing how effectively a written time plan organizes our minds and our work and allows us to become truly successful individuals.

Begin at once your own time study. Write it on a sheet of paper headed "Test of Time." The sooner you gain control of your time, the sooner you will experience a big boost in personal productivity in your job and your life.

If you have been wasting time, if you have been unorganized in the past, forget it. There is no way to change that. Tomorrow? Well, that's different. It isn't here yet, so you can plan the entire day. Remember, time is speeding away. Don't delay. The journey will be worth your life, a life of happiness and true success. This is motivation. It can be accomplished day by day.

* * * *

The third five-year plan began taking shape. Our sports programs were at an all-time high. In addition to our successes in football and basketball, both baseball and golf earned No. 1 rankings. Women's basketball swept the National Invitation Championships, and volleyball captured its first ACC championship. And an achievement as meaningful as the others came from the NCAA's decision to use our Student-Athlete Total Person Program as a model for the "Champs" program which the national body carried to 177 universities.

The question, of course, was how to maintain this level and continue growth? The first five years, starting in 1980, set the standard for increasing the programs, and the next five escalated the prestige as well as size of Georgia Tech's programs. The third time period would test our program and determine whether our efforts were a blip on the screen or a real, long-term trend.

As I analyzed each sport's components and needs, I realized that the athletic program's plans had to be made compatible with the Olympic Village blueprints. To say that involved a lot of conferences and planning sessions understates the situation. I found myself engrossed in meeting after meeting about Olympic planning, spending hours finding the right combination of answers to meet complicated training, living, transportation, and security requirements. The one thing that remained clear during the conferences was that the 1996 Olympics had to be successful, no matter the cost in time. Understanding that success involves hills and valleys helped me take each problem as an opportunity to get up and start again.

Six areas stuck out in my mind, and I pondered and worked on them constantly. First, state-of-the-art dormitories for the Village and for future Georgia Tech housing would be constructed. ACOG would pay one-fifth of the cost. Georgia Tech would amortize a $90 million mortgage over a long term through student occupancy. The

debt incurred was undoubtedly a huge burden. But it also represented a plus just as large for the campus and the athletic program.
The Athletic Association leases more than 200 rooms from Georgia
Tech each year, and a sore spot in our recruiting had been the antiquated student housing. Now we could display the best housing
available: single bedrooms, cozy living areas, and full kitchens. The
Ritz Carlton had moved on campus!

Second, President Crecine expressed a keen interest in hosting
the swimming and diving venue on campus. ACOG would build the
Aquatic Center for $19-20 million. But making it compatible with
the needs of the university's student body after the Olympics would
be expensive. Georgia Tech would have to reshape the facility for
the recreational needs of students, costing more than $30 million.
Third, the Alexander Coliseum had been slated to serve as the boxing venue. ACOG offered to pay to air condition the facility only.
Fourth, I also considered the condition of our athletic facilities and
the needs of the Olympic community. Olympic athletes needed to
train, practice, and have sports treatment readily accessible at
Bobby Dodd Stadium at Historic Grant Field, Chandler Baseball
Stadium, George Griffin Track and Morris Bryan Stadium (track
and field), the Bill Moore Tennis Center, the Hugh Spruill
Fitness/Strength Center, and our sports medicine facilities.

The fifth and sixth items on my list included the Student-Athlete
Total Person Program and our national reputation. We needed to
make the nationally acclaimed success program available to students across campus, and Georgia Tech had to keep its sports programs on the highest level. We had the best coaches, a tremendous
support system, and a strong administrative staff to put this six-
point program into place. We needed action to implement it.
Naturally, I wrote these goals down, because a written plan provides
the key to action. Putting goals down on paper makes ideas more
permanent and creates a vision of what you want to achieve.

Our facilities were competitive in the ACC, and the Olympics
gave us the opportunity to go far past that stage to be in a class all our
own. Writing out the dream plan, the vision came into focus. Bobby
Dodd Stadium at Historic Grant Field, the oldest on-campus stadium
in the NCAA Division I-A, would claim my attention first. With
Bobby Ross as coach and a national championship on record, the
design followed: a complete renovation of the stadium proper. New
seats, electronic scoreboard, press box, a president's box, 36 executive

suites, concourse in the west stands, and other improvements such as switching from artificial playing surface to natural grass would comprise the elements of the grand plan. The design was ambitious. It would cost somewhere between $15 million and $20 million — a steep price tag, even including the upgrade to our fitness/strength center in the Wardlaw Building.

My long-time dream of a total person program continued to occupy my thoughts. I had learned the Total Person concept from Paul Meyer of the Success Motivation Institute (SMI). My focus on the categories of excellent health of mind, body, and spirit derived from my familiarity with Dr. Kenneth Cooper, the famous cardiologist who developed the Aerobics Center in Dallas, Texas. I met Dr. Cooper at a seminar in 1968 where we were both scheduled to speak. His motivational speech about health, fitness, and preventative medicine probably saved my life.

As head football coach at the University of Cincinnati that year, I paid very little attention to my personal health. Believing that I could outwork my opponents, I slept only a few hours a night and became a workaholic. While undergoing a medical exam for a life insurance policy, however, my blood pressure went off the board. I became aware of my unhealthy lifestyle. When Dr. Cooper gave me one of his books, I read it cover to cover in one sitting. His advice convinced me that at age 38 I had to begin a rigorous fitness program. Nutrition had to be a priority, and I needed to sleep at least six hours a night.

I combined this change with Paul Meyer's motivation program, which taught me how to plan my time. I wrote down my schedule by the hour each day and became amazed at how much more I accomplished in shorter periods of time. With my health returning and my time under control, my entire life took on a different color. Even though detailed organization had always been difficult for me, once I made a habit of following Paul's SMI guidelines they became a part of my life. Later I took a right brain-left brain test to analyze my thinking process, and the results indicated that my greatest strength lay in envisioning large goals. I could see the big picture. This explained the hard time I had dealing with details. But by writing down everything and keeping score of my activities, I strengthened my organizational skills. I learned to not only visualize a completed goal but to apply the principles and details which could implement that vision.

I realized that the Student-Athlete Total Person Program needed a home. A good friend, Hank McCamish (founder and chairman of the McCamish Group, a billion-dollar life insurance company) was instrumental in helping me to realize this dream. He worked for 40 years in the life insurance business and also served as president of the Million Dollar Round Table. We needed a center for sports performance which could encompass a sport psychologist, motion analysis lab, sports physiology, sports medicine and rehabilitation, and sports vision and nutrition. Lawton Hydrick, associate director for facilities, served as point person to direct this plan. Bill Reynolds and the architectural firm of Smallwood, Reynolds, Stewart and Stewart became invaluable in creating the facility's design. The estimated cost of fulfilling this dream was $8 million to $10 million.

What about the Alexander Memorial Coliseum? We had to answer many questions about whether to renovate or to build a new structure. There was little interest in replacing the coliseum. Could we combine the Olympic swimming and diving venue with a new coliseum, as one person suggested? ACOG would pay 20 percent for the pool, and we could add about $20 million and find ourselves with a new arena. Yet another plan involved building the new coliseum with a pool in place of the gym floor. After the Olympics, the pool could be removed and a gymnasium floor inserted. The Olympic regulations that stipulated a separate pool for warm-ups would require an adjacent practice area which could be built next to the arena and left as a competition pool for Georgia Tech's swimming program. With each concept we studied, the price escalated.

The problem that remained, though, was determining what to do with the old Alexander Memorial Coliseum and where to construct its replacement. We could level the present structure and build on the present site, but that would erase the Olympic venue for boxing and put our basketball program without a gym for at least two years, and playing all our games off campus for that length of time was not acceptable. This required serious thinking.

I asked Julian LeCraw, a notable real estate developer and member of the Georgia Tech Foundation Board (then treasurer and in the future to be president), to aid us in this undertaking. With a committee appointed by President Crecine, we studied various ways of tackling the problem. The Georgia Tech Foundation owned property on Fourteenth Street near campus, and that could be considered for a possible site. Locked in to an urban location in downtown

Atlanta, Georgia Tech had very little space for expanding. Across Interstate 75/85 was a large vacant lot owned by the Coca-Cola Company. We met with their representatives to study an option to purchase or lease the space and a proposal for joint partnership. Ted Turner's NBA team, the Atlanta Hawks, was considering a move from its downtown Omni Arena home court, and we examined the possibility of becoming partners. So many avenues were developing that a firm decision had to be made, I realized.

To learn the facts about big-time arenas, I visited six arenas across the nation. The information I gathered convinced me that we were headed in the wrong direction. The cost of building and maintaining a large arena was overbearing. It also meant we would need to engage in the "event" business. Finding potential conventions, circus shows, and big sporting events to pay for new facilities would get complicated — and fast. Event hosting meant we would have to apply for a liquor license. The proposal was simply over the top. This was not our mission.

I pleaded the case against a new coliseum in a meeting with the Athletic Board of Trustees. When explained in detail, the facts made them agree with me. A complete renovation of the present Alexander Memorial Coliseum could better serve our future needs while staying consistent with our mission, I suggested.

A meeting with Earl Shell, president of Hardin Construction Company, followed. Earl and Bill Reynolds mapped out a plan. Taz Anderson, a member of the Athletic Board, gave us firm backing for renovation. Alexander Memorial Coliseum would need to be gutted for a new structure to be built under the existing roof. The design finally approved lowered the floor six feet to increase seating and create better sight lines for courtside boxes. With all new seating, a new concourse, 12 executive suites, a large entertainment hall named the Whack Hyder Room for pre-game events, and a new pressroom, the resculpted facility would be every bit as good as new. It would be a showcase – with brass railings, air conditioning, and all the extras — for $12-14 million. That was a fraction of the $60 million or more a new arena on an as-yet-undetermined site would have cost. Both men's and women's basketball, volleyball, graduation exercises, and assorted campus events could use the coliseum when completed. Recreating an improved Alexander Memorial Coliseum was set.

The Olympics facilities blueprint was laid out in a clear and concise form, with three goals: renovating Bobby Dodd Stadium at Historic Grant Field, building the center for sports performance, and improving Alexander Memorial Coliseum. Other areas had to be shored up as well, including baseball, the track, and the tennis center. As each plan moved forward, several illnesses sidelined me temporarily. After finally getting myself checked out thoroughly, I was told I had prostate cancer. After my first operation to rid myself of the disease, Alice Ross, the head football coach's wife, brought a turkey dinner with all the trimmings to my home. She even produced an apple pie for dessert, making her generosity a memory I'll never forget. Not long after, I underwent additional surgery, this time removing my gall bladder, followed by a double hernia repair. My daughters joked that I'd gone too far in living a triplicate life: three daughters, the triple option, and three surgeries.

After five months I returned to the office, and we began by focusing on renovating the stadium. Seeing the blueprints of the design for making the stadium first class gave me an idea. Our Student-Athlete Total Person Program had been so successful in producing outstanding people. Why not make the concept available to all students on campus? President Crecine and I discussed the concept. He championed student rights and expressed constant interest in their welfare. I suggested that we construct a building inside the stadium to provide space for presenting life skills programs to our entire student body. A fellow big-picture man, he quickly came up with a plan. A structure to recruit students to Georgia Tech, provide financial aid and career placement, and to house the Total Person Program would make our dream possible. The complex would be called the Student Success Center. We had never heard of this type of concept in place at any major university. President Crecine and I put together a steering committee to assist fundraising for this truly academic/athletic effort. Charles Brady, a graduate of both Georgia Tech and Harvard University and the founder of INVESCO served as a trustee of the Georgia Tech Foundation Board. He and Kim King served as co-chairmen of the committee. Members included Eugene M. Clary, founder of Clary and Associates, as honorary chair; Ray Anderson, chairman and CEO of Interface, Inc.; Lawrence L. Gellerstedt Sr., chairman of Beers Construction Co.; Wade Mitchell, executive vice president of Trust Company Bank; Tazwell Anderson, president of Taz Anderson Realty Co.; Jack Johnson, president of Entry Systems, Inc.; M. Lamar Oglesby of

Kidder, Peabody and Co., Inc.; Charles R. Yates, president of the Robert Woodruff Arts Center; L. Travis Brannon Jr., partner of Jones, Day, Reavis and Pogue; George Mathews Jr., chairman and CEO of Intermet Corp.; and Claude A. Petty Jr., senior partner of P.C. Association.

Jim Langley, vice president for external affairs, joined with me for several meetings to push the project forward. He was an expert in communications and development, with years of experience serving Georgia Tech. The old Knowles Building, adjacent to the west side of the stadium, became part of the plan. The design architect recommended leveling the Knowles Building and replacing it. The new structure would open up into the president's suite, the new press box, and the 36 planned executive suites. With regret, we contemplated the history that the Knowles Building represented. It had opened as a dorm in 1947 and later became the campus business office. Its transformation into the Success Center came in 1993.

The Student Success Center developed into a unique undertaking. For 350 days a year it would be used for academics. On the remaining six, which were football game days, it would be turned into an entertainment center. Executive suites could be used by the career placement center for corporations to interview Georgia Tech students for future employment. On game days, the boxes were leased to individuals, groups, or corporations. The Success Center would complete the first phase of stadium renovation. It needed to succeed.

That meant raising the necessary capital, of course. We needed an enormous contribution to get the campaign off the ground.

It is my conviction that if you really believe in something strongly enough, you can sell your belief to others. Caring for the student athletes and their personal attainment through our total person program and extending that effort into the entire campus was worth the effort to build the Success Center. I remembered the early 1980s and developing the sport programs with the outside help of key alumni and friends of Georgia Tech. Albert "Bud" Parker had impressed me with his attitude and leadership while building the tennis program. We learned that raising funds from former tennis lettermen was the key. In the drive for tennis funding, Bill Moore surfaced. He believed in our direction and came through for us.

Bud, Bill, and I became close friends in the process, and starting in 1982 we participated in two fishing tournaments a year. In early

December we traveled to Marco Island, Florida, where I still keep my Grady White boat, and entered the Marco Island Fishing Classic. Bill usually left as champion, pulling in large amberjacks, kings, grouper, and occasionally a trophy-lane snapper. In August Bud Parker and I traveled to our friend's ranch in Augusta, Montana, for the Broken O Ranch Fishing Derby. An eight-pound rainbow trout I still have displayed in my office reminds me of the thrill and pride we took in our fishing challenges.

On one of our trips, we discussed with Bill the proposed Student Success Center. Bill Moore believed in the Total Person Program for all students and immediately pledged a gift to not only start the funding process but to ensure that we would go forward. His generosity represented the largest single gift in Georgia Tech's history at the time of his pledge. In my opinion, Bill Moore himself is the epitome of the total person. He shuns the spotlight. But we insisted that the complex be named the Bill Moore Student Success Center, giving students a model in that 1938 graduate to follow.

The gift stimulated others to come forward. Gene Clary, a great friend of Georgia Tech, provided a contribution for the Gene Clary Theatre, a 100-seat auditorium for special programs. Nelson Abell, another former tennis letterman and chairman of the board of the Abell Corporation in Louisiana, stepped up. Thanks to my good friend Walter Dunn and others in the company, Coca-Cola Company made a very large gift. Committee co-chairman Charles Brady and Bud Shaw, chairman of the board of Shaw Carpet, cemented the effort. Revenue from the 36 suites would also provide funding, as would gifts from many other contributors. The Bill Moore Success Center became a reality.

The Russell Corporation sponsored a new press box with up-to-date electronic equipment to be added to the building. The old, dingy concourse under the west stands turned into an attractive New Orleans style area provided by the family of the late Roy Richards of Southwire Company in his memory. With all the other new improvements to the stadium, we now had one of the most attractive facilities of its kind in the country. Bobby Dodd Stadium at Historic Grant Field became a fitting honor for Bobby and Alice Dodd and their children, Linda and Bobby Dodd Jr. Coach Dodd was loved by his players more than any other coach in the game, and his legacy would endure in both the record books and in the memories of those whose lives he touched.

As the stadium property took shape and came close to being finished, more change took place in the sports program. Our football season under National Coach-of-the-Year Bobby Ross entered the season against Joe Paterno's Penn State Nittany Lions in the Kick Off Classic at the New Jersey Meadowlands. Although we fell short of a victory, Bobby took his team through another flourishing season, accumulating eight wins in regular season play and a victory over Stanford in the Aloha Bowl in Hawaii. And then it happened — the call that a director of athletics never wants to receive.

Bobby Beathard, general manager of the San Diego Chargers of the NFL, called to ask permission to talk with Bobby about the club's vacant head coaching position. Bobby and I visited back and forth several times about the issue, but it was inevitable. Another chance to coach in the pros interested Bobby. His step to the next level of coaching was natural, and he left Georgia Tech after five productive years. Bobby brought us our first ACC championship in football and our fourth national title. He could have stayed at Georgia Tech for the remainder of his career, but he opted for the next challenge. And he continued his winning ways by taking the Chargers to the Super Bowl in 1993.

President Crecine put together a search committee to select the next coach with Dr. John White, dean of the Engineering School, as chair. George O'Leary, defensive coordinator, and Ralph Friedgen, offensive coordinator, were perhaps the two strongest in their fields in college football, and they were instrumental in our team's success. George and Ralph were the first to be interviewed. Another young coach with a Georgia Tech background, Bill Lewis, was having unbelievable results as head coach at East Carolina University. In a coincidence, his team was selected to compete against North Carolina State in the Atlanta Peach Bowl and would practice at Georgia Tech in preparation for the big game. The hottest coach in Division I-A, Bill was the coach sought by every school with a job opening. He was on our list, too, but the code of ethics in intercollegiate athletics requires a call to the director of athletics to gain permission to speak to a coach. I refused to call until his season was completed. Once East Carolina defeated North Carolina State in a dramatic come-from-behind finish, I placed a call to Dave Hart Jr., director of athletics at East Carolina. As it happened, I had coached with Dave Sr. at the University of Kentucky when Dave Jr. was a small lad. It seemed strange that I was now conversing with the next generation.

Dave Sr. was a skilled high school coach in Johnstown, Pennsylvania, when I was coaching Highlands High School in Fort. Thomas, Kentucky. We were both scheduled to speak at a clinic in Hollywood, Florida, one year — the same clinic at which Bear Bryant invited me to visit with him at his summer home in Alabama. Although more than a thousand coaches attended the clinic, promoter Tony Leone needed three or four times that many to break even. He was losing his shirt on the investment. That year, to wrap up the events and close out the clinic, he arranged a huge banquet with the grand prize of an automobile to one person holding a lucky prize number. I had that number! After the exciting announcement, I had my picture taken with the keys to the new Buick.

Unfortunately, there was no automobile for me to pick up at the end of the clinic. Tony had to write me an IOU that year because of the clinic's financial problems. Several years later when I returned to Hollywood, Florida., where the clinic was held for an NCAA convention, I related the story at the dinner table. Who should walk in but Tony Leone, wearing a large Texas hat and smoking what looked like a foot-long cigar. He spotted me and bellowed out, "Homer, I am going to get you that car!" The car never showed up and the IOU never got honored, but Tony certainly gave me the gift of a funny story and a memory I still laugh at — which might be worth just as much.

With David's permission, I talked with Bill Lewis. He was interested. George Mathews offered his private jet to fly me to Raleigh, North Carolina, where I could meet with Bill before bringing him to be Atlanta for the interview with the search committee. At the same time that I was talking with Bill about the Georgia Tech position, he was selected as National Coach-of-the-Year, one year after our own Bobby Ross. Bill Lewis had the right credentials, and having served two seasons as assistant coach at Georgia Tech, he was familiar with the school and its environment.

I first met Bill while coaching at the University of Oklahoma. Dave Hart Sr. was head coach of the University of Pittsburgh, and he sent Bill, then an assistant coach under Dave Sr., to scout Oklahoma's game with Notre Dame. As offensive coordinator, I explained our plan of attack against Ara Parsegian's Fighting Irish team, which would sweep the national championship in 1966. Bill heard my strategies then and again in 1975, when Frank Broyles, head coach at the University of Arkansas, invited me to lecture to his staff on leadership. Bill was Frank's assistant at the time. When Bill left Broyles's organization, he went on to become coach at the University of Wyoming, then made a stop at the University of Georgia to coach under Vince Dooley. Vince was high on Bill and chose him as defensive coordinator when Erk Russell left the Bulldogs for the head post at Georgia Southern. From the University of Georgia, Coach Lewis accepted the head position at East Carolina in Greenville, North Carolina, under athletic director Dave Hart Jr. Over his career, Bill would serve under father and son!

I had more than a general interest in Greenville, North Carolina. One of my first assignments as director of athletics at the University of North Carolina was to speak to the alumni in that community. Eddie Smith, a graduate of UNC, invited me to spend the night at his home. The next morning he escorted me to his new business: building the Grady-White boat. Housed in an old tobacco barn, his shop proved too enticing. I bought one of his first boats and quickly became friends with Eddie and his wife, Jo. After the purchase of my fifth Grady-White boat, I was even asked to write an article for his national newsletter.

In three seasons, Bill Lewis had assembled a national power at East Carolina. He came across superbly in the search committee interview and was offered the job as head coach at Georgia Tech. George O'Leary and Ralph Friedgen planned to leave Georgia Tech to join Bobby Ross with the San Diego Chargers. Ken Riley, captain of the Cincinnati Bengals during my last year coaching in the NFL, topped the list of remaining candidates.

Ken played his collegiate career as the quarterback for the famed Jake Gaither, head coach at Florida A & M University. Ken also had numerous brilliant years in the Cincinnati Bengal organization and as assistant coach with the Green Bay Packers before he returned to Florida A &M to replace his old coach.

I had the privilege of knowing Coach Gaither. Speaking at his annual football clinic in Tallahassee, I emphasized the importance of the quarterback's snap count in focusing the center snap on the moment the offensive unit rolled off the line of scrimmage. Coaches packed into the clinic. When I asked Coach Gaither if I could demonstrate with one of his defensive coaches, Jake sent his defensive end coach to the front, calling him "the quickest cat in the room." I put a quarter in my volunteer's hand and told him I could snatch it out before he closed his fist. "No way, man!" he remarked. At that moment I grabbed the coin and held it up to the watching coaches. The defensive end coach wanted another chance. I did it again. The crowd really got a laugh out of the trick. The demonstration prompted Coach Gaither to say that I had the slickest hand movement he'd ever witnessed. Coach Gaither and I later served on several NCAA national committees together.

Gaither's protégé, Ken Riley, missed the opportunity at Georgia Tech, however. Bill Lewis, national coach of the year, accepted the head coaching position and found himself in the early stages of our third five-year plan. From Bobby Ross's national championship team we still had quarterback Shawn Jones and running backs William Bell and Dorsey Levens, the latter to achieve fame by playing a key role in the Green Bay Packers' 1997 Super Bowl victory. Defensive standout Coleman Rudolph led his squad with the experience of a national championship behind him, too.

Early victories over North Carolina State and Clemson University set the stage for a big game with Florida State University in Atlanta. Ranked No. 1 one at the time, Florida State was competing in its first season as a member of the ACC. The conference's make up was certainly changing. Television served as a catalyst, driving schools and conferences to strategically align their positions to earn top dollar. The SEC added the University of South Carolina and Arkansas to form a twelve-team league splitting football into two divisions. The east and the west division winners competed in a playoff game to represent the SEC in the Sugar Bowl. In the ACC, independent Florida State looked like an attractive candidate for membership. Commissioner Gene Corrigan saw clearly that adding perennially strong Florida State would give the ACC more national prestige. We needed a greater national presence to ensure that our football league wasn't left out in the cold when it came time for major bowls to offer their bids.

Gene Corrigan probably was one of the most astute leaders in the NCAA. A popular and well-informed man, he had a complete knowledge of the inner workings of intercollegiate athletics. When I became director of athletics at UNC in 1969, Gene Corrigan greeted me at the university. At the time, he served the ACC as assistant commissioner under Jim Weaver. Gene left the conference office to take the job of athletic director at Washington and Lee for a short time before moving on to the University of Virginia. He had been an outstanding athlete at Duke University, and at Virginia he put together a competitive program that brought the school into the national spotlight. After several years at Virginia, he left to take over the reins at Notre Dame. I knew from an off-the-record conversation with ACC Commissioner Bob James that Bob planned to retire in a couple of years, and I soon talked with Gene about his plans and future interests.

Gene had one of the premier positions in the country at Notre Dame. He, his wife Lena, and their family enjoyed South Bend very much. However, they felt a tug for the ACC, which had always been home for the Corrigans. Gene hinted that he might be interested in a return to the conference in the days ahead. Unfortunately, Bob James passed away in 1987, leaving a conference he had brought to a nationally competitive level in all sports in a period of unexpected transition. Thanks to Bob's work, the ACC had become one of the country's top conferences. Finding a replacement was impossible, but I knew where to locate a man with the skill and love of the ACC to carry on Bob's tradition of excellence. After I was appointed to help select the next ACC commissioner, we summoned Gene for an interview, and he accepted the position. In the meantime, Nancy Thompson, first secretary of the ACC, kept business matters moving along until the new commission came on board. Nancy provided an anchor for the conference, keeping athletic directors in line and aiding the conference office with her knowledge of each program.

Florida State remained a symbol of the conference's transition. Georgia Tech's upcoming game with FSU presented a chance for the Yellow Jackets to reassert their national standing and to capture a place in the top five. For top-ranked FSU, a defeat would knock the team out of its No. 1 position, but a win meant a showdown with Notre Dame and Coach Lou Holtz for the national championship. During the first three quarters, Georgia Tech showed the team was mentally, physically, and strategically prepared for the match-up. Leading 24–10 going into the final

quarter, an exhilarating Tech victory seemed possible. FSU quarterback Charlie Ward had been benched after throwing five inter-
ceptions in the tense game. Coach Bobby Bowden gave him
another chance, though, and the FSU shotgun, no-huddle offense
made a last effort. FSU closed the gap to 24–20 with 1:40 left on
the clock, then lined up for an on-side kick. And what happened
next is still a vivid memory.

FSU kicked and Georgia Tech recovered the football, with two
players clearly in possession on the ground, both hugging the
pigskin. A head linesman aligned on the far side of the field had
position to make the call, but by the time he approached the scene,
FSU had managed to secure the football. The referee awarded FSU
the ball with a first down at Georgia Tech's 39-yard line.

With FSU out of time-outs, Georgia Tech could have easily run
out the clock to win the big game if the call had gone for the Yellow
Jackets. Instead, a touchdown pass and a safety that Georgia Tech
gave up in order to negotiate better field position gave Florida State
the 29–24 victory. The defeat devastated the Yellow Jacket squad.
They didn't win again in 1992, enduring a losing season. Florida
State continued on to win the national title, defeating Nebraska in
the Orange Bowl. Bobby Bowden developed Florida State into a
powerhouse. As a member of the ACC, Florida State made a
tremendous impact, putting the conference in bowl position when
alliances were created to declare a national championship game.

While Bill Lewis worked to get the football program back on
track, I faced my own dilemma. In 1993 Bobby Cremins's own
school, South Carolina, approached him with a plea to bring his
alma mater back to respectability and competitiveness. Bobby's own
thrilling career as captain of the Gamecocks made for a greater
temptation to leave Georgia Tech than any offer he'd yet received.
Through the years, he had turned down the chance to coach at Ohio
State, Kentucky, Arkansas, Washington, and Notre Dame to stay at
Georgia Tech. But South Carolina was his own school. His former
teammates attempted to convince him to return for the program's
sake. Bobby continued coaching at Georgia Tech, wining another
ACC championship, until it was finally time to make a decision. On
March 23, 1993, Bobby called to tell me he had decided to go to
South Carolina. It was time for Georgia Tech to act quickly.

I swiftly met with President Crecine to form a search committee. Dean John White again accepted the offer to chair the group.

We met that afternoon and laid out a plan of action. As usual, we knew we had to be prepared at all times for replacing coaches. And just as predictably, I caught a flight later that afternoon for Marco Island. I had to get out of town to work on this problem from a different location. George Mathews again generously offered to have his jet stand by for flying me around the country for the search if necessary. Phyllis had preceded me to Marco Island, and when I arrived that evening she reported that Bobby Cremins was calling to speak to me. We finally talked that evening. He didn't sound at all happy with his decision. I encouraged him, telling him to hang in there while the process played itself out. He was very concerned about whom Georgia Tech might hire, however, and even more about what would happen to his staff, Kevin Cantwell and Sherman Dillard. He suggested that I consider Kevin Cantwell for his replacement. In the meantime, I had talked with Dean Smith at North Carolina and C.M. Newton at Kentucky, compiling a list of prospective candidates before going to bed. I was exhausted.

At 2 a.m. on March 25, Bobby Cremins woke me up from my sleep with a call. He wanted to come back. Still groggy from traveling and the hard work, I wasn't sure if I was dreaming. I asked Bobby to call back in the morning to discuss the saga. At 6 a.m., I got another phone call. It was Bobby, again. He really did want to return to Georgia Tech as head men's basketball coach. Earlier I had felt that Bobby had been placed in an uncomfortable position of having to choose between his loyalty to his former school and teammates, and the program he was coaching. Georgia Tech had become his home, though. Now he was loyal to Georgia Tech, and he wanted to stay on. He had brought Georgia Tech from a program on the bottom of the league to one at the top of the nation. He had persistently chosen Georgia Tech over any job offers that came his way, and he had just as consistently taken the team to 11 straight NCAA appearances. He was one of the top five coaches in the nation. But I had to know if he had signed a contract with South Carolina. When he answered that he hadn't, I could tell him the good news.

"Bobby, your contract at Georgia Tech is still in force," I replied. I told him that technically a letter of resignation was required to release him from his duties to the Georgia Tech Athletic Association, and he had never turned in one. We would love to have him back. But first he had to inform Mike McGee, director of athletics at South

Carolina, of his decision. After meeting with Mike McGee and performing that duty, Bobby wanted to leave immediately to come home. He didn't have any transportation, so his wife, Carolyn, drove from Atlanta to Columbia, South Carolina, to pick him up and bring him back to Atlanta. The episode almost resembled a cloak-and-dagger story, and Bernie McGregor, associate athletic director at the time, kept me posted via a three-way hook up. I also returned to Atlanta, pleased to no end to inform President Crecine, the search committee, and the athletic board that we would retain Bobby Cremins. We were all overjoyed. Bobby would be back home with his Georgia Tech family.

Now was the time to focus my attention on our Olympic facilities campaign, meant to ensure that everything would be in place prior to the Summer Games in 1996. The Games would coincide with the culmination of the third five-year plan and my own stepping down as director of athletics at this school I had fallen in love with. Its people, traditions, and integrity combined better than in any institution in the world. To this day, I am convinced that Georgia Tech is unique.

We set up endless meetings to help us reach our goal, going through first designs, then cost estimates. And then the reality set in. We would need contributions of cash and pledges of $40 million or more. For two years, I met almost every day with corporations, foundations, and individuals to sell the plan. The staff put together an attractive video program to spell out our objectives. We got an unbelievable response. At the same time that we were trying to gain support for Olympic facilities, however, Georgia Tech was positioning itself to become a world-class university in the twenty-first century. Part of that effort was a campus-wide campaign to meet objectives for disciplines across the breadth of the university. Fortunately, President Crecine paved the way for the Georgia Tech Athletic Association to become part of the university's campaign. Unlike the earlier 1985 effort, this time the Athletic Association was written into the project, and I was formally asked to serve on the steering committee.

The Olympics were two years away. During this period, Dr. John Patrick Crecine resigned. The institution began its search for its tenth president, with Dr. Mike Thomas, a highly capable administrator serving as vice president for academics, acting as interim president. Mike was a good friend and supporter of our program, and he took charge of the multitude of issues facing Georgia Tech. The campus-wide campaign would be put on hold until a new president had been selected.

In meeting with Dr. Thomas, I explained the urgency of continuing the Athletic Association's plan to have facilities in place before Georgia Tech became the Olympic Village. The acting president agreed. We had to move forward immediately. We broke down the project into the Bobby Dodd Stadium at Historic Grant Field, the center for sports performance with a conference center and museum to display Georgia Tech's past, and the Alexander Memorial Coliseum. In addition, we would add a new track and shore up the Bill Moore Tennis Center.

The first person to step forward was my good friend, Hank McCamish. Hank's major gift, however, stipulated that the new center for sports performance be named the Homer Rice Center for Sports Performance. In addition, Mrs. Dot "Polly" Poole, a professional artist, insisted on painting my portrait for the new center. These things went against my belief that a person had to be deceased before receiving such recognition. Hank is one of my close friends, and I tried to convince him not to attach my name to the new center — but to no avail. As Hank asserted, "I am writing the check. No name — no check." My name and portrait would go on record. I didn't know how to thank those who shared my vision for bestowing such an honor on me. Despite their deep belief in me, for some reason I never felt I deserved to be singled out in that way. I was just doing my job the best way I knew how, and the satisfaction I gained from that had always been good enough for me.

After Hank came forward with another major gift, J. C. "Bud" Shaw and John Williams, CEO of Post Properties joined my friend Bud Parker in a visit to me regarding the Olympic facilities plan. Bud Shaw's keen interest in young people produced another major gift, in appreciation of which we named the complex of the Arthur B. Edge Jr. Center and the new Center for Sports Performance the J. C. "Bud" Shaw Sports Complex. John Williams made an additional donation to ensure that the landscaping always remained in top shape, and Bud Parker continued his consistent gifts to the Athletic Association to meet specific needs.

In the early 1980s when Bobby Dodd and I drove to LaGrange, Georgia, to meet with Fuller Callaway Jr. about the Callaway Foundation's gift for the Arthur B. Edge Jr. Intercollegiate Athletic

Center, I realized that I was meeting one of the giants of the textile industry. Each year from that day until his death I wrote Fuller a letter of thanks for the gift. He always replied with a short note of appreciation. So many developments and successes would not have been possible without his support. During the Olympic facilities campaign, I approached the Callaway Foundation for a gift to honor Fuller Callaway's memory. None of our athletic facilities was ever named for this great man, and now was the time to change that. John O'Neill, although retired and then associate athletic director emeritus on the Athletic Board, led the way. We met with Tommy Gresham, chairman of the Callaway Foundation Board, Charles Hudson, and other members of the board. We filed an official request for a major gift to honor Fuller Callaway, and we designed the Fuller Callaway Plaza as the gateway to Bobby Dodd Stadium at Historic Grant Field. The gateway would be adjacent to the new Center for Sports Performance. An attractive obelisk with Fuller's likeness, flags from each Atlantic Coast Conference member flying from atop the structure, and a special VIP parking lot would comprise the Fuller Callaway area. At the dedication ceremony, Alice Callaway, Fuller's widow, expressed her approval of the honor.

The Callaway Foundation's major matching gift was instrumental in providing funds for the stadium renovation, the Center for Sports Performance, and the re-creation of the Alexander Memorial Coliseum. Bronze plaques in Fuller's honor were placed at the entry point of the west stands in Bobby Dodd Stadium and the Alexander Memorial Coliseum as well as to the Callaway VIP Parking lot, where personalized spaces for 21 individuals, corporations, and foundations represented a veritable Who's Who of Georgia Tech's history. Each had made special major gifts to Georgia Tech athletic facilities, and the combined group represented a total of more than $70 million contributed to secure the program's future.

Georgia Tech's athletic heritage became a focal point in the design of the Center for Sports Performance. The Athletic Heritage Center was a museum but needed a personalized name connecting it to someone who linked Georgia Tech's past and present. We approached the Intermet Corporation. Its founder George Mathews had retired, but the powers-that-be remaining in the corporation were receptive to the opportunity to honor George. Always a utility man in meeting the Athletic Association's needs for emergency support, George had a long history as a superior athlete at the institution as well. At the dedication, we began by honoring one of Georgia Tech's greatest athletes and ended on a humorous note recognizing his continual support. "This is one time George cannot contribute funding to the program," I concluded at the ceremony. It was long past time to honor him for his overwhelming generosity over the years.

We kept driving toward improving facilities, and the attractiveness of our coaching staff to other colleges meant that we had to continue seeking out the best coaches for our programs. I lived by the old adage, "If you hire good people and they do well, other schools will want your people." To our credit and dismay, our coaches and staff were in great demand. In football, Bill Lewis resigned to move to a position with the Miami Dolphins. Charles Mosley, a good friend and strong supporter of the Georgia Tech athletic program, had kept in contact with Bobby Ross and suggested that Bobby might be interested in coming back. However, although Bobby missed the college campus, his life was now the NFL.

We turned to one of his assistants. George O'Leary had been popular with players and fans as a top assistant to Bobby Ross during our national championship period, and we had seriously considered naming him head coach when Coach Ross left for the Chargers. The years George spent in the NFL gave him the added ingredient of experience needed to move into the head coaching slot.

In the Chargers' organization, George worked alongside Bill Arnsparger, defensive coordinator of the professional team. A friend of mine from our Kentucky days, Bill had developed the "no-name" defense for the Miami Dolphins with Don Shula during the team's Super Bowl championship era. I talked to Bill about George and the young man's capabilities; I trusted Bill's assessments. He was high on George and informed me that George would be the right choice for Georgia Tech. And Bill was correct, as usual.

George's first three years as head coach produced two winning seasons and a trip to the Carquest Bowl in Ft. Lauderdale, Florida, defeating West Virginia 35 to 30. I felt comfortable with George at the helm. His methodical approach created a system that would put the football fortunes back on top. He also managed to bring Ralph Friedgen back to campus. Ralph had been Bobby Ross's offensive coordinator during the national championship run at George Tech, and his coaching had been a catalyst in the Chargers' march to the Super Bowl in 1993. George and Ralph were a great tandem in collegiate football. Having them team up again created a lot of excitement with Georgia Tech fans. Yellow Jacket football was back. The fourth year (now under the directorship of my successor Dave Braine) improved to ten wins, an ACC championship, and a win over arch rival University of Georgia to close out the regular season, and the defeat of Notre Dame in the Gator Bowl. George was rightfully awarded Coach of the Year honors.

In baseball, Jim Morris received an unbelievable offer to coach the University of Miami Hurricanes. The Miami team was arguably the best collegiate baseball program in America. Coach Ron Fletcher built the Miami program into a perennial national contender. He was retiring, but he recommended Jim Morris as his successor. Jim's good fortune presented me with the challenge of finding an equally competent replacement. I called on my friend, Randy Carroll. He not only had been a member of the Athletic Board during my tenure and chairman of the finance committee but was considered an inside expert in baseball circles. Randy also did color commentary on our radio network for our baseball games, and his traveling with the team kept him aware of the best coaching prospects in collegiate play. I asked Randy to chair the search committee.

Several calls to friends in baseball around the country produced solid leads. A key call to Cam Bonifay, former outstanding player at Georgia Tech and general manager of the Pittsburgh Pirates, presented me with the name of a young coach who had impressed all the scouts: Danny Hall, head coach of Kent State. Danny had attended the University of Miami at Oxford, Ohio, planning to study medicine. The talented student became a baseball all-conference infielder, staying on in graduate school to become a graduate assistant coach. He moved to the University of Michigan as an assistant, and during his eight years there the Wolverines earned one of the country's best records. Making a move to become a head coach himself, Danny took over a down-and-out Kent State University program and promptly brought his team to the front with Mid-America Conference championships and appearances at the NCAA regional playoffs.

When Georgia Tech decided to offer Danny the job, he accepted. Danny's coaching combined well with the talents of shortstop Nomar Garciaparra and Jason Varitec, who both play professionally now with the Boston Red Sox, and center fielder Jay Payton of the New York Mets. In his first season with the Georgia Tech team, Danny took the players to the finals of the College World Series, barely missing the national championship. The same year, he was also named Coach of the Year.

Puggy Blackmon made his own move to another program a year later. One of the NCAA's most successful golf coaches, Puggy decided to accept the University of South Carolina's coaching offer. An immeasurable asset I had by serving intercollegiate athletics as president and chairman of several national committees over the years was knowing coaches and administrators throughout the country. That familiarity with personnel allowed me to pick up the phone and talk with just about anyone — and that is what I did. Jack Nicklaus, whose son was a member of the Georgia Tech golf team, added his advice to that of others I called. Making these contacts allowed me to compile a list of six top golf coaches. One name kept popping up more frequently than any other, however – Bruce Heppler. Bruce was a young assistant coach at Oklahoma State University, which was one of the dominant programs in the NCAA. Bruce himself had played collegiate golf at Brigham Young University.

When we shaped the program under Puggy Blackmon, we had formed a golf committee called the Tee Club, made up of some of the most successful and influential men in Atlanta and throughout the state of Georgia – Charlie Brown, Charlie Yates, Jon Martin, Jim Dellinger, Andy Bargeron, Jimmy Cleveland, Hugh Spruill, among others. They joined an even longer list of members, including NCAA Player of the Year Stewart Sink, the team captain who was turning pro, Dan Yates, Neil Riley, Jack Zeigler, John Imlay, and Tommy Barnes. From Tee Club members we formed a search committee, and Bruce Heppler emerged as their choice. He accepted the position.

With the committee's assistance, we raised the funds necessary to complete the "new" facilities. The home course at the beautiful Golf Club of Georgia in Alpharetta enhanced our national recruiting efforts. With a driver, pitch, and putt training course just off campus on Georgia Tech Foundation property on Fourteenth Street and a new golf center, Bruce promptly recruited several outstanding young players. In three years, his team pursued the national title, finishing third in the NCAA finals ahead of Bruce's former team, Oklahoma State. Freshman Matt Kuchar won the United States

National Amateur Championship, giving Atlanta its first victory since Bobby Jones in 1930. In Bruce's second year, another freshman named Brice Molder earned honors as NCAA Player of the Year while playing on the team that captured the ACC championship. To say the future looked bright would be a gross understatement. In Bruce Heppler, Coach of the Year, we had hit the jackpot!

Buddy Fowlkes decided to retire after 30 years as head track coach. Buddy had been loyal to Georgia Tech throughout his career. He had produced several national champions. A stickler for details, he always kept on top of the strict NCAA regulations. Fortunately, Buddy's loyal assistant, Grover Hinsdale, was waiting in the wings. Georgia Tech filled out the men's track coach position by naming Grover, and completed the program's leadership by selecting former track champion Alan Drosky as women's track and cross country coach. By the end of 1997, 12 individual national champions had been recorded in the Georgia Tech track program in addition to three Olympic gold medalists.

The sports program had reached championship caliber in the ACC. In the first five-year plan (1980-1985) we had set the program back on track. In the second plan (1986-1990) we gained national recognition. We continued the competitive challenge for championships when the Olympics came to Atlanta in 1996 as the culmination of the third five-year plan (1991-1996).

Bobby Cremins had taken the Jackets back to the NCAA "Sweet 16" and regular season ACC championship. Agnus Beranato directed the Lady Jackets basketball team to its first NCAA appearance. George O'Leary had the football program on the upswing. Shelton Collier moved the volleyball program to a high level in the NCAA. I admired the coaches at Georgia Tech. Coaching at a technical school is challenging. However, Georgia Tech's tradition carried on in high fashion because of community support and the school's family atmosphere. Our coaches simply were the best in the nation.

The Olympic facilities campaign continued. The "new" Alexander Memorial Coliseum began to take shape. Members of the Alexander-Tharpe Fund were asked to consider contributing to place their names on the Wall of Fame or other naming opportunities. The resounding response totaled more than $8 million. That amount provided a good start, but we needed another really, really big gift. Frank Beall, head of the advertising area of our operation, had discussed with John Fletcher (a Georgia Tech graduate with ties to the McDonald's Corporation) the possibility of approaching McDonald's to explore the company's interest. Our marketing director Kevin Bryant picked up the ball and brought the proposal front and center. We arranged a time for me to meet with McDonald's officials, including regional head Lynn Crump and others from the company's headquarters in Chicago. Our discussions went smoothly. The corporation was interested in the Alexander Memorial Coliseum at the McDonald's Center concept.

However, convincing McDonald's of the feasibility of our idea was only the beginning. Gaining acceptance for a facility with a corporate name on campus would not be an easy task. I asked Jim Murphy, our treasurer and chief financial officer, to lead the charge. We met first with the State of Georgia Board of Regents, where I explained to Chancellor Steven Portch and his board members that we were not asking the state to finance any of our Olympic facilities. We merely wanted them to understand our intentions and to grant their permission to follow the direction we outlined. General Bill Ray, the gentleman brought in to build the Olympic Village, was also serving as chief administrator and finance officer of the campus during the search for a full-time president. He helpfully guided us through the protocol of handling the corporate naming proposal. As it turned out, several buildings on the Georgia Tech campus had corporate names hidden in the background of the official structure's title. Even the president's office building had a connection with the great entrepreneur Andrew Carnegie.

The Board of Regents members agreed to our plans and were pleased enough to give us the go-ahead even though we had no sitting president at the time. We then had to seek the approval of several state agencies as we made our way toward the final hurdle: the state attorney general's office of Mike Bowers. By this time the story had reached the media, adding more unnecessary complications. However, it was my judgment to take the process to the next step, which would involve the in-coming president.

Several years earlier, Col. Hugh Hardison retired as chief of the Georgia State Highway Patrol. A former Georgia Tech letterman, Hugh was hired by the Athletic Association as our security officer. He gave helpful advice to me on many occasions, particularly when it involved the state system. I asked him about our plan. His advice this time was indeed critical.

While continuing my duties in the athletic program, consulting about the Olympic Village, and being involved with the ACC and national intercollegiate athletics, I paid close attention to the search committee that would select Georgia Tech's new president. Committee chairman Dwight Evans and member Kim King updated me as the process went along. On a July day in 1994, I received word that the new president would be Dr. G. Wayne Clough.

President Clough officially took over the reins as Georgia Tech's tenth president in September of 1994, becoming the first Georgia Tech alumnus to serve as president of the institution. President Clough had served the University of Washington as provost and Virginia Tech as dean of the College of Engineering, with terms at Duke University and Stanford University as a member of their respective faculties. He and his lovely wife Anne became very popular with the Georgia Tech family. Dr. Clough proved to be a tremendous leader and brought Georgia Tech through the Olympics with accolades. His leadership shaped Georgia Tech into a premier institution recognized around the world. His energy and drive picked up the capital campaign with unbelievable success. The campaign was "dying on the vine" until he moved it into the $500 million-plus range. He is also one of the finest presidents I have had the opportunity of serving under. I felt blessed!

With the new president on board, I wanted to complete the Olympic Facilities Campaign. The attorney general finally gave his approval to the McDonald's Center, and the major gift followed. The McDonald's partnership was the first of its kind on a major university campus. President Clough proved instrumental in completing the arrangement, allowing the facilities for the Athletic Association to be completed prior to the 1996 Summer Olympics in Atlanta. I reviewed the projects on my list as each became a reality:

- Bobby Dodd Stadium at Historic Grant Field
- The J. C. "Bud" Shaw Sports Complex
- The Fuller Callaway Jr. Plaza
- The Homer Rice Center for Sports Performance
- The George Mathews Jr. Athletic Heritage Center
- The Alexander Memorial Coliseum at the McDonald's Center
- The Olympic Track at the George Griffin Track and Morris Bryan Stadium
- A facelift for the Bill Moore Tennis Center

One thing remained to be added, and with it a major gift to cover a significant part of the cost of the package — otherwise the Georgia Tech Athletic Association would be saddled with a financial burden for many years.

While I was serving as director of athletics at UNC, a young man by the name of Bill Cobey became my top assistant. When I departed, Bill replaced me as director. Bill grew up in a sports-centered family. His father, William Cobey Sr., was director of athletics at the University of Maryland when the great Jim Tatum produced a national football championship under the Cobey administration's direction. Bill Jr. earned his undergraduate degree at Emory University in Atlanta, majoring in chemistry, and added an MBA from Wharton College. His love of athletics was too strong for him to stay away, however. He came to North Carolina to head up our academic program. It didn't take long for anyone to realize that Bill was a sharp young man. I moved him up the ladder quickly until he became my right hand, and together we developed some of the early operating procedures of a model athletic program. In 1973 ours was recognized as the No. 1 sports program in the nation.

After serving as UNC's director for several years, Bill embarked upon a career in politics and was elected to the U.S. Congress. On a visit to Atlanta, Bill introduced me to his uncle and aunt, the delightful Mr. and Mrs. Randolph Thrower. Little did I know at the time that this pleasurable encounter would eventually lead to the largest gift in Georgia Tech history. Randolph Thrower was a prominent Atlanta attorney and had been head of the U.S. Internal Revenue Service. He introduced me to Mrs. Lee Candler, widow of Howard Candler Jr. Of course, when you think of Candler the next thing that comes to mind is Coca-Cola. And the history of Coca-Cola usually is tied to Emory University. Lee Candler expressed her desire to contribute to the athletic program. Her husband had been fond of Coach Bobby Dodd, and they were frequent spectators at Yellow Jacket football games when it was the only game in town.

We added a conference center to the Center for Sports Performance in memory of her late husband – the Howard Candler Jr. Football Conference Center. The center contained the latest video and electronic communications equipment in addition to adjacent meeting rooms. This contribution served the entire Olympic facilities project, and having the cost covered gave me huge relief. I could leave the program upon my retirement knowing that everything was paid for. All of the new facilities and additions were completed, dedicated, and ready for the 1996 Olympic Games. In addition to the facilities, I felt that one other part of the program needed to be secure: the Student-Athlete Total Person Program. Mrs. Candler agreed to take care of this, also. Her pledge to endow the total person program in perpetuity meant that the Lee and Howard Candler Student-Athlete Total Person Program would affect students' lives forever.

The Summer Olympics arrived in Atlanta in July 1996, and Georgia Tech hosted the Olympic Village through the Games' conclusion in August. Athletes from 197 countries used our athletic facilities. The world's largest sporting event finally was in progress! The long hours of meeting, negotiating, planning, and plotting had produced the real thing. It was excitement plus. Our newly re-created Alexander Memorial Coliseum at the McDonald's Center served as the venue for the boxing events. The swimming events took place at the new aquatic center on campus. Our other facilities saw thousands of athletes practicing and training for their events. The Homer Rice Center for Sports Performance offered sports medicine testing and rehabilitation services. Jay Shoop, associate director for sports medicine, placed a world map on the wall, and as the athletes entered, a pin was placed on the chart to note their home nations. It was a sight to see the hundreds of pins stuck all over that world map. Dr. John Cantwell, a prominent Atlanta cardiologist, directed all the physicians serving athletes of the Olympic Village and at each venue, and afterward he agreed to become medical director of the Homer Rice Center for Sports Performance. The Hugh Spruill Strength and Fitness Center proved to be a popular location with the athletes. Under Jay Omar's direction, the strength and fitness center was one of the country's best and offered state-of-the-art equipment. Olympic athletes trained incessantly there to gain an edge on their competition.

During the Games, I not only served as Senior Administrator for the Athletic Facilities and director of our nationally recognized athletic program, I was involved in several local services. At Peachtree Road United Methodist Church, I taught a Sunday School class under my good friend, Don Harp Sr., minister of the church and fishing companion on several trips – including, of course, Marco Island. I co-chaired the Tobacco Free Kids (Oral Health America) Program with Bishop Bevel Jones, who was later to develop a golf tournament (in my name) to educate our young people about the dangers of tobacco. I also served on the governing board of the Capital City Country Club with A. J. Land, board president, a Georgia Tech man and good friend. It was an interesting time for the Club, especially during the Olympic festivities. It was a pleasure to serve with Oscar Davis, Thomas Powell, Dale Harmon, Stewart Long, Tommy Hills, Harry Thompson (a former Georgia Tech tennis great and helpful to me in building the tennis program), Jack Stahl, General Manager David Pflieger, and others. Due to my busy schedule, I needed an exercise program to get away and to maintain my physical condition, and the Club furnished that – especially the men's exercise class under leader George Schisler.

After it was all over, no post-Olympic letdown marred our return to the business of running the Georgia Tech Athletic Association. After coming through the Games with flying colors, we didn't have time to rest. The new fiscal year was upon us.

But the year after the Olympics brought mixed emotions for me. For the first time in a decade and a half, I would not be the person planning the next five-year program. I planned to retire before the end of 1997. The post-Olympic year and my last months as director of athletics and executive assistant to the president presented a dramatic turning point for me. After 55 years as a student athlete, coach, and administrator, my always interesting and consistently rewarding career was at an end. Before I could think much about how to close out this process, I received a call from the president of Davidson College in North Carolina. Jim Murphy, our chief financial officer and the athletic board treasurer, was being called back to his alma mater to take over the position of director of athletics. With his long years of experience, he was a solid choice for Davidson. For us, losing him would create a void. We understood what a wonderful opportunity the new job was for Jim, though. We knew he had to accept such a tempting offer, and he did.

The chief financial officer's position was crucial in the athletic center's operations. As Jim prepared to leave, I studied the situation thoroughly and prepared to find a replacement. I looked carefully at a young man from Virginia Tech in Blacksburg, Virginia, named Jeff Bourne. Virginia Tech Athletic Director Dave Braine discussed Jeff with me and recommended him very highly. In the back of my mind, I wondered if I could convince General Bill Ray to consider the position, however. I weighed the two options in my mind. I'd kidded Bill Ray off and on about joining us after he finished his job with the Olympic Village. It was time to think seriously about that prospect.

Lawton Hydrick had handled the facilities for us for several years, but he needed to spend every bit of his time developing the new Center for Sports Performance and the George Mathews Athletic Heritage Center. I needed Bill Ray to head up both finance and facilities. Once those areas were in place, then he could pass them on to younger people who would only have to handle either finance or facilities under Bill's overall supervision. Bill had been working with this for the entire campus. He had taken charge of all facilities in addition to his task of building the Olympic Village. And he'd done all that without a president while dealing with a university deficit. He turned the situation around and took facilities and finance into the black before joining us at the Georgia Tech Athletic Association.

Major General (Ret.) Bill Ray, a graduate of the U.S. Military Academy with advanced degrees from Ohio State, the University of Texas, and Harvard University, was called to Georgia Tech by President Crecine to serve as vice president for Olympic Planning. He would be responsible for planning, programming, the design, and construction of the $240 million infrastructure project on the Georgia Tech campus. Prior to coming to Georgia Tech, the decorated general served as company commander of the 25th Infantry Division in Europe, following that assignment with a tour in Vietnam. As special assistant to General Colin Powell, he led an interdepartmental team to Saudi Arabia and successfully negotiated a $4 billion host nation arrangement. During Desert Storm, he worked with his close friend General Norman Schwarzkopf and oversaw the completion of a $14 billion construction program.

Bill was a pleasure to work with and would serve the athletic association very well during the next several months.

My final responsibility for the ACC was to help select the next commissioner by serving on the search committee for a third time. Eugene Corrigan was retiring. In addition to being commissioner of the ACC, during the last two years he had presided over the highest office of the NCAA as its president. The combination of leadership positions gave a fitting closure to one of the great administrators of our time. Gene excelled in creating a positive attitude in all his endeavors, infecting those around him with a can-do spirit that brought out the opportunity in any situation. We were personal friends and enjoyed our close relationship, jokingly naming ourselves "Big E" and "Big H" as time went by.

Dr. Thomas Hearn, president of Wake Forest University, served as chairperson of the search committee. After going through the usual investigations and recommendations, we narrowed the field to three or four candidates. John Swofford, director of athletics at the University of North Carolina, led the pack of nominees. He had been a student athlete at UNC during my tenure as director of athletics. As quarterback, John produced a memorable three-touchdown victory over Vanderbilt. The next day, he flew to New York to join his brother, who was a guest on the Ed Sullivan show. Introduced from the TV audience as the North Carolina quarterback whose throwing arm had defeated Vandy the day before, John gained his bit of fame from the entertainment world as well as sports early in his career.

One day at North Carolina, my secretary and special assistant Susan Strobel informed me that a young student-athlete wanted a conference with me. John Swofford came to my office and questioned me about what it would take to become an athletic director. He was interested in an athletic director's career. When he graduated, I paved the way for him to attend graduate school at Ohio University. At the time, Ohio offered the only graduate program for athletic administration. John completed his advanced degree and worked at an internship at the University of Virginia under Gene Corrigan, who was the school's director of athletics at that time. As an intern, John so impressed Gene with his effectiveness that the director offered him a full-time job.

As I began planning to leave North Carolina, Bill Cobey and I set up a plan to bring John Swofford back to UNC. John stayed with Bill at UNC until he replaced Bill, who was leaving to run for the U.S. Congress. The new athletic director at UNC, John Swofford had reached his goal.

In 1997, John Swofford reached even higher, accepting the commissionership of the ACC. John was only the fourth commissioner in the conference's 43-year history, and in my long career, I'd had the honor of serving on search committees for three of those officers. John's appointment, however, would be my last involvement with the Atlantic Coast Conference.

My plans to leave Georgia Tech went forward as President

Clough and I plotted my retirement. We set the final date as December 31, 1997. This wouldn't be good timing for hiring a new director, however, because our fiscal year began July 1. We moved the date up to May 1997, allowing President Clough and the search committee to begin the process when a director could begin the year with a fresh start. And President Clough and Georgia Tech hit the jackpot. Dave Braine, the highly successful athletic director from Virginia Tech was interested. He eventually accepted the position at Georgia Tech, becoming the school's sixth director of athletics. A proven top NCAA Division I-A administrator with a sound track record, he would not be a trial-and-error choice. He would step in and know what to do in his job.

Naturally I'd been concerned about who would follow me. Dave's choice to come to Georgia Tech left me ecstatic. And in an interesting twist of fate, he brought with him Jeff Bourne as his chief financial officer, the same young man we had seriously considered to replace Jim Murphy. We'd gotten two picks for a single offer! I had known Dave since 1968 and followed his career from that time on.

Dave Braine grew up on a farm in Pennsylvania. An outstanding high school quarterback, he won a scholarship to the University of North Carolina where his athleticism allowed him to excel as a defensive back and kicker. He entered the coaching ranks on the high school level, moving quickly to the college ranks to take positions at Virginia Military Institute, Richmond, Georgia Tech, and the University of Virginia. At Virginia, Athletic Director Gene Corrigan persuaded Dave to shift into an administrative role. From there Dave moved on to Fresno State as associate athletic director, and then to director of athletics at Marshall University before heading to Virginia Tech as director to build of one of the strongest intercollegiate programs in the country. Georgia Tech was fortunate to lure this strong leader to Atlanta to become the sixth director in Georgia Tech's athletic history. I can't think of another person who fits the program at Tech more than Dave Braine. His legacy will ensure a success that will take the program I left to a much higher level. Knowing that his wife, Carole, represented an additional asset to the Georgia Tech community and strength to the program, my mind was at ease. I knew that we were in good hands. As a bonus, Dave also was an avid fisherman. In fact, he was an expert "fly" caster. We built on our friendship when he could break away from Georgia Tech by fishing the streams of Montana and from my boat in Marco Island.

As I prepared to pass on the baton to Dave Braine and leave Georgia Tech after 17 years, I reflected on my career, which ranged from coaching in high school, college, and the pros to athletic director at major universities. One foundation for my success was my service in the U.S. Navy. Serving my country during World War II was an honor. At the time, the media projected a positive message: we had to defeat Adolph Hitler's Nazi Germans and Japan, unconditionally. I was anxious to do my part. We had to win the war to preserve the peace for generations to come. It was a time of real personal values, and a strong family was the cornerstone. The victory saved America and made it possible for all of us today to enjoy the many benefits our society has to offer. We are fortunate to live in the greatest land on the face of the Earth. We must always protect this life, and in time erase the negatives that threaten our livelihood.

CHAPTER SIX

RETIREMENT
AND THE FUTURE

President Clough announced my retirement at a press conference on May 9, 1997. My 17 years as director of athletics and executive assistant to the president had ended. By late February of that year, I'd known it was time to step down. My daughters presented me with a joke t-shirt on my seventieth birthday on February 20, reminding me that I'd heard it all, seen it all, and done it all — but just couldn't remember it all!

When I arrived at Georgia Tech nearly two decades earlier to accept a task that others thought was impossible, Coach Bobby Dodd had presented me with three envelopes labeled "One," "Two," and "Three." He told me that each time a crisis developed I should open up an envelope but to do so in order. After a few weeks on the job, it was already time to open up the first one. It read, "Blame me and move on." I certainly didn't blame Coach Dodd, but I handled the situation and followed his advice to move on. Years later, another crisis occurred. The second envelope advised, "Blame yourself and reorganize." I again followed his instructions, handled the circumstances, reorganized my administrative staff, and carried on. After receiving the t-shirt from my daugh-

ters on my seventieth birthday, I decided it was time to open up
envelope number three. It read, "Prepare three envelopes." It was
time to retire.

I'd always thought retirement should be similar to the saying
about old soldiers: just fading away without fanfare. This was not
to be. President Clough was intent on organizing a dinner in my
honor. At first I was skeptical and tried to dissuade him from setting
up the event, but the plans progressed for a banquet at the Grand
Hyatt in Atlanta on October 29. The next day a half-time presenta-
tion during our game with the University of North Carolina was
planned. It seemed only fitting that this be the game because I had
served both schools as director of athletics.

Bob Harty, director of communications for Georgia Tech, put
together a video. Wes Durham, new voice for the Yellow Jackets
replacing the retiring legend, Al Ciraldo, had been asked to M.C. the
event. Hiring Wes had brought back a flashback of my days at UNC.
Twenty-five years before bringing Wes on board, I had hired his
father, Woody Durham, to become the voice of the North Carolina
Tarheels. Woody became a legend in his own right and set a standard for broadcasters across the U.S. Wes had some big shoes to fill
in replacing Al Ciraldo and living up to his father's reputation. Wes
showed he could hold his own, though, as he became highly respected and a very fine game-day broadcaster.

The dinner was a black-tie affair. The banquet room overflowed
with family, friends, and associates from the years. I had no way of
knowing what to expect, and Phyllis had warned me not to prepare
a canned speech. If I were called upon, I would have to "wing it."

After Joe Siffri, a member of the 1990 national championship
football team and then director for the Alexander-Tharpe Fund,
returned thanks, I glanced at the head table. Dr. Ray Bardill, my first
quarterback from the 1951 Wartburg Central High team and now a
college dean at Florida State University, sat at the head. Scattered
around the table were others I'd known so well and worked closely
with over the years.

There was Grant Teaff of Baylor University, president of the
American Football Coaches Association and one of our outstanding
coaches of all time. Gene Corrigan, who had just stepped down as
commissioner of the Atlantic Coast Conference. John Swofford, the
new commissioner of the ACC, who had just left his athletic directorship at the University of North Carolina. Hank McCamish,

chairman and CEO of the McCamish Group, who had been responsible for the funding that initiated the construction of the Homer Rice Center for Sports Performance. Brad Nessler, who announced play-by-play programs for ABC and ESPN. Bobby Cremins, our head men's basketball coach, who had become the winningest coach in Georgia Tech history. And our youngest daughter Angela Rice Miller, who had come to share this night with us.

As Angela approached the podium, we were not sure what she might come up with. She began by saying, "Now everyone will know who Dad's favorite daughter is — I always knew but I'm sorry sisters Nan and Phyl had to find out." She then presented me with two plaques, the first with a poem.

Dear Dad,
The time has come for you to step down.
Some will shed tears, other will cheer.
But let's take a moment and reflect
On those years that have brought us all together here.

Wartburg, Tennessee, is where it all began.
You said you would do anything to be given a chance
To teach, to mold, to fulfill your dream.
But Dad, did you really have to coach a prison team?

It was a start, you were on your way.
And you finally had 11 — enough to play.
You went undefeated your first year out.
Now that is something to brag about!

It was time to move on to a bigger high school
Where crew cuts, bike riding, and attending church were your
    rules.
A tradition had been started, a legend you became,
And Highlands will always remember your name.

By now, three lovely daughters had blessed your home.
Mom, you were kind of in this all on your own.
The story's been told — all we know is what we've heard,
But Dad, did you really not make it to any of our births?!!

Now the colleges were knocking at your door.
Here was an opportunity you hadn't had before.
Kentucky was the school that lured you away,
I'll never forget that moving day.

We stood in a circle and said a prayer
That the path we were taking would lead us where
We would grow as a family and always stay strong,
For some football seasons seem to last too long!

Oklahoma, Cincinnati, Rice, and Carolina.
Steven Owens, Greg Cook, Tom Kramer, Jim O'Brien.
What great years those were, what fine young men.
But Dad, why wouldn't you let me date any of them?

Dad, you've made it to that final game.
Montana and Marco are calling your name.
You've earned the praises, the awards, the fame.
Your Georgia Tech legacy will always remain.

From high school, to college, the pros and AD,
It's been an exciting life for my sisters and me.
The games, the trips, the boys, and yet,
Our hearts will always stay at Georgia Tech!

The second plaque gave me a send-off cheer for my retirement:

R – is to remind you that you are Retired!
E – is for Extra Vitamins!
T – is for Take Your Daughters on a Vacation!
I – is to bug Mom with "Is dinner ready yet?"
R – is for Rest, Read, Relax.
E – is for Extra Vitamins!
M – is for Marco and Montana
E – is for more Extra Vitamins!
N – is for "No, you can't take Ann with you. She stays at Georgia Tech!"
T – is for Take Your Grandkids on a Vacation!

As Angela was going through her surprise tricks, my mind faded to flashback of her marriage and then further back to the day Phyllis and I were married on August 12, 1950.

On August 27, 1983, I marched down the aisle at Highlands United Methodist Church in Fort Thomas, Kentucky, with my daughter Angela on my arm. I was taking her to the altar to marry Jeff Miller, an architect from Cincinnati. What an emotional moment! This was my third and final daughter to give away.

It was difficult with the first two, Nancy and Phyllis, but this was our baby! I managed my part well, however. The experience of two previous performances made me a veteran. So I said, "Her mother and I," and turned and sat in the pew next to my lovely wife, Phyllis. Perfect.

I felt the strain as Phyllis and I joined hands to witness the ceremony.

It was a typical wedding. The church was crowded with friends of both families. Our minister and close friend Reverend Don Herron from Southern Hills Methodist Church in Lexington, Kentucky, was performing the ceremony.

During the service it came time for Reverend Herron to light the three unity candles. He reached for one of the larger candles placed on the altar to light the traditional candles. But he had considerable difficulty getting the large candle out of its holder. He finally broke the candle out and lit the three small candles. But now the large candle did not fit back in its holder. As he wrestled with the candle while continuing the ceremony, I recalled my own marriage to Phyllis Wardrup in Middlesboro, Kentucky, 33 years earlier.

Our wedding was also a traditional procedure, much like the one taking place at this moment in Fort Thomas. We went through the rehearsal at the church and then the dinner. Afterwards I drove my friends and my brother, who was to be my best man, to my parents' home, an hour's drive from Middlesboro, to spend the night. The wedding was scheduled for the next day at 4:30 in the afternoon.

At one o'clock it was time for us to drive to Middlesboro, to a guest house about a mile from the church to dress and prepare for the wedding. We arrived at the guest house at two — and that's where this story begins.

As we were climbing out of the automobile, my brother and I reached for the same tuxedo. I had picked up his suit and put it in the car, and he, knowing I had put his tux in the car, assumed mine

was in the car, too. But my tuxedo was back at my parents' home.
It was time to make a game plan.

*First, we would not tell anyone, so no one could panic. I would
drive back and pick up my tux.*

*My brother stepped in and said, "You can't drive back.
Something might happen, and you might not make it back in time."
He then volunteered to drive back for my tux. The group went into
the home to dress for the wedding. They were all my good friends
— former football teammates from Centre College and my best
friend from Fort Thomas, my hometown. Naturally they thought all
of this was very funny, so I endured quite a bit of gallows humor
during the next hour and a half.*

*We had a few calls to see if everything was going all right, and
we reported, "Fine," not wanting to start a panic.*

*At 3:30 the ushers left for the church, and I was left at the house
alone to await my brother's arrival which, I hoped, would be soon.
The ushers were instructed not to tell anyone because we believed we
would make it in time for the 4:30 ceremony. I waited impatiently as
the minutes ticked off — 4:05 . . . 4:10 . . . 4:15 . . . 4:20 . . . and still
no sign of my brother.*

*At the church, everyone was seated, ready for the ceremony to
begin. One of the ushers finally decided it was time to make a move.
He sent the florist truck for me, and alerted some of the local people of our dilemma.*

*The florist truck arrived in a few minutes, and I hopped in and
started for the church with no idea how this was going to work out.
I did have my shirt, my black tie, my shoes, and my socks.*

*Wearing an old pair of pants, I ran into the church as everyone
was scurrying around to handle the situation. My wife's brother,
Tom Wardrup, and one of my Centre College friends, John Acton,
decided that John would give me his pants because he was my size,
and Tom would give his pants to John. Tom seemed a little relieved
at this point to be out of the wedding party. Brothers-in-law! John
took off his pants to bring them to me, but, unfortunately, he went
through the wrong door and ended up in the sanctuary with no
pants on. It didn't take John long to realize his mistake. He quickly
ran into another room.*

*By this time, the organist had played "Here Comes the Bride"
over and over, changing music, looking around, not knowing that
there would be a delay because no one had told her. Phyllis's mother*

and my mother were puzzled as to the reason the ceremony had not started on time. Other friends had run up the street to pick up a jacket that they draped on me as we started into the sanctuary to our appointed places, to finally begin the ceremony, 35 minutes late.

My brother was to have been best man, but since he had still not arrived, another friend, Jim Harris from Fort Thomas, was switched to this position. When he marched in with me the mothers of the bride and groom thought there had been a big mistake and realized at this point that something was wrong. Finally Phyllis's father, Leo Wardrup, brought Phyllis down the aisle. My father, a Methodist minister, began the ceremony, having been informed the changes that had taken place.

Although my pants were several inches short and the sleeves on the jacket a little too long, I held up the best I could, and we arrived at the point where it was time to place the ring on Phyllis's finger. I reached into the pocket of my jacket, but found no ring – of course. As I looked down the altar at the attendants, only one, Loretta Wardrup, wife of brother Tom, was married and had a ring. I then began a whisper campaign for Loretta to pass her ring up to me. The chain reaction worked successfully, and I received the ring just in time to put it on my wife's finger and be pronounced man and wife.

Until she got to the altar, Phyllis was never aware there was anything wrong and, although we started late, no one in the sanctuary actually knew what happened. As we were running out of the church, my brother finally arrived with the tux. It has still never been worn. He had driven back on schedule and was two miles from the church when he was stopped on the other side of the railroad tracks by a freight train. The train stopped, backed up, and went forward for more than 35 minutes, which kept him from getting to the church on time.

Phyllis' mother commented that it was one wedding that was much more interesting from the outside than from the inside!

All of those details came back to me as I watched Reverend Herron struggle with that stubborn candle. Just as my mind returned to the present, the minister in his frustration handed the candle to our daughter Nancy, who was Matron of Honor. By a single and spontaneous act Nancy made me realize how good and productive the marriage created by that confused ceremony 33 years earlier has been. Nancy calmly blew out the candle and laid it aside, and the ceremony continued.

If I had never known it before, I realized then that the young can meet and conquer adversity because they see the solutions, not the obstacles. And if I had never known it before, I realized then that Phyllis and I had given the world three beautiful, poised, competent, and sensible young ladies.

So when Nancy politely blew out the candle at Angela's wedding, it broke the tension, and I was able to accept the reality of my final daughter's marriage with a little humor and a great amount of joy.

Others from my life at Georgia Tech surrounded me at the dinner, including Dr. G. Wayne Clough, president of Georgia Tech, along with Dave Braine, the new director of athletics at Georgia Tech. With all of these people and more present, it was a grand evening — truly a gala affair.

Bob Harty and Julie Rhame of the Georgia Tech Communications Department had assembled a terrific video featuring friends and celebrities from all over the country. The large-screen event featured Tom Landry, head coach of the Dallas Cowboys and one of the greats of our time, and Jim Host, founder and C.E.O. of Host Communication of Lexington, Kentucky. Jim Harris, my longtime friend and former Highlands High School classmate, joined Rick Norton, my first collegiate All-American quarterback from the University of Kentucky. Others so important to me personally and professionally appeared, including Woody Durham, the voice of the North Carolina Tarheels; Archie Griffin, two-time Heisman Trophy winner and halfback on my Cincinnati Bengals team; Jack Thompson, my friend and chief fundraiser for Georgia Tech athletics; Jeremiah McClary, co-captain of the 1990 Georgia Tech football team that captured the national championship; Bernadette McGlade, my selection to begin the varsity women's program and Georgia Tech's caretaker of the Student-Athlete Total Person Program; George O'Leary, the Georgia Tech football coach I had hired to head the Yellow Jackets back to winning ways. The parade went on with Bill Cobey, my good friend and right hand at the University of North Carolina; former president Jimmy Carter, a long-time Georgia Tech supporter; Dean Smith, the greatest collegiate basketball coach from the North Carolina regime; Ken Anderson, my All-Pro quarterback of the Cincinnati Bengals as well as president of the organization; Mike Brown, Paul Brown's son and the person who had introduced me to the giant of football coaching while I was in boot camp at Great Lakes Naval Station; Gil Brandt, former scout director of the Dallas Cowboys; Jack Lenygel, Naval Academy athletic director; daughters Nancy, Phyllis, and Angela; and my wife Phyllis, whose remarks stole the show.

As the program continued, President Clough and Athletic Director Dave Braine called me to center stage to respond to everyone who had reached the dais. I was overwhelmed. President Clough even read a proclamation from Georgia's Governor Zell Miller. (See Appendix D.)

Dave Braine presented me with a gift of the finest fly-fishing rod and reel I had ever seen. Then the president presented me with a book of letters. He read the first letter, which was from my 11-year-old grandson, David Miller:

If I could be anyone other than myself, I would be my grandfather Homer C. Rice. He has accomplished so many things in his life and touched many hearts. He made Georgia Tech one of the best colleges ever. He is so bright and active. He always is helping people out, and teaching people new things. He never brags or shows off. He never thinks he is the best. He is one of the greatest leaders I have ever known, and I wish I could be just like him.

Coach Braine came back with an announcement that I would be added to the Wall of Legends at the entryway to the Arthur B. Edge Jr. Intercollegiate Athletic Center, inscribed along with Bobby Jones, John Heisman, Bill Alexander, and Bobby Dodd upon Georgia Tech's history wall. My daughters Phyllis and Angela unveiled a bronze plaque at a later ceremony. The honor overwhelmed me. I'd never dreamed of such a reward, and I felt a little reluctant to accept the recognition of being placed alongside these great people of Georgia Tech's history. The recognition must be passed on to the many who made it possible to achieve what successes we accomplished during my time as director of athletics.

As I stood behind the podium at the Grand Hyatt and looked out over the packed ballroom, I made my remarks as quickly as possible. How in the world could one say thanks to so many people for all these wonderful things? The one person I simply had to recognize was Ann Harrell, my long-time administrative assistant. She was so loyal, totally dependable, and such a great friend as we met the day-to-day challenges of the program. She rightly received a standing ovation

That evening brought to a close my 55 years as an athlete, coach, and administrator. And I felt very fortunate for the time I'd spent on the campus of Georgia Tech. The evening really meant the recognition, in my opinion, of all of those with whom I'd been associated and whose continuing efforts made the evening possible.

Ceremonies were also held at half-time of the Georgia Tech-UNC football game. Flanked by President and Athletic Director Dave Braine, Phyllis, and my three daughters, I hurried to midfield for recognition of my 17 years of service at Georgia Tech. The Georgia Tech Chorus, directed by Gregory Colson, stood by. Gregory had been head of the Georgia Tech Music Department for the past 20 years and reminded me of another story.

I lived in Middlesboro, Kentucky, during my junior high school years when I met my wife to be, Phyllis Callison Wardrup. Greg Colson was also from Middlesboro. A friend of ours named Bobby Rush, who was an accomplished drummer, organized a dance band. Gregory played piano, Bobby the drums, and I played the trumpet. An African-American friend named Fred Peck provided vocals. This was in 1939, and I did not see Gregory again until we arrived at Georgia Tech in 1980 – 41 years. It was quite a surprise to see him as Georgia Tech's director of music. Back in Middlesboro, we had been asked to play for a nightclub called the Silver Slipper. My father, the local Methodist minister, heard of this. As expected, that contract with the Silver Slipper ended up being a one-night stand. However, later on as a junior in high school living in Fort Thomas, Kentucky, I auditioned for Jimmy Dorsey's band and played for three nights at the famous Moonlight Gardens at Coney Island in Cincinnati. As times changed, I was permitted to perform. However, World War II and concentration on a sports career ended my ventures into music.

Growing up through the years, sports was my obsession. My father was a baseball player, and my older brother, Robert Cecil Rice, was an outstanding athlete. It was natural for me to play every sport that existed or was available, season by season. My dear mother was always concerned that I would be seriously injured. To deal with this fear, she never saw me play.

When I wasn't playing a sport, I would pick up an odd job to earn enough income to make it from one season to the next. A newspaper route, digging ditches, being a cave guide – whatever was

*available. I was always busy, which I sincerely believe helped me
cope with my hectic schedule in the sports business.*

At the half-time ceremony for my retirement, I was presented with a
trophy in recognition of my service to Georgia Tech. I looked at the
inscription, which read, "A man's life matters only in how it impacts
others." The quote by Jackie Robinson took me back to 1947.

*I returned home after World War II in August 1946. Before heading
for college, I played baseball for the American Legion. As a catcher,
I was selected to participate in an all-star game at the old Crosley
Field, home of the major league Cincinnati Reds of the National
League. After the game I was approached by a Brooklyn Dodger
scout, Frank Rickey, from Portsmouth, Ohio. Frank was the brother of Branch Rickey, president of the Dodgers in Brooklyn. Branch
Rickey made a bold move in 1947 by bringing in Jackie Robinson,
the first African-American in the major leagues, against much opposition from owners of the other major league clubs. I traveled to a
Dodger tryout camp with a good friend, Harold Wiggins, from my
hometown. Harold, an outstanding second baseman, also had the
power to swing for the fences. His home run clouts made a big
impression on the scouts. As for me, Frank Rickey put me in foot
races against the other players trying out. I won heat after heat,
which also made an impression. Catchers are not known for speed,
but as a sprint champion I knew how to run. The Dodgers were
looking for speed, and my quickness won me an opportunity with
the Dodgers.*

*I spent three years in the organization before I entered the
coaching profession, which was my true career goal. During that
time, however, watching Jackie Robinson created an indelible
impression. A college man from UCLA, Jackie was an outstanding
running back before joining the Negro Baseball League and ultimately the major leagues. In my opinion, Jackie Robinson advanced
the cause of uniting the races more than any other person at that
very difficult time. I will never forget Peewee Reese, captain and
shortstop of the Dodgers, putting his arm around Jack during a
heated game before a capacity crowd, as if to say, "Jackie, everything is OK."*

Sports pave the way for all people to work and play together in
harmony and peace. As Jesse Owens represented the U.S. in the

Olympics in the early 1940s, Jackie Robinson opened the gates
for all major sports. What a tribute to have Jackie's words on the
trophy I received at half-time.

The Brooklyn Dodgers moved to Los Angeles but kept their
spring training camp in Vero Beach, Florida. I lost contact with most
of the Dodgers until 1990, when I visited another good friend,
Harry Figgie from Cleveland, of Figgie International, Inc., on St.
Johns Island near Vero Beach. One of his companies was Rawlings
Sporting Goods, which supplied uniforms and equipment for the
Dodgers. Harry and I visited the Dodger camp, and it was like old
home week. At least 10 former Dodgers, then working as scouts or
just friends of the organization, were there, as was manager Tommy
LaSorda. Tommy invited us to sit next to him during the intra-squad
game. He is definitely one of the great men in the sports world.

I should mention that prior to the retirement celebration, the Homer
Rice Center for Sports Performance was dedicated on Thursday,
May 9, 1996. With that dedication, a dream I'd had for so many
years became a reality. I'd always wanted to put the components
together for providing our student-athletes with every conceivable
program for developing themselves to their highest capacities. And
it happened! But this venture took tremendous funding and the
belief of many people that this courageous step forward could —
and should — be taken.

Jim Langley, vice president for external affairs, served as master
of ceremonies for the evening. As always Jim handled the program
with class. He first introduced Bishop Bevel Jones, who provided the
opening prayer for such a special event. Bishop Jones, an outstanding Methodist bishop and an ardent Georgia Tech fan, provided
inspiring thoughts that brought the program into focus during this
special event. Then a line of speakers came forward that would have
impressed the Queen and King of England!

J. C. "Bud" Shaw, the gentleman who provided the funds for the
creation of the J. C. "Bud" Shaw Complex, joined with John
Williams of Post Properties and with Drew Hearn, who contributed
funding for the Andrew Hearn Sr. Academic Center. Frank Broyles,
the former great athlete and coach at Georgia Tech and later himself
a national championship winner at the University of Arkansas
where he now serves as athletic director, spoke on behalf of the
Intermet Corporation, which provided funds for the George

Mathews Jr. Heritage Museum. Lee Candler received an introduction to the group for her contribution toward the Howard Candler Jr. Football Conference Center. Tommy Gresham, chairman of the Callaway Foundation, was on hand to represent the organization that had contributed to building the Fuller Callaway Plaza.

Hank McCamish was the no-longer anonymous friend who started the ball rolling with an initial gift making it possible to move the sports performance center project forward. And there was Sammy Huntley, one of our former athletes and now an executive with Russell Athletics, along with Lynn Crump, regional vice president for the McDonald's Corporation, and Bill Reynolds, who put the architectural design together for Smallwood, Reynolds, Stewart & Stewart Architectural Firm. John Aderhold, president of Winter Construction Company, had handled the facility's construction. Lawton Hydrick became the first director of the Center for Sports Performance, and Russ Chandler served as Olympic Village mayor.

Dr. G. Wayne Clough provided extraordinary remarks at the dedication ceremony, and Polly Poole, class of 1942 and husband of renowned artist Dot Poole, unveiled my portrait which would be hung in the new facility. Dot had graciously spent countless hours working to perfect the portrait. Polly asked Phyllis to aid him in the unveiling, and Phyllis thanked everyone for our family. To my relief, I wasn't called upon to make remarks myself. All three of our daughters attended, and with Nancy, Phyllis, and Angela together with my wife and the wonderful guests, it was a great evening. We all realized this was the first and only such facility in intercollegiate athletics. I have to note further that Georgia Tech was the only university which had stepped forward with a complete program to build the student-athlete into a total person for a lifetime of success.

Thanks to the great generosity of friends of Georgia Tech, more recognition followed. Henry and Helen Maddox, who had set up the W. Henry Maddox III Foundation, made the initial contribution to the Homer Rice Scholarship for All Georgia Tech Sports. Kelly Spiggle of the Alexander-Tharpe Fund put together a program that brought in hundreds of thousands of dollars to the scholarship fund. Thousands of friends joined the Maddoxes in contributing.

Another Homer Rice Scholarship for All Sports was contributed by my good friend Jere Goldsmith, with whose family my own made trips abroad. The Goldsmiths also had a Kentucky Derby party at their home each year in early May that we looked forward to. I must admit that as we watched on a huge TV screen, with the horses parading in and the band playing "My Old Kentucky Home," my pride in my Kentucky heritage brought tears to my eyes.

In addition, Jon and Merrilee Martin and Hugh and Gerry Spruill contributed generously to endow the Homer and Phyllis Rice Golf Scholarship, given to a worthy student-athlete in golf.

One of my favorite spots on campus was the library. When I wanted to get away from my office to avoid interruptions to study job-related topics, a short walk up Bobby Dodd Way was my course. Browsing the volumes of books and research-related material, I would eventually find a quiet table to write reports or to read the many NCAA legislative reports that the library offered. The library was my place of choice for such studying, so I was surprised but also pleased at another contribution. The Homer Rice Center for Information Competency section added to the library in my honor helped students to gain skills in locating and evaluating information, then in synthesizing and integrating that information to produce new knowledge. The discoveries of tomorrow belong to those who master the information available today, after all. Miriam A. Drake, dean and director of the library, made the announcement of the new section. (I should add that if my "reading times" did not produce enough information, I could always call Tony Barnhardt, collegiate editor of the *Atlanta Journal-Constitution*. Tony was always keen on the latest information from the NCAA, and he and I would meet for lunch at Mary Mac's restaurant and hash out the world of inter-collegiate athletics.)

Many other events conveyed a thank-you for my service to Georgia Tech. One I will always remember: Dave Braine and Jack Thompson escorted me across the street from the Georgia Tech campus to the World Headquarters of the Coca-Cola Company, where we met Charles Wallace and Jim Terry for a luncheon. After the lunch, Charles Wallace presented me with a large, framed Norman Rockwell painting from my friends at Coca-Cola. There are only three copies of this famous edition of a young lad fishing, which was used on the cover of *Saturday Evening Post* in the 1930s. Now I had one of the three copies, and it would take center stage in our Broken O Ranch, Montana, home – bordered by four other Norman Rockwell prints of four young boys in a sports scene given to me by my good friend Boonie Fennell. The Coca-Cola Company, along with Ron Allen's Delta Airlines, were great friends of the Georgia

Tech athletic program.

Then, as the ultimate recognition, I was inducted into the Georgia Tech Hall of Fame, joining the many great athletes, coaches, and administrators in Georgia Tech's long and storied history.

It has always been my nature to shun the spotlight – just as I was reluctant to recount my own life in this volume. But I must take this moment to note the many people who helped me achieve my goals in life. The fact that honors and awards followed actually pays tribute to those who helped me along my path. It is always the team that succeeds, never the individual. And it is not the individual competitor, but the cause, or purpose, that prevails.

I sincerely appreciated the large plaque the student-athletes presented to me during my last year. The plaque expressed their thanks to me for my commitment to student-athletes as unique individuals even before their roles as athletes. That they honored the supreme effort necessary to conceive, develop, and implement the Student-Athlete Total Person Program was, in the end, the most rewarding recognition of all. The time came to close the book. For 17 years, with the assistance of many, we had laid the building blocks in place at Georgia Tech to construct the program. We grew into a $20 million budget, built a program with $100 million worth of new and expanded facilities, and created the Candler Fund and endowments approaching $50 million. This lasting and solid achievement would outlive my own career. At the end of that project, it was time for me to retire. I left a career that began in 1951 at a small rural school in Tennessee with only seven players reporting for the first practice and cluminated in 1997 after being involved with the world's largest sports spectacle: the 1996 Summer Olympics. Such highs and lows! With both wins and losses behind me, I had more than enough memories from a highly motivating, always interesting career for my family and me.

After retiring as director of athletics and executive assistant to the president of Georgia Tech, I pondered what the future might bring. In the first week I received call after call — hundreds of letters and several job offers. I definitely was not interested in permanent employment, but within two months I had recorded 17 job offers. Then future plans fell into place. President G. Wayne Clough invited me to serve as a development consultant to Georgia Tech, both for the campus and the Athletic Association. At the same time Dr.

Gary Schuster, dean of the College of Sciences, along with Dr. Bob
Gregor, director of the Health and Performance Science department,
called me to a meeting to discuss a possible teaching position. The
conversation led to an offer to teach a program on the Attitude
Technique Philosophy as a scientific approach to succeeding in life
for Georgia Tech students. Overnight I became an adjunct professor.
I asked Dean Schuster what the *adjunct* meant, and he jokingly
replied, "It means you don't get paid."

This was the perfect way for me to continue to contribute to
young people. I titled the course "Leadership Fitness – Striving
Toward the Total Person-Total Success Concept." Using the Attitude
Technique Philosophy, the course directed students to balance their
lives in the four basic areas mentioned earlier:

- Creating a positive self-image
- Achieving optimal health
- Pursuing a successful career
- Securing financial independence

I asked my good friend Bud Parker to assist me with the class. As
always, he jumped into the ring and became an instant admirer of
the class members. Phyllis and I join Bud and Robin Parker on occa-
sional trips and sometimes a vacation to Bermuda.

The class was designed to instruct students to live life as positive, self-motivated persons. I believed it would help students to
develop a successful plan for their complete lives. In addition to the
regular course materials, I invited highly successful professionals to
speak to the class. This was an exciting plus for the students.
Speakers included –

- Gary Azar, Vice President, Coca-Cola North America
- Arthur Blank, Founder, The Home Depot
- Charles Brady, Executive Chairman, Invesco
- Dr. Alexander Bralley, Founder, MetaMetrix Laboratories
- Dr. John Cantwell, Chief Medical Officer, 1996 Olympics
- Russ Chandler, President, Wilson Engineering
- Don Chapman, CEO, TUG Manufacturing Corp.
- Dr. G. Wayne Clough, President, Georgia Tech
- Mark Dash, Partner, Goldman Sachs & Co.
- A. D. Frazier, CEO, Invesco

- John Imlay, President, Imlay Investments
- Dr. L. Bevel Jones, Methodist Bishop
- Carolyn Luesing, President, Luesing & Associates
- Hank McCamish, Founder, The McCamish Group;
- Dr. Randy Martin, Associate Dean, Emory Clinical Development
- Shirley C. Mewborn, Vice President, Southern Engineering Co.
- William E. "Bill" Moore, Founder, Kelly-Moore Paint Co.
- Dr. William Osher, Director of Success Programs, Georgia Tech
- Pete Petite, Chairman, Healthdyne Inc.
- Dr. Chris Rosenbloom, Associate Professor of Nutrition, Georgia State
- Catherine Ross, Executive Director, GRTA
- Dr. Gary Schuster, Dean, Georgia Tech College of Sciences
- Julius "Bud" Shaw, Chairman, Shaw Industries
- W. Thomas Smith, Vice President, IBM
- Leland Strange, Chairman, Intelligent Systems
- John Wallace, Senior Partner, King & Spalding
- John Williams, Founder and CEO, Post Properties
- Rick Worsham, President, Worsham and Sammons
- Ambassador Andrew Young, Chairman, Good Works International

Appropriate to the mission of the course, the class was held in the Bill Moore Student Success Center's Gene Clary Theatre.

What a wonderful opportunity for me! The best measurement of success I know is this: to have done that which has benefited the largest possible number of people and has left the world a better place because you lived in it. Just think of the tremendous opportunities we have in the competitive world to give of ourselves for the betterment of mankind. By becoming goal-oriented, and then passing that philosophy on to others, we have created a lifetime of constructive work. By taking a personal interest in others and by passing on the "Attitude Technique," we can build a legion of believers strong enough to revolutionize the thinking of mankind. What a fantastic achievement! What perfect success.

Teaching the course also gave me a chance to emphasize the importance of goal setting, which is at the heart of the Attitude Technique Philosophy. Yale University produced a study of graduates who had been out of school for 20 years. Three percent committed their goals to writing and changed them as they went along. Ten percent knew what they wanted to do with their lives, but did not write their goals. Eighty-seven percent had never bothered to write down their goals because they had not yet thought them out. The result? The 3 percent had achieved more than the 97 percent combined. It doesn't take a Ph.D. in statistical analysis to understand this study. The initial step in goal setting is to write out your goals. Ben Franklin said, "Living without a goal is like shooting without a target." By writing your goal down, you develop a positive attitude. The greatest key to success is a good attitude.

My position as an adjunct professor deepens my gratitude for all that I have had an opportunity to achieve in my long career. I have had the good fortune to dedicate my life and time and effort to a cause greater than myself, and that dynamic purpose has made my life a truly glorious adventure. Success comes by consistently progressing toward a worthy purpose. In the words of Andrew Carnegie, "No man can become rich himself without in turn enriching others."

Another great motivator whom I enjoy quoting to my students is Booker T. Washington, who said, "I have begun everything with the idea that I could succeed." Your attitude determines your action. You must have courage to begin and to follow through. My experience is not to wait for inspiration. Begin. Take the first step. Set a deadline and meet it. Action stimulates the thought processes. It brings from the subconscious mind the real truth and the greatest inspiration. Success must be continually practiced, and it begins by setting goals in order to achieve desires.

And of course, as the name of the course implies, becoming a "total person" is, as I see it, the ultimate goal. I emphasize that striving for this goal is not an easy task, but one well worth every ounce of energy you can muster. You will be more effective as a leader, and you will be able to fulfill your high purpose in life.

As I define it and teach it in my course, a total person develops three high qualities. First, he or she is a free individual. He or she is one who has literally found God, one who no longer has a vacuum in his or her life, one who follows God's command.

Second, he or she is positive. He or she has developed a positive mental attitude technique. This is the sixth sense whereby the subconscious mind reacts positively to any and every situation without any demands. This requires deep thinking.

Third, he or she must be a "giver." My father once told me, "Never judge anyone, but you will be able to recognize the grabbers from the givers." The giver gives of himself – his time, his service, his talents, and his possessions – to God's plan. Only a "giver" can become a total person.

I remind my students that the total person concept developed in my life and studies while I was seeking the path to total success. Everything I researched kept falling into those same four basic areas: spiritual, family and social life; health and fitness; career; and financial well-being. These remain the components of the total person, and the bedrock of my teaching.

In addition to the teaching position, I became chairman of the Candler Trust Fund Committee, working with Randolph W. Thrower of the Sutherland, Asbill and Brennan law firm and Ray Jones, Mrs. Candler's special accountant. Lee Candler's gift to endow the Student-Athlete Total Person Program, as well as other special programs, resulted in one of the largest gifts in Georgia Tech's history. A grand lady who enjoyed Georgia Tech football and basketball games from her executive suite and wore the Yellow Jacket colors proudly, Mrs. Candler passed away on February 13, 1999.

I set up a campus office in my football skybox. On game days, it converted into the original box for the game – where my family and friends joined Phyllis and me. Frequent guests were Polly and Dot Poole, Hayne and Katherine McCondichie, Jere and Barbara Goldsmith, Jack and Peggy Johnson, Taz and Gregory Anderson, Emily Sessions (Phyllis's travel companion for overseas trips), and Reverend Don and Mary Ellen Harp. (Don is our minister at Peachtree Road United Methodist Church – and an expert fundraiser. Whenever Don and Mary Ellen visited the box to see Tech play football, Don would disappear. I became suspicious. Sure enough, he was going from box to box visiting other spectators. I had to explain to him that this was my side of the street. Since Don is building a new sanctuary for our church, I often wondered if he crossed the line, but I never challenged the popular minister. He is a unique church leader, and always available for counseling help when you need him.)

Consulting, teaching, and serving on boards have become my profession, but I always find time to "play." Phyllis and I plan to spend more of the winter months in Marco Island, Florida, where I keep my Grady-White Boat, named 'Attitude Technique V.' Fishing, cruising along the water, taking walks along the beach, bicycling, playing tennis, and eating plenty of fresh seafood fill our days in Florida.

We keep our Atlanta home for the fall (football) and springtime, but head to Montana for the summer—thanks to the wonderful generosity of Bill Moore and his lovely wife, Desiree, who have become our close friends. Bill saw how much I enjoyed fly-fishing on the Sun River on his Broken O Ranch, and now he invites us to live there for the summer. Phyllis and I have adapted to the double-wide trailer on the clear, rushing Sun River, and our Montana family – Dan Freeman, president of the ranch, and his wife Tina, daughters Cari, Chris, and Kim, and his parents Dave and Dee – adopted us and taught us to be real ranch hands. The fly fishing equipment Dave Braine presented me with at my retirement dinner proved to be among the best poles I'd ever flicked over a stream. Marco Island, Florida, in the winter and the Broken O Ranch in the summer — not bad! The leisure has also given me special time to enjoy my family. Three daughters and seven grandchildren (Ryce Hetherington, Leigh Hetherington, Drew Hetherington, Jamie Ingle, Brian Ingle, David Miller, and Andrew Miller) and, when they can break away from their jobs, sons-in-law Steve Hetherington, Jim Ingle, and Jeff Miller visit us at Marco Island and the ranch, bringing back the kid in me, too. What a joy they are.

Thinking back over the long career in sports, I fully realize the importance of athletic competition. The self-discipline, hard work, and dedication necessary to become a champion fully prepare young people for a better life outside of sports, too. Experience in sports competition, enduring coach-player relationships, and academic achievement combine to produce a winning person for our society. What better way to serve others than to help develop this successful, total person. It has been a privilege to be part of it all. I shall always be indebted to those responsible for the opportunity.

GEORGIA TECH: A HISTORY OF INTEGRITY

During my childhood in the state of Kentucky from 1927 to 1944, I heard little about Georgia Tech as an institution of higher learning. But I heard plenty about the school's football prominence. John Heisman, Bill Alexander, and Bobby Dodd — each coach became a legend contributing to the school's extraordinary tradition. How did such a legacy of excellence begin?

The school's faculty bears responsibility from the start. In 1903, Georgia Tech fielded only a makeshift football team, lacking a full-time coach. When John Heisman brought his Clemson Tigers to Atlanta and defeated Georgia Tech 77–0, the Tech faculty decided it was time either to hire a competent coach or to drop the sport forever. "We must field a team representative of our high ideals," the professors unanimously declared.

The school was fortunate to lure John Heisman to Atlanta to become Georgia Tech's first football coach. Coach Heisman eventually also became the first director of athletics to develop a broad program of sports for the university's men. From the moment of Heisman's arrival, Georgia Tech was destined to become a famous — and in some circles notorious — champion football program.

Recognition as an athletic powerhouse brought attention to Georgia Tech's academic prowess as well, spotlighting its reputation as a leading engineering school. Heisman led the way for the School of Technology to become a national and eventually a world leader.

A genius at devising innovative plays and outmaneuvering opponents, Heisman led Georgia Tech to its first national football championship in 1917. His team, nicknamed "The Golden Tornado," was the first national champion hailing from the South. On the way to building the champion team, the 1916 squad defeated Cumberland College 222–0, the most lopsided score in the history of the game.

Meanwhile, a substitute player from Mudriver, Kentucky, had warmed the bench on Coach Heisman's 1908-1911 teams. Although not a regular on the team, the young lad possessed such a deep knowledge of the game that Chip Robert, the team's captain, advised Heisman to hire "Old Alex." Heisman took the advice, and Bill Alexander quickly made his mark as an assistant coach.

When Heisman departed from Georgia Tech in 1920 to return to his alma mater, the University of Pennsylvania, his name had already become synonymous with gridiron excellence. Each year the New York Downtown Athletic Club names the outstanding collegiate football player of the year as winner of the "Heisman Trophy Award" in honor of Georgia Tech's first coach.

Before leaving, Heisman led the 1919 Georgia Tech team to a victory over my own school, Centre College. The crowd of 20,000 was the largest ever to watch a game at Grant Field. The reigning Southern Conference Champion in 1919, Centre would win the national championship in 1921 with a brilliant 6–0 win over Harvard. When playing Heisman's team in 1919, however, even Centre's Bo McMillan, Matty Bell, Red Roberts and Company were no match for the "Golden Tornado," which swept to a 24–0 victory.

After serving in World War I in France, Bill Alexander took over the mantle of head coach and director of athletics in 1920. Later on he combined an appointment by President Blake Van Leer to teach mathematics with a commitment to expanding the school's athletic horizons. The first coach to schedule intersectional games, including Knute Rockne's Notre Dame, the University of Pittsburgh, and other national colleges, Coach Alex directed Georgia Tech to its second national championship. In 1928, Georgia Tech won an 8–7 victory over California in the Rose Bowl, which featured the bizarre but famous wrong-way run by California's Roy Riegels.

Through those years as a player and assistant coach with Heisman and then as head coach and athletic director, Coach Alexander emphasized high sportsmanship. If one individual can be pinpointed as the person responsible for Georgia Tech's consummate integrity, Bill Alexander undoubtedly is that person. He himself was a man of the highest integrity, and he passed on this gift to all with whom he came into contact. Georgia Tech can look back to its beginnings and praise this man for being the source of a tradition that continues today.

In 1945, Bill Alexander turned over his coaching duties to another young assistant coach named Bobby Dodd. An All-American under General Neyland at Tennessee, Bobby Dodd served Coach Alex for 14 seasons before being named head coach. Although sought by many outstanding universities, Dodd stayed at Georgia Tech, eventually assuming the duties of director of athletics in 1950. Dodd not only continued in the footsteps of Heisman and Alexander, but he also accelerated the pace, becoming one of the most outstanding and winningest football coaches of all time. His 1952 team produced Georgia Tech's third national title, and his teams' bowl game appearances converted into wins that remain on national record books today.

The three giants of Georgia Tech produced extraordinary young men who would carry on the great tradition of sportsmanship and integrity that has forged a unique past and present for Georgia Tech. Without exaggeration, I can say that this magical strength of character, which has put Georgia Tech at the forefront of scholastic institutions, can also serve as a building block for making this country a better place.

Here's a short roster of names that embody that character, starting with Coach Heisman's captain of 1908, Chip Robert, and followed by such outstanding athletes as Pup Phillips, Bill Fincher, Red Barron, and Stump Thomason. Clint Castleberry, who after an outstanding freshman season, departed in 1942 to serve in the Air Force in World War II, might have been the best of them all. Pilot of a B-26 on a mission off the coast of North Africa, his plane was lost over the Mediterranean, and he never returned. Howard Ector and Buck Flowers, Paul Duke, Coach Dodd's first captain, and George Mathews, whose 99-yard runback of a Navy fumble gave Georgia Tech the victory. Frank Broyles, later to become a legend in his own right as football coach and athletic director at the University of

Arkansas, Bobby Davis, George Brodnax, Ray Beck, Pete Brown, Maxie Baughan, Smiley Gebhart, and Billy Martin.

Coach Dodd's teams featured many great players and All-Americans: running backs Leon Hardeman and Billy Tees; All-American linebackers George Morris (often mentioned by Bobby Dodd as his best all-around football player) and Larry Morris; quarterback Darrell Crawford, whose famous "Kingsport" play stunned Auburn with four touchdown passes; quarterback Pepper Rodgers, whose last-minute place-kicking won the Orange Bowl. In fact, Tech's string of outstanding quarterbacks runs right up to the present day: Billy Lothridge; Wade Mitchell, who represents Tech in the National Hall of Fame as an Academic All-American; Kim King; Eddie McMahan; John Dewberry; Shawn Jones; and Joe Hamilton. And so many other great players! W.J. Blane, Lucius Sanford, Lenny Snow, Ted Roof, Bobby Moorhead, Danny Rhino, Willie Clay, Ken Swilling, Coleman Rudolph, Marco Coleman, Jimmy Robinson, Drew Hill, Harvey Middleton, Gary Lee, Robert Lavette, Eddie Lee Ivery, Scott Sisson, John Davis, and Keith Brooking. There are literally too many to mention — men whose character on and off the field has made Georgia Tech one of the greatest institutions of all time.

I felt the presence of this tradition of positive integrity when I arrived on campus on April 1, 1980, to direct the athletic program. My responsibility was to preserve that heritage and build upon that past. My job was to direct the program, to train student athletes in total development. And in the process, I would be part of preparing leaders for our society — a greater and even more worthy cause.

THE STUDENT-ATHLETE TOTAL PERSON PROGRAM

BY BERNADETTE MCGLADE

Bernadette McGlade arrived at Georgia Tech in 1981, becoming Georgia Tech's first female varsity coach for an NCAA Division I team. She quickly moved from head of the women's basketball program to serve as senior associate athletic director. During her years as coach and with the Athletic Association, she nurtured and developed the Student-Athlete Total Person Program. The program's success paved the way for that of the GTAA as well, and the Total Person concept won national acclaim, forming a model that eventually transferred to 177 universities. Bernadette made her next career jump to the Atlantic Coast Conference offices, accepting the post of assistant commissioner in 1997. Along the way, she kept up her academic studies and earned a master's degree from the University of North Carolina. In this selection based on her thesis, she describes the Georgia Tech Student Athlete Total Person Program.

In 1980, Dr. Homer Rice accepted the positions of assistant to the president and director of athletics at Georgia Institute of Technology. He pledged to develop a support program to enhance each student-athlete's opportunity for life-long success. The Total Person Program balances all areas of a student's life, bringing together academic and athletic excellence, spiritual and emotional development, career planning and placement, and social and personal success. The Total Person Program bridges the gap between a student-athlete's collegiate sports career and the professional and personal goals that shape life after college. The National Collegiate Athletic Association and the Division I-A Directors of Athletics Association adopted this visionary program, helping numerous student-athletes to become winners both on and off the field.

The Total Person Program enhances a young person's growth and maturation, focusing on mental, physical, spiritual, and social development. Based on the philosophy of balance in a "four-square model," the program improves a student-athlete's adjustment to success in adult life. Within the formal educational structure, only sport provides the opportunity to teach each individual to integrate physical and cognitive awareness in a way that enables full personal development. This holistic approach places exercise and competitive sport firmly within the educational arena.

Dr. Rice intended the Total Person Program to provide student-athletes with the greatest opportunity to grow in all aspects of their lives, not just athletically and academically. Even very disciplined intercollegiate athletes whose high level of commitment generates success in athletics and the classroom may not be fully prepared for life after college. Student-athletes have a particularly difficult transition period after completing their competitive amateur careers in college sports. Many find it hard to quickly and successfully manage the adjustment, regardless of whether they embark on professional careers in athletics, go to work in corporate America, become entrepreneurs, or start their own families.

Dr. Rice noted that it took as long as two years for student-athletes to become comfortable in a chosen career. They had to learn to manage personal finances, be comfortable in social and business environments, and transfer athletic leadership skills to life situations. Naturally, a certain number of high achievers make the transition very well. But this wasn't true for all student-athletics. Witnessing this phenomenon over 40 years, Homer Rice increasingly focused on the problem. As a teacher, coach, and administrator at high school, collegiate, and professional levels, he analyzed the trend from different perspectives. He committed himself to improving accomplishment beyond athletics and the classroom, while building on those two areas.

Competitive sports at times can seem like a big business. Many argue that it should be taken out of the educational system. However, within the framework of education, competitive sport can provide an opportunity for teaching personal growth and developing long-term skills. These coping strategies last a lifetime because the principles of coping with stress are the same, whether dealing with competition, deadline pressures, workplace conflicts, or threats to one's self-esteem because of personal or job loss. The holistic four-square approach provides the model program Homer Rice envisioned.

Student athletes often need more support and education in acquiring these life skills, for many reasons. Managing stress, time, family, career issues, or finances can be overwhelming. Adjusting to lifelong pressures that lack intense competition may be uninteresting and physically unchallenging to student-athletes. This lack of interest limits an individual's appreciation for — and participation in — recreational sports and non-competitive activities. Running out of collegiate eligibility presents a similar problem for student-athletes. Additionally, proper nutrition, health maintenance, and overall physical care have to be renegotiated as personal tasks. A coach, trainer, or conditioning staff member usually manages this area to maximize a student athlete's competitive performance. Assuming this responsibility and customizing these areas for meeting the needs of a student-athlete's post-competition life presents its own challenge to an individual.

The student-athlete's social life changes dramatically. Training schedules leave little time for engaging in campus social events, denying student-athletes the full range of opportunity to interact with diverse groups of people or to gain exposure to rules of etiquette in social or business situations. While undergraduates at the university may learn these things as a matter of course by joining professional or academic clubs, fraternities, or sororities, student-athletes have to catch up on the opportunities they missed because of their commitment to practice and the team's traveling schedule. Student-athletes also need more support for spiritual and emotional growth. It's been said that the mind and heart may make the difference between winning and losing on the field, and this is just as true in other areas of life. Handling emotions, creating a positive attitude, and learning productive psychological traits enhance cooperation and competitiveness in sports, business, and everyday life. Research supports the importance of developing an individual's spiritual and emotional sides for better psychological well-being and a successful life.

No one had seriously attempted to address these needs on the collegiate level before Homer Rice began the Total Person Program at Georgia Institute of Technology. Inspired by the Total Person Concept he himself followed, Dr. Rice set the goal of creating a model program for supporting student-athletes in their personal and professional growth while engaged in intercollegiate athletics. He needed not only to develop a program but to educate his staff and professional peers about the Total Person philosophy to make his plan work. Further, he needed to find the financial resources and personnel to let him make the program a priority within his own athletic department and the university in which he worked. Finally, the program had to be supported and carried out for several years in order to gauge its actual potential. In his second year at Georgia Tech, Dr. Rice began constructing this program and putting it into place.

Dr. Rice had developed a philosophy of success at an early age after his father presented him with a book titled *I Dare You* by William Danforth. Danforth emphasized a balanced approach to developing mental, physical, social, and religious well-being, resulting in the four-square concept. The author posed the question that Dr. Rice himself later asked: "Who will be content today without striving for all the four-square life has to offer — physical strength, mental alertness, a magnetic personality, and a religion that fits us for the highest service?"

Growing out of the model that he had found so useful for himself, Dr. Rice outlined for athletic administrators and coaches an educational program to teach the principles of success. Using cassette tapes, lesson and planning manuals, and an instruction booklet, he formulated "The Attitude Technique," stressing the importance of total balance in a professional's work and personal life. Planning, goal-setting, attitude, and positive-thinking techniques, along with follow-up evaluations as contained in his program, became part of training programs for university coaches as well as continuing education programs for athletic administrators. The program served as the foundation of the Total Person Program for student-athletes at the Georgia Tech Athletic Association.

Dr. Rice surveyed the literature available for helping individuals find success as he began working on his own program. A short list his sources includes *As a Man Thinketh* by James Allen, *Successful Living* by Nelson Boswell, *The Magic of Believing* by Claude M. Bristol, *Life Is Tremendous* by Charles E. Jones, *Secrets of Mind Power* by Harry Lorayne, *Psycho Cybernetics* by Maxwell Maltz, *The Greatest Salesman in the World* by Og Mandino, *You Can Become the Person You Want To Be* by Robert H. Schuller, *The Magic of Thinking Big* by David J. Schwartz, *On Becoming Human* by Ross Snyder, and *The Success System That Never Fails* by W. Clement Stone. After studying, researching, digesting, and adapting their lessons to his own goals, Dr. Rice realized that they all supported his fundamental premise: "Control your mind, and in turn control your life in a positive mental attitude." That became Dr. Rice's Attitude Technique.

Dr. Rice adjusted, revised, and improved his model as it developed. The written material he designed for GTAA student-athletes and staff reveals continual evolution in the program, but six areas of concentration resulted:

1. Personal growth
2. Academic growth
3. Career planning and placement
4. Health and nutritional wellness
5. Spiritual fulfillment
6. Emotional stability

These components were discovered in phases. In 1982, personal growth seminars along with academic and mental enhancement programs and seminars were developed. The wellness program arose in 1985, career planning and placement in 1986, and leadership opportunities in 1988. As the program grew and became refined from 1982 to 1990, institutions including the University of Arizona, the University of Tennessee, the University of Missouri, and others contacted the Georgia Tech Athletic Association to learn about the program. Dr. Rice consulted with many organizations, sharing his knowledge and distributing the program to a wide audience. With increasing pressure being placed on the NCAA to look after the welfare of student athletes, a program like the Total Person Program was needed on a national scope. In 1990, the NCAA enlisted the member schools which had most successfully implemented the Total Person Program to assist with developing of a national model.

The NCAA *Life Skills Program*, developed by the National Collegiate Athletic Association in 1993, provided a comprehensive tool kit for schools seeking to implement this kind of program. The final package consisted of a series of materials, program models, suggested topics of interest, and suggestions for initiating and carrying out a balanced life skills program for student athletes. Focusing on personal growth, health, social development, academic enhancement, and career development, the program recognized Georgia Tech's contributions in leading the way to a national program.

"The challenge that today's college student-athletes face, both on and off the playing field, is unparalleled in the history of education. Unfortunately, many college student-athletes are unprepared to face the biggest challenge of all – life after graduation, or what the rest of us call 'real life,'" noted the NCAA in 1993. The NCAA Life Skills Program uses principles similar to the Total Person Program, with five individual components:

1. Commitment to academic excellence
2. Commitment to athletic excellence
3. Commitment to personal development
4. Commitment to service
5. Commitment to career development

The NCAA provides significant support for member institutions that choose to implement a Life Skills Program, offering the opportunity to initiate the program in phases tailored to specific campuses. This flexible approach, along with a well-developed Life Skills kit that includes extensive material from the NCAA, has allowed the Total Person Program to be integrated into many college campuses across the country.

APPENDIX B

ORIGINS AND DEVELOPMENT OF THE ATTITUDE TECHNIQUE PHILOSOPHY

The story is personal, but I want to tell it to you because sharing the "Attitude Technique" has become my high purpose in life. To clearly explain the plan to you, however, I must pass on the personal experiences I have had, together with the personal experiences of many others who have utilized these "secrets" to reach their goals successfully.

Like many high school coaches, I found it necessary to supplement my income. I accepted a part-time position with a life insurance company. During a sales program, I learned the basic principles of management and motivation. Before six months had elapsed, I led the company in sales. In fact, the insurance job potential was so lucrative, it became necessary to decide which path I wanted to follow, professional selling or a career in athletics. I now know that that with the program I developed I would have been successful in any profession.

By faithfully practicing the "Attitude Technique," I advanced from that small high school to a large one, to the college ranks, to the National Football League as one of the 28 head coaches, and on to the position of director of athletics at one of the leading universities in the nation. It did not come by accident. It was planned. I trained myself, and I was prepared for each opportunity when it came.

By utilizing goals and plans, I found it possible to achieve exactly what I wanted. The results have been amazing. More importantly, while charting my own course, I began developing a program that could be shared with others.

The birth of the "Attitude Technique" actually took place during my early years, perhaps when I was a high school student or even before, because I wondered why some people were successful and others were not. I was strongly influenced by a book my father gave me when I was a young boy, *I Dare You* by William Danforth. It stimulated me to search for the secrets to a successful life. Later on, someone gave me the book *Think and Grow Rich* by Napoleon Hill. From it I learned to put down in one, two, three order the ideas that I could use to challenge myself to continue to seek what I really wanted to know.

My curiosity was keen. At first most of my interest revolved around athletics. Why were certain football players better than others? Finding the answer to that question helped me to become a better player, so I was encouraged to continue seeking information. During my college days I began to read anything I could find that dealt with success or motivation — the works of Andrew Carnegie, for example.

As I began my coaching career on the high school level in 1950, my curiosity was even stronger. I made a trip to Massillon, Ohio, considered to have the best high school football program in the nation. After going over their program from top to bottom, I realized they were winning because of one thing – a planned positive attitude. That made an indelible impression upon me.

Shortly after my return from Massillon, I listened to a record by Earl Nightingale entitled "The Strangest Secret." It wrapped up the works of Andrew Carnegie, Napoleon Hill, and Norman Vincent Peale all in one package. Tremendously powerful, it led me to read the works of Norman Vincent Peale: *The Art of Living*, *The Power of Positive Thinking*, and *The Amazing Results of Positive Thinking*. I analyzed Dr. Peale's philosophy and integrated it into my own.

Later I met a man named Paul J. Meyer, president of Success Motivation Institute. He encouraged me to further my study in this field. I began taking the management and goal-setting courses that were offered by his company. I would start early each morning and study for only 30 minutes, but I gained something from those 30 minutes each morning that probably has made the difference in my life today. I developed an attitude with which to start the day, an attitude that enabled me to control my thoughts and eventually my life. I went through four cassette tape programs offered by Paul Meyer's company. They were sensational.

With an enthusiasm that seemed inspired, I continued to read other books: *The Magic of Thinking Big* by David J. Schwartz, *Psycho Cybernetics* by Maxwell Maltz, *On Becoming Human* by Ross Snyder, *Life Is Tremendous* by Charles E. Jones, *Secrets of Mind Power* by Harry Lorayne, *Successful Living* by Nelson Boswell, *The Magic of Believing* by Claude M. Bristol, *You Can Become the Person You Want to Be* by Robert H. Shuller, *As a Man Thinketh* by James Allen, *The Success System That Never Fails* by W. Clement Stone, *The Greatest Salesman in the World* by Og Mandino, *See You at the Top* by Zig Ziglar, *The Blueprint* by Carl Stevens, *Upward Bound* by Jack Kinder, and other books by Kinder and Roger Staubach (NFL Hall of Fame quarterback). All of these were valuable and instructive. Each of them contributed to my thinking. I recommend them to you. What they all said was, "Control your mind, and in turn, control your life with a positive mental attitude."

When did the first opportunity develop to apply the technique? After I began my personal program, I decided I wanted to utilize it with young men, working through athletics. The stage was set to apply the series of study and success theories to a particular football coaching position early in my career. The experiment would be a "live" test since the work I was engaged in would be judged by thousands of people, and measured by its effect on the members of the squad.

The secret of all successful people is setting a predetermined goal. The fact that the odds are as high as 95 percent against a person's becoming successful means that the field is wide open. The potential is present in each of us, and we only have to know how simple it is to use our valuable resources. Anyone can reach a plateau of mediocrity, but "achievers" will decide how high above that plateau they want to rise by setting goals. The amount of success a person achieves is the direct result of how well that person plans each and every minute. So long as the thinking is good and worthy and clearly defined in the mind, the individual is on the way to some very happy moments. On the way, in fact, to total success.

In my first application of the Attitude Technique, I had each member of the squad work out his personal plan for life. Then we set our goal for the football season. Our goal was to establish the *best* record in the history of the school. The plan was made. The action began.

It wasn't easy, but the "Attitude Technique" was soon causing some changes in the lives of our players. Not many people really believed we would achieve the success we were shooting for because few understood our plan. It was our secret, and we had pledged not to reveal our team goal to anyone outside the squad family. As the season opened that particular year, there was no doubt in our minds that we would play each and every minute exactly according to the plan. We thought of each member as a link in the chain. That is how important each member of the squad was to become. This put tremendous responsibility on each person, for if one member failed, it would jeopardize the entire organization. The plan involved the entire squad, not just the first 11, in a strong sense of dedication and concentration.

After the first game, the score indicated the plan would work. It was a great feeling, a fine start, but the battle was only beginning. We had to realize that to continue meant to improve each day. This is motivation, growing as an individual and improving as a player each day. We had taken the first step. Now it was time to dig in and work even harder for the next opponent.

During the next week, we worked for improvement. Each day we strove to be just a little bit better than the day before. But despite our hard work and despite the fine start, the season had its tough moments. At times, it was a season of frustration, fear, and worry. Several players developed a negative attitude. Many quit the squad, not because of the hard physical work, but because they would not allow themselves to accept the positive mental attitude each individual had to assume to succeed in this undertaking.

The next season brought back several young men who were dedicated in their willingness to think positively, and several new players who were ready to learn. It was a new life. We capitalized on the mistakes, trials, and tribulations of the past season and again started our work for the new season in the same manner as the previous year. We worked and thought positively, even more than before, and the season rolled on. When it was completed, we found ourselves just one point and 30 seconds short of our goal. Although we had not reached the perfect season, it proved to everyone the important fact that our goal could be obtained. It was possible. All we needed was just a little more effort. We came so close. Yet hardly anyone was satisfied because now each one realized we could have made it if each had believed strongly enough. The "chain" was forming. It was becoming stronger.

When the following year began, our athletes were ready. They had talked about their intentions, and they had worked very hard to be in the best condition possible. When fall practice opened, these players were not going to be denied. They parked their automobiles and began riding bicycles. They were off the streets at 8:30 and in bed each night by 10:00. They lived the life of the true athlete. The chief of police remarked to me about the effect this program had on the entire community. He noted how peaceful his job became when football season began. When classes opened, our players were the leaders. Many of our young men held offices in their classrooms and in student government. They not only went to church each Sunday, they also influenced their parents to go if they had not been attending regularly. A feeling of respect pervaded the entire community. This squad had found the key and had gone to work. That year we became state champions. We achieved that best season.

The squad received accolade after accolade. While they were flushed with this success, I took the opportunity to remind our athletes that this was just the first step toward a complete life of success. They had accomplished their goal as a result of their planning. They had simply decided to be something in life. The ones who stayed with it realized fully that they could continue and achieve their life's ambition. They understood the secret. It was so simple. Why only a few actually make the grade is difficult to understand. We can stumble around it, but if we never pinpoint our objective, we will continue to think negatively and give up easily. Through participation in sports, an individual finds out about himself. He learns to win the battle over self, to submit to self-discipline, to believe.

This approach to the game of football was amazing. It brought about a season that was considered the best in the history of the school, and a claim to the state championship. Remember, however, that I am not talking about that first season. It was two seasons later before the goal was accomplished.

This team reached the top. Could we stay on top? Most of the team members were graduating, but the "AttitudeTechnique" was still present. These young men had planned beyond the football season. Their careers for life had been planned. So those who graduated carried with them the benefits of what they had learned, and in addition, the foundation was built for those who came after them.

The "program," as it was often referred to, was highly respected in the area and gained outside prominence. I was asked to lecture at many clinics and to write articles on our football techniques for national sports magazines. Attendance at our games began to soar. An undefeated string that carried through 50 straight games was underway. It wasn't easy, but the next four seasons were championship years.

Looking back to that first year, I can see that it would have been easy to give up our goal. Sometimes we nearly did. There *were* some frustrating moments, but this is a part of any climb toward excellence. There will always be frustrating moments. We knew we would never find out what was inside of us if we did not strive to do our best and even more. There were times when we had only a thread to hang on to, but we proved that we all must hang on and on until we regain the momentum to carry up to the top. Each contest must be played this way. It may take until the last second, but this is what we prepare for — the complete game — the complete game of life.

The players at that high school learned the important principle of giving. A person gets back from life what he puts into it. In business, a person's earnings are measured by service. If he wants to earn more money, he must provide more and better service. Conversely, if he gives poor service, his earnings will fall. The principle holds in every form of human endeavor. It is true in our spiritual life, in marriage, in athletics, in business, in everything. The return is in proportion to the investment.

The seven-year test with a high school football program proved that the "Attitude Technique" theory was valid. I share that one example with you because it was early in my career, and because it had a wonderful impact upon my life. It is important to emphasize, however, that I could not have directed such a program without first planning my complete life and developing the proper technique for mental attitude.

In my own search for the higher goal, I often use the Bible.

God is the source of supply for all of our needs. In the seventh chapter of Matthew, the seventh and eighth verses, are the familiar words: "Ask and you will receive; seek and you find; knock, and the door will be opened to you. For everyone who asks will receive, and he who seeks will find, and the door will be opened to him who knocks."

That is the "secret" of the "Attitude Technique." You may decide to stay right where you are now and make your job and your life very meaningful and successful. You may decide you want to move to a higher position in another locality. Whatever path you decide upon, it can be a very happy, exciting adventure if you utilize the "Attitude Technique" principles, but *you* are the key. That is the first and most important principle.

The second is that you must start now. The rewards have been waiting for you. The Architect of the universe did not design a ladder leading to nowhere. The Carpenter from the plains of Galilee gave us the only tool we need, the advice of His teaching: "As you sow, so shall you reap. We become what we plan. We are at this very moment exactly what we have planned to be — nothing more, nothing less. All of the philosophers, prophets, teachers and wise men throughout history have disagreed on many things, but on this one point they are in unanimous agreement. Marcus Aurelius, the great Roman emperor and philosopher said, "A man's life is what his thoughts are made of." Ralph Waldo Emerson said, "A man is what he thinks about all day long." And Dr. Norman Vincent Peale said, "If we think in negative terms, we receive negative results. Conversely, if we think in positive terms, we receive the positive results." Therefore, we can control our lives by controlling our thoughts. We become what we plan.

After learning these principles, applying them first to my life and then to the young men I coached, I realized it was possible to be successful in whatever task I decided to undertake, whether it be in education, coaching, administration, or business.

As the years went on , there were times when I lost control, but it was simple to reread, restudy, and regain my objective thinking. Each and every time it put me back on the right track.

The "Attitude Technique" enabled me to plan each step until I reached my goal. It is literally amazing how I have worked out my life by carefully planning each step up the ladder. My experiences have taken me from a small rural school up through two succes-

sively larger high schools to positions as chief football assistant on
the major college level, head coach at major colleges, director of
athletics at major universities, head coach of a professional football
team in the National Football League, and the assistant to the president at a major institution. I have not stopped planning or studying the motivation field because I realize it is the only way to stay at
my level or have any hopes of improving on my plans. Therefore, I
must concur 100 percent with all the great people from whom I
have learned. We can be what we want to be if we learn to write out
our plans, control our thoughts in a positive manner, and believe
strongly enough in the outcome.

There is an affirmative, scientific approach to becoming a winner — a complete winner. True, problems exist throughout the
world — poor economic conditions, hunger, racism. To attempt to
predict the future is presumptuous. Nevertheless, a positive, planned
personal program is still clearly necessary and viable. Man can control *his* future. This has been true throughout all history. Success can
be yours as it has been for others.

What I am talking about is having a winning career, living a
vibrant life, developing inner happiness, and retiring independently.
The "Attitude Technique" program is a complete life.

THE BANQUET PROGRAM

Heisman, Alexander, Dodd. These legendary figures embodied Georgia Tech's rich athletic heritage, dating back nearly a century. Now a new name was being added to this prestigious list: Dr. Homer C. Rice. With his retirement as Georgia Tech's athletic director in 1997, Homer Rice concluded a stellar 47-year career during which he became one of the most respected men in collegiate athletics. Dr. Rice's long career has been varied, extending past even his administrator experiences.

He was a star high school athlete in football, basketball, and track in his native Kentucky. After joining the U.S. Navy during World War II, he earned All-American honors as a quarterback at Centre College, while spending his summers playing professional baseball with the Brooklyn Dodgers. (Dr. Rice earned A.B., M.S., and Ph.D. degrees from Centre College, Eastern Kentucky University, and Columbia Pacific University.) His 27-year coaching career included high schools in Tennessee and Kentucky; the universities of Kentucky, Oklahoma, and Cincinnati; and the Cincinnati Bengals of the National Football League.

He served as athletic director at the University of North

Carolina at Chapel Hill before becoming athletic director and head football coach at Rice University and then moving to Cincinnati to coach the Bengals.

In February of 1980, Dr. Rice accepted the position of athletic director at Georgia Tech. Many considered his mission of rebuilding the institution's athletic program impossible. Everyone considered it at least extremely challenging. Yet the results he brought out have been nothing short of remarkable. The complete list of Georgia Tech's athletic achievements under Dr. Rice's leadership is too exhaustive to catalog, but highlights include:

- 1990 national championship in football
- 1990 NCAA men's basketball Final Four
- 1992 national women's basketball invitation tournament champions
- 1993 NCAA runner-up in golf
- 1994 college baseball World Series runner-up
- Three Olympic gold medalists in track

Perhaps Dr. Rice's most enduring contribution to Georgia Tech Athletics is his "Total Person Concept," a philosophy that emphasizes student-athletes as complete persons, helping them to acquire the skills necessary to become successful in today's extremely competitive marketplace. Rather than valuing student-athletes exclusively for their athletic prowess, the Total Person Concept strives to set the student-athletes on a course for a lifetime of success. Many athletic departments across the country have embraced Dr. Rice's vision, which is the model for the NCAA's Champs Program.

Another manifestation of Dr. Rice's vision is found in the Homer Rice Center for Sports Performance, a facility that uses the latest technology and research in physiology, nutrition, sports medicine, sports psychology, sports vision, and motion. This holistic approach will be invaluable in bringing Georgia Tech's athletic program into the twenty-first century.

In addition to his administrative and coaching work, Dr. Rice is also a noted author. He has published five books and written numerous articles on topics ranging from triple-option football to leadership and motivational techniques in athletics.

With Dr. Rice's retirement, Georgia Tech honors the career of a man who is much more than a skilled athletics administrator. More important, Tech honors a "total person," a man who not only strives for excellence in all that he does but also strives to bring out the best in others.

A PROCLAMATON

BY THE GOVERNOR OF THE STATE OF GEORGIA

A PROCLAMATION
DR. HOMER RICE

Whereas: Dr. Homer Rice is recognized for his years of service and as one of the most respected collegiate administrators in the nation; and

Whereas: During his distinguished career, Dr. Rice has made a significant impact on the lives of others through playing, coaching, and leading athletes at all levels; and

Whereas: Dr. Rice has served as an outstanding football coach at the University of Kentucky, Oklahoma, Cincinnati, and Rice, as head coach of the Cincinnati Bengals, and in 1961 was voted the "Winningest Football Coach in America"; and

Whereas: Dr. Rice has served as Director of Athletics at the

University of North Carolina, Rice University, and the Georgia Institute of Technology; and

Whereas: Dr. Rice guided the re-emergence of Georgia Tech as a national intercollegiate power, producing a national championship in football, a Final Four and a Sweet Sixteen appearance in men's basketball; a N.W.F.T. championship in women's basketball; two College World Series appearances in baseball; and three Olympic gold medalists in track; and

Whereas: Dr. Rice's greatest contribution has been the development of young men and women through his Total Person Concept, a program that has been modeled by the NCAA and adopted by scores of universities around the country; and

Whereas: It is indeed fitting to honor Dr. Rice for his outstanding contributions and service to professional and collegiate athletics; now

Therefore: I, Zell Miller, Governor of the State of Georgia, do hereby commend Dr. Homer Rice on a job well done.

In witness whereof, I have hereunto set my hand and caused the Seal of the Executive Department to be affixed this 30th day of October, 1997.

INDEX

A

Abell, Nelson, 72, 124
ACOG. *See* Atlanta Committee for the Olympic Games (ACOG)
Acton, John, 154
Adams, W. B., 42
African Americans, 159-160
Air Force Academy, 20
Alexander, Bill, 20, 27, 36, 57, 70, 101, 170-171
Alexander Memorial Coliseum, 46, 68, 120, 121, 142
Alexander-Tharpe Fund
assets of, 77
dues for, 56
establishment of, 47
as fundraising institution, 34, 36, 43, 91
officers of, 100
Aloha Bowl, 125
American Football Coaches Association, x, 21
Anderson, Bobby Joe, 56
Anderson, Ken, 23, 24, 156
Anderson, Kenny, 97, 100
Anderson, Ray, 122
Anderson, Tazwell, 63, 68, 121, 122
Andrew Hearn Sr. Academic Center, 75
Angelucci, Ralph, 10-11
Arey, Norman, 94
Arizona State University, 20
Arledge, Roone, 44
Arnsparger, Bill, 135
Arthur B. Edge Jr. Intercollegiate Athletic Center, 42, 43, 63, 133-134
Atkins, Derick, 98
Atlanta Committee for the Olympic Games (ACOG), 103, 118, 120
Atlanta Falcons, 17, 86
Atlanta Hawks, 121
Atlanta Journal, 88
Atlanta Journal-Constitution, 30, 85, 94, 162
Atlantic Coast Conference, 18, 29-30, 39-77
Attitude Technique Philosophy
application of, 35, 79

concepts of, 50-55, 165
origins and development of, 179-186
time management and, 115-117
Auburn University, 12

B

Ball, Sam, 13
Baltimore Colts, 17, 82
Banquet program, 187-189
Bardill, Ray "Bubby," 1, 3-5, 8
Bargeron, Andy, 137
Barnes, Tommy, 137
Barnhardt, Tony, 162
Barrett, Gerald, 18
Baseball, 76, 97, 136, 159
Basketball
basketball facilities at Georgia Tech, 68-69
men's team at Georgia Tech, 46, 57-60, 82, 97
Homer Rice as coach of, 3
televised basketball games, 49
ticket sales, 76
women's basketball at Georgia Tech, 117
Baylor University, 21
Beall, Frank, 94, 138
Beathard, Bobby, 125
Beavers, Bill, 46, 99
Beers Construction Company, 66
Bell, Richard, 56
Bell, William, 128
Bengals (Cincinnati), 7, 18, 23-24, 25, 26
Bennett, Leeman, 17, 86-87
Berenato, Agnus, 98, 138
Beringause, Gary, 69
Bernstein, Don, 44
Big Eight Conference, 16
Bills (Buffalo), 84
Bird, Roger, 13
Bisher, Furman, 88
Blackmon, Puggy, 61-62, 71, 77, 101, 137
Blane, W. J., 27
Blue-Gray Game, 22
Bobby Dodd Stadium, 95, 124-125
Bonifay, Cam, 136
Boone County High School, 11

Bortell, Earl, 71
Boston College, 20
Bourne, Henry, 65, 87, 88
Bourne, Jeff, 143, 146
Boutselis, George, 17
Bowden, Bobby, 130
Bradshaw, Charlie, 11, 83
Bradshaw, Terry, 24
Brady, Charles, 122, 124
Braine, Carole, 146
Braine, Dave, 97, 112, 136, 143, 146, 156-158
Brannon, L. Travis Jr., 123
Bridges, Billy, 55
Bridges, Tom, 42
Brigham Young University, 20
Brodnax, George, 68
Broncos (Denver), 35
Bronzan, Bob, 20
Brooklyn Dodgers, 159
Brown, Charlie, 63, 71, 137
Brown, Jim, 10
Brown, Kevin, 97
Brown, Mike, 9, 23, 26, 156
Brown, Paul
    as Bengals' owner, 18, 26
    children of, 156
    as Cleveland Browns coach, 9-10
    as Cleveland Rams coach, 9
    photograph of, 110
    Homer Rice and, 11, 23-24, 28
Brown, Pete, 26
Browns (Cleveland), 9-10, 18, 23-24, 82
Broyles, Frank, 13-14, 21, 90, 127, 160
Bryan, Morris, 63
Bryan, Rebecca Alexander, 70
Bryant, Bear
    at University of Alabama, 11
    career moves of, 10
    coaching staff of, 13
    protégés of, 14
    retirement of, 82
    Homer Rice and, 83-84, 126
    as speaker, 21
Bryant, Kevin, 94, 139
Buccaneers (Tampa Bay), 17
Buffalo Bills, 84
Byrne, Bill, 20

C
Callahan, Ray, 17
Callaway Foundation, 41
Callaway, Fuller Jr., 40-41, 133-134
Cameron, Eddie, 13

Candler, Howard Jr., 141
Candler, Lee, 141-142, 161, 167
Candler Trust Fund Committee, 167
Canham, Don, 20
Cantwell, Kevin, 131
Carlen, Jim, 60
Carnegie, Andrew, 139, 180
Carnevale, Ben, 20
Carroll, Randy, 63, 69, 136
Carson, Bud, 36
Carter, Hugh, 40
Carter, Jimmy, 40, 156
Carter, John, 56
Casey, Willis, 46, 49
Cassada, Eddie, 102
Centre College, 11
Chandler, Russ, 64-65, 69, 103
Chapman, Don, 56
Chargers (San Diego), 125
Chesley, C. D., 49
Cincinnati Bengals, 7, 18, 23-24, 25, 26
Ciraldo, Al, 40, 93, 150
Citadel, 13
Claiborne, Jerry, 86
Clark, Perry, 100
Clary, Eugene M., 122, 124
Cleary, Mike, 20
Cleveland Browns, 9-10, 18, 23-24, 82
Cleveland Indians, 9
Cleveland Rams, 9
Cleveland, Jimmy, 137
Clough, Anne, 140
Clough, G. Wayne
    Homer Rice Center for Sports Performance and, 161
    as president of Georgia Tech, 140
    and Homer Rice retirement, 146, 149, 150, 156, 157, 163-164
Clune, John, 20
Cobey, Bill, 93, 141, 145, 156
Cobey, William Sr., 140
Coca-Cola, 141
Coleman, Marco, 101
Coleman, Tom, 27
Collier, Blanton, 9-10, 11, 18, 23
Collier, Shelton, 99, 138
Colts (Baltimore), 17, 82
Commitment, 80
Confidence, 80
Cook, Greg, 15, 82
Cooper, Kenneth, 119
Corrigan, Eugene, 90, 128-129, 144-146, 150
Corrigan, Lena, 129

Cosell, Howard, 7
Cotton Bowl, 14, 21
Covington, Thomas, 99
Cowboys (Dallas), 14, 34, 82
Cox, Darrel, 12
Crecine, John Patrick
   Bobby Dodd Stadium and, 95
   coach recruitments, 130-132
   fundraising activities of, 94
   Olympics and, 103-104, 120
   as president of Georgia Tech, 90-91
   resignation of, 132
   Student Success Center and, 122
   swimming and, 98
Cremin, Carolyn, 132
Cremins, Bobby, 76, 92-93, 100-101, 130-
   132, 138
   background of, 59-60
   championships of, 82
   as coach of year, 76
   recruitment by University of South
   Carolina, 130-132
   success of, 97
   winning teams of, 92-93, 100-101, 138,
   151
Cross, Pete, 94
Crump, Lynn, 139
Cunningham, Gary, 20
Curry, Bill
   as coach of year, 76
   evaluation of, 45
   fees increases at Georgia Tech and, 48
   as head football coach for Georgia Tech,
   44, 57
   as head football coach for University of
   Alabama, 81, 84-86
   as quarterback, 83
Curtis, Isaac, 24

D
Dallas Cowboys, 14, 35, 82
Danforth, Dan, 50, 180
Daniel, Tom, 27
Davidson, David, 30, 85
Davidson, Fred, 90
Davidson, Rick, 98
Davis, Doug, 13
Deadlines, 80
Decision-making, 52, 80
Degree Completion program, 99
Dekalb Junior College, 60
Dellinger Golf Center, 71
Dellinger, Jim, 71, 137
Dempsey, Ced, 20

Denver Broncos, 35
Desdunes, Jean, 97
Desert Storm, 144
Desire, 51
Devaney, Bob, 14
Dickey, Frank Graves, 10
Dillard, Sherman, 131
Dillon, John, 2
Dodd, Alice, 124
Dodd, Bobby
   "140 Rule" and, 32
   Bobby Dodd Stadium, 95, 124
   death of, 95
   as football legend, 57, 171
   friends of, 141
   fundraising for Georgia Tech, 40-41,
   133-134
   as Georgia Tech coach, 31, 33, 36, 101
   recruitment of Rice as player for George
   Tech, 27-28
   Homer Rice and, 149-150
   speeches of, 34
Dodd, Bobby Jr., 95, 124
Dodd, Linda, 124
Dodgers (Brooklyn), 159
Dolphins (Miami), 7, 12-13, 135
Dooley, Bill, 81
Dooley, Vince, 44, 127
Drake, Miriam A., 162
Dryman, Tal, 56
DuBose, Rem, 56
Duke, Paul, 42, 43, 64-65, 67
Duke University, 13, 20
Dunn, Walter, 124
Durham, Wes, 150
Durham, Woody, 150, 156
Duval, David, 98
Dyer, Ben, 56

E
East-West Game, 22
Edge, Arthur B., Jr., 41
Ellis, Ray, 28
Ethics, 36-37, 80
Evans, Dwight, 140
Explosive Short-T (Rice), ix

F
Fairbanks, Chuck, 14
Faith, 51
Falcons (Atlanta), 17, 86
Feller, Bob, 9
Fellowship of Christian Athletes, 21, 35, 82
Felton, George, 100

Fennell, Clem, 8-9
Fennell, Gloria, 8-9
Fennell, Jenny, 9
Fennell, Kent, 9
Ferst, Alvin, 42
Figgie, Harry, 160
Finn, Mike, 94
Fletcher, John, 138
Fletcher, Ron, 136
Florida Marlins, 97
Florida State University, 4, 129-130
Flynn, Bill, 20
Ford, Gerald, 89
Formations
    short "T," 83
    single-wing formation, 5, 12
    split-T formation, 5
    "T" formation, 28
49ers (San Francisco), 13
Fowlkes, Buddy, 46, 61, 70, 77, 98, 138
Fresno State University, 20
Friedgen, Ralph, 125, 127, 135-136
Frnka, Henry, 20-21
Fry, Hayden, 21
Fulcher, Bill, 36
Fuller, Dick, 48

G
Gaither, Jake, 127-128
Garciaparra, Nomar, 136
Gellerstedt, Larry, 66
Gellerstedt, Lawrence L. Sr., 122
Gender equity in sports, 48-49, 62-63, 73,
    89, 96
George Griffin Track, 71
Georgia Tech
    "140 Rule" and, 31-33
    Atlantic Coast Conference and, 39-77
    chapel building, 43
    coaches of year at, 76-77
    coach recruitment at, 60, 130-132, 135-
    138
    ethical violations at, 36-37
    financial issues, 27, 30, 31, 33-35, 39,
    47-48, 66-67, 87, 92-94, 117-118, 132
    football income, 47-48
    football legends of, 169-172
    gender equity and, 48-49, 62-63
    graduation rate, 73, 89-90
    national championships of, 101
    national recognition and, 79-104
    Olympics and, 87, 90-91, 99, 103-104,
        117, 132-134, 138-143
    parking issues, 42-43

practice fields, 63-64
Homer Rice five-year plans for, 39-77,
    79-104, 115-147
    See also Specific associations, buildings
    and sports
    separation of church and state and, 43-44
    skyboxes, 66, 67
    stadium renovations, 46, 64
    student fees, 48
    televised games, 44-45
    tutorial programs, 74-75
    world attention for, 115-147
Georgia Tech Alumni Association, 56
Georgia Tech Athletic Association, 26-27,
    33, 42, 57, 88, 132
Georgia Tech Foundation, 120
Georgia Tech Hall of Fame, 163
Gill, Geoffrey, 56
Gilman, Sid, 17
Glass, Bill, 82
Goals, 79, 80
Goldin, Sid, 42
Goldsmith, Jere, 161-162
Golf, 61-62, 71, 77, 98, 117, 137
Goodman, Ralph, 3
Gordy, Frank, 65
Gosdin, Janice, 29
Goslimond, Gary, 77
Grambling University, 22-23
Gray, Billy, 14
Green Bay Packers, 45, 128
Green, "Mean" Joe, 24
Gregor, Bob, 164
Gresham, Tommy, 134
Griffin, Archie, 24, 156
Griffin, Dean George, 69-70
Groh, Al, 81
Groslimond, Gary, 62
Guthridge, Bill, 16
Gymnastics, 73, 99

H
Hall, Danny, 136-137
Hall, Galen, 14
Hardin Construction Company, 68
Hardison, Hugh, 139
Harp, Don Sr., 142
Harrell, Ann, 31
Harris, Hubert, 56
Harris, Jim, 155, 156
Harrison, Morris, 68
Hart, Dave Jr., 125-126
Hart, Dave Sr., 83, 125-126, 126
Harty, Bob, 150, 156

Hauck, Owen, 11, 17
Hawks (Atlanta), 121
Hearn, Drew, 42, 75, 160
Hearn, Thomas, 145
Heeman, Warren, 40-41, 65
Heisman, John, 57, 101, 169-171
Henry Frnka Clinic, 22
Heppler, Bruce, 137-138
Herren, Don, 14
Herren, Pat, 14
Herron, Don, 153
Hetherington, Nancy Rice, 112, 151, 153, 155, 161
    See also Rice, Nancy
Highlands High School, 8-9, 11, 83, 126
Hill, Napoleon, 102, 180
Hinsdale, Grover, 138
Hogan, Francis, 63
Holloway, Fred, 42
Holtz, Lou, 129
Homer and Phyllis Rice Golf Scholarship, 162
Homer Rice Center for Information Competency, 162
Homer Rice Center for Sports Performance, 133, 142, 160
Homer Rice Scholarship for All Georgia Tech Sports, 161
Host, Jim, 156
Howard Candler Jr. Football Conference Center, 141-142
Howell, Arthur, 67
Hudson, Charles, 134
Hudson, Don, 10
Hugh Spruill Strength and Fitness Center, 142
Hullings, A. M., 8
Hunsinger, John, 45
Hutchinson, Sue, 98
Hyder, Whack, 47, 69
Hydrick, Lawton, 50, 96, 120, 144

I

I Dare You (Danforth), 50, 180
Imagination, 51-52
Imlay, John, 137
Immediate goals, 79-80
Income Plus Program, 100
Indians (Cleveland), 9
Ingle, Phyllis Rice, 112, 151, 153, 161
Intermediate goals, 79
Intermet Corporation, 134-135

J

James, Bob, 29-30, 49, 84, 129
James, Carl, 20
James, Pat, 14
J. C. "Bud" Shaw Sports Complex, 133, 160
Jenkins, Daryl, 101
Jets (New York), 17
Jobe, Ben, 100
Johnson, Jac, 122
Johnson, Walter, 46
Jones, Bevel, 142-143, 160
Jones, Bobby, 61, 138
Jones, Gomer, 13
Jones, Jim, 20
Jones, Ray, 167
Jones, Shawn, 101, 128

K

Kaiser, Roger, 47
Kansas State University, 16
Kehoe, Jim, 93
Kelly, Jim, 17
Kelly-Moore Paint Company, 72
Kent State University, 136
Kessner, Rick, 13
Keyo, Jim, 49
King, George, 20
King, Kim, 27, 39-40, 63, 90, 93, 122, 140
Kirwan, Ab, 10
Kirwan, Brit, 10
Klompus, Lenny, 49
Knight, William, 56
Kramer, Tommy, 15, 22
Kuchar, Matt, 137-138

L

Lacewell, Larry, 14
Land, A. J., 143
Landry, Tom, 21, 23, 35, 82, 156
Lange, Lowell, 46, 99
Langley, Brian, 3-4
Langley, Jim, 123, 160
Langley, Paul, 3-4
LeCraw, Julian, 94, 120
Lee and Howard Candler Student-Athlete Total Person Program, 142
Leeman, Brad, 98
Lee, "Swede," 14
Lengyel, Jack, 20
Leone, Tony, 83, 126
Levens, Dorsey, 128
Levy, Marv, 86, 87
Lewis, Bill, 125, 126-128, 130, 135
Long-range goals, 79

Love, Erskine, 42, 77
Lowe, Lowell, 3, 4
Luck, Jim, 46, 50, 60, 69
Lude, Mike, 20

M
McAuley, Herb, 98
McCamish Group, 120
McCamish, Hank, 120, 133, 150-151
McCarty-Roper, Joan, 99
McCauley, Herb, 46
McClary, Jeremiah, 101, 156
McCoy, Ernie, 26
McDonald, Bill, 50, 86, 87
McDonald, Jerry, 42
McDonald's Center, 140, 142
McDonald's Corporation, 139
McGee, Mike, 131-132
McGlade, Bernadette, 63, 76, 98, 156, 173-178
McGregor, Bernie, 99, 132
McKay, Antonio, 98
McKeever, Dan, 42, 104
McKenna, John, 46-47, 85-86
McKenzie, Jim, 13-15, 17
McMath, Bob, 104
McMurry College, ix
Madden, John, 7
Maddox, Henry III, 42
Maier, Frank, 56
Majors, Johnny, 16
Markwalter, Jack, 56-57, 100
Marlins (Florida), 97
Martin, Jon, 137, 162
Martin, Merrilee, 162
Massillon High School, 11
Mathews, George, 42, 67, 123, 126, 131, 134-135, 143, 160-161
Matthews, W. L., Jr., 10
Mayfield, Clarkie, 12
Mewborn, Shirley, 56
Meyer, Paul J., 96, 102, 119, 180
Miami Dolphins, 7, 12-13, 135
Michigan State University, 26, 81
Mickel, Buck, 42
Miller, Angela Rice, 112, 151, 153, 155-156, 161
    See also Rice, Angela
Miller, David, 157
Miller, Fred, 20
Miller, Jeff, 153
Minnesota Vikings, 22
Mitchell, Wade, 122
Mize, Larry, 61

Modell, Art, 10, 23, 24
Moore, William "Bill," 72, 114, 123-124
Morris Bryan Stadium, 71
Morris, Jim, 60, 69, 70-71, 77, 93, 97, 101, 136
Morris, Warren 87
Morrison, Dwane, 46
Mosley, Charles, 135
Motivation, 51
Murphy, Jim, 96, 139, 143, 146
Murray, Bill, 13
Myers, Paul, 20

N
NACDA. See National Association of Collegiate Directors of Athletics (NACDA)
National Association of Collegiate Directors of Athletics (NACDA), 20
National Collegiate Athletic Association, 36, 44
National Invitation Championships, 117
Naval Academy, 20
Navy. See U.S. Navy
Neal, Ida, 98
Nease, Lawton "Mac," 56
Negro Baseball League, 159
Neinas, Chuck, 89, 90
Nelson, Dave, 26
New England Patriots, 14
Newton, C. M., 131
New York Downtown Athletic Club, 170
New York Jets, 17
Neyland, Bob, 5
Nicklaus, Jack, 137
Nightingale, Earl, 102
Noll, Chuck, 24
"No name" defense, 135
Norton, Rick, 12, 13, 15
Notre Dame University, 16, 33, 44

O
Oakland Raiders, 7
O'Brien, Jim, 82-83
Oglesby, M. Lamar, 56, 122-123
Ohio State University, 9, 11, 20
Oklahoma State University, 137
O'Leary, George, 125, 127, 135-136, 138, 156
Ole Miss. See University of Mississippi
Oliver, Brian, 97, 100
Olympics
    African Americans and, 160
    coaches for, 98-99

medical team, 87
negotiations for, 103-104
preparations at Georgia Tech, 90-91, 99,
    117, 138-143
Homer Rice responsibilities for, 115, 132-
    134
"104 Rule," 31-33
O'Neill, John, 33, 36, 50, 134
Oral Health America, 142
Orange Bowl, 7, 15, 20, 130
Osborne, Tom, 15
Owens, Jesse, 159-160

P
Pace, Bill, 16
Packers (Green Bay), 45, 128
Parker, Albert "Bud," 42, 63, 71, 72, 114,
    123-124, 164
Parker, William, 71
Parking, 42-43
Paterno, Joe, 90, 125
Patriots (New England), 14
Payne, Billy, 90, 103
Payton, Jay, 136-137
Peachtree Doors, 42
Peale, Norman Vincent, 180
Peat, Marwick & Mitchell, 96
Peck, Fred, 158
Pennsylvania State University, 26, 33, 125
Performance, 81
Perkins, Ray, 82, 83, 86, 87
Perry, George, 8
Persistence, 52-53
Petros Prison, 2, 5-7
Pettit, Joseph M.
    athlete recruitment and, 74
    Atlantic Coast Conference and, 47
    coach recruitments and, 60
    death of, 65, 87
    football continuance at Georgia Tech
        and, 34
    fundraising for Georgia Tech, 41
    Homer Rice relationship with, 24, 26,
        27, 29, 45, 49-50
    separation of church and state and, 43-44
    stadium renovations at Georgia Tech and,
        64
    student fees and, 48
Petty, Claude A. Jr., 123
Phinney, Susan, 100
Pittsburgh Steelers, 24
Planning, 52
Plaxico, Tommy, 46
Poole, Dot, 161

Poole, Polly, 43, 64-65, 94, 133, 161
Pope, Ewell, 39-40, 64
Portch, Steven, 139
Potts, Russ, 93
Powell, Colin, 144
Price, Mark, 76, 97
Prison football teams, 2, 5-7
Proclamation of Governor of the State of
    Georgia for Dr. Homer Rice, 191-192
Propst, Dean, 95
Purdue, 20
Purvis, James, 98

Q
"Quarterback Corner," 93

R
Raiders (Oakland), 7
Rams (Cleveland), 9
Rams (Los Angeles), 9
Rawlings Sporting Goods, 160
Ray, Bill, 139, 143-144
Ray, Dee, 49
Ray, John, 16
Redskins (Washington), 23
Reedy, James, 70
Reese, Peewee, 159
Reeves, Dan, 35
Reynolds, Bill, 68, 120, 121
Rhame, Julie, 156
Rice, Angela, 8, 112
    See also Miller, Angela Rice
Rice, Bob, 55
Rice Center for Information Competency,
    162
Rice Center for Sports Performance, 133,
    142, 160
Rice Golf Scholarship, 162
Rice, Grace, 105
Rice, Home, Attitude Technique Philosophy
    and, 35, 50-55, 79, 115-117, 165, 179-
    186
Rice, Homer
    as adjunct professor at Georgia Tech, 164
    as assistant to president of Georgia Tech,
        45
    banquet program for retirement of, 187-
        189
    as basketball coach, 3
    as Bengals coach, 7
    Paul Brown compared with, 11
    Bryant and, 83-84, 126
    as chairman of Candler Trust Fund
        Committee, 167

church attendance, 14, 142
coach recruitment for Georgia Tech, 84-
89
daughter's marriage, 153, 155-156
Bobby Dodd's relationship with, 149-150
ethical violations and, 36-37
five-year plans for Georgia Tech, 39-77,
79-104, 115-147
friends of, 8-9
as Georgia Tech director of athletics, 25-
37
governor of Georgia's proclamation for,
191-192
health problems of, 122
as Highlands High School coach, 8-9, 83,
126
Homer and Phyllis Rice Golf Scholarship,
162
Homer Rice Center for Information
Competency, 162
Homer Rice Center for Sports
Performance and, 133, 142, 160
Homer Rice Scholarship for All Georgia
Tech Sports and, 161
inducted in Georgia Tech Hall of Fame,
163
as life insurance salesman, 102
marriage of, 1, 153-155
musical ability of, 158
Olympic games and, 115, 132-134
as Petros Prison coach, 2, 5-7
Pettit's relationship with, 24, 26, 27, 29,
49-50
photographs of, 105-114
public speaking and, 95-96
as quarterback, 27-28
retirement of, 101-102, 143-147, 149-
168, 187-189
as Rice University athletic director, 21-23
salary of, 29
sports complex at Georgia Tech and, 41-
43
as University of Cincinnati coach, 16-18,
119
as University of Kentucky coach, ix, 11-
13
as University of North Carolina director
of athletics, 16, 19-21, 25-26, 29, 44, 46,
129
as University of Oklahoma coach, 13-16,
126-127
as Wartburg Central High School coach,
1-5, 7-8
World War II and, 147

Rice, Nancy, See also Hetherington, Nancy
Rice
Rice, Nancy Kathryn, 1, 112
Rice, Phyllis (daughter), 7, 112
Rice, Phyllis (wife)
church attendance, 14
education of, 19
family vacations, 82, 84, 88, 131
football game attendance, 167
friends of, 8-9
Homer and Phyllis Rice Golf Scholarship,
162
Homer Rice Center for Sports
Performance and, 161
husband's career and, 7, 16, 27, 28-31,
158
marriage to Homer Rice, 1
photographs of, 112, 113
Rice, Robert Cecil, 10, 105, 158
Rice, Sam, 105
Rice Scholarship for All Georgia Tech
Sports, 161
Rice University, 15, 21-23
Richards, Roy, 124
Rickey, Branch, 159
Rickey, Rank, 159
Riley, Ken, 127-128
Riley, Neil, 137
Robbins, Clyde, 68
Robert, Lawrence W. "Chip" IV, 39, 170
Robert, L. W. "Chip", Jr., 39
Roberts and Company, 39
Robinson, Eddie, 22-23
Robinson, Jackie, 159
Rockne, Knute, 88, 170
Rodgers, Pepper, 36, 45
Roper, Frank, 74
Ross, Alice, 85
Ross, Bobby, 84-89, 91, 91-93, 125-128,
135
Royal, Darrell, 14, 21
Rudolph, Coleman, 128
Rupp, Adolph, 47
Rush, Bobby, 158
Russell Corporation, 124
Russell, Erk, 127
Rutland, Guy, 43

S
Salaries, 29
Sale, Oliver, 56
Salley, John, 76, 97
San Diego Chargers, 125
San Francisco 49ers, 13

Sangster, Bill, 26-27, 87, 88
San Jose State University, 20
Saturday Evening Post, 162
Schaffer, Bill, 104
Schembechler, Bo, 16, 18
Schnellenberger, Howard, 83
Scholastic Aptitude Test, 73, 90
Schultz, Dick, 20
Schultz, Jim, 50
Schuster, Gary, 164
Schwarzkopf, Norman, 144
Scott, Dennis, 97, 100
SEC. *See* Southeast Conference
Shaw, J. C. "Bud," 124, 133, 160
Shealy, Dal, 21
Shell, Earl, 68, 121
Shelton, Brian, 77, 97
Shepherd, Dan, 42
Shively, Bernie, 10, 11, 19
Shoop, Jay, 87, 142
Short "T" formation, 83
Shula, Don, 7, 12, 135
Sieple, Larry, 12-13
Siffri, Joe, 101, 150
Single-wing formation, 5, 12
Sink, Stewart, 137
Sitterson, Chancellor, 21
Skyboxes, 66, 67, 167
Slayton, George, 50, 74-75
Smallwood, Reynolds, Stewart and Stewart, 68, 120
Smith, Dean, 16, 19, 57-59, 131, 156
Smith, Deen Day, 43
Smith, Eddie, 127
Smith, Frank, 56
Smithgall, Charlie III, 64, 93
Softball, 98
Southeast Conference, 13, 128
Southern Hills Methodist Church, 14
Southwest Conference, 21
Southwire, 42
Split-T formation, 5
Spruill, Gerry, 162
Spruill, Hugh, 67, 137, 162
Stanford University, 125
Stansbury, Todd, 99
Starr, Bart, 45
Staton, Charlie Brown, 94
Staton, John, 56
Steelers (Pittsburgh), 24
Stevenson, Jim, 104
Stewart, Craig, 93
Stewart, Milton, 56
Stith, Buck, 94

Stith, Hammond "Buck," 56
Storey, Fred, 70
Strangest Secret (Nightingale), 102
Straub, Ralph, 17
Strobel, Susan, 145
Student-Athlete Total Person Program
    advocates of, 46
    building for, 120
    as "Champs" model, 117
    development of, 8
    Olympics and, 91
    overview of, 173-178
    promotion of, 55-57
    purpose of, 50
    success of, 101, 122
    women and, 76
Student Success Center, 122
Stumberg, Bert, 43
Subconscious mind, 53-55
Success Motivation Institute, 20, 96, 119, 180
Sugar Bowl, 20, 128
Super Bowl, 13, 125, 128, 135
Swilling, Ken, 101
Swimming, 73, 98
Switzer, Barry, 14
Swofford, John, 145, 150

T
Tampa Bay Buccaneers, 17
Tarkenton, Fran, 22
Tatum, Jim, 141
TCU. *See* Texas Christian University (TCU)
Teaff, Grant, x, 21, 150
Tee Club, 71, 137
Television, 44-45
Tennis, 62, 71-72, 77, 96-97, 98
Terry, Don, 3-4
Texas A & M, 10
Texas Christian University (TCU), 20
Texas Tech University, 21
"T" formation, 28
Tharpe, Bob, 104
Think and Grow Rich (Hill), 102, 180
Thomas, Mike, 132-133
Thompson, Jack, 36, 50, 57, 94, 100, 156
Thompson, Nancy, 129
Thorne, Kenny, 77, 97
Thrower, Randolph, 141, 167
Thuesen, Gerald, 104
Timberlake, Cammy, 63
Time management, 115-117
Title IX, 48-49, 62-63, 73, 96
Tobacco Free Kids, 142

Todd, Dee, 98
Tomasila, Regina, 98
Total Person Concept, 35-36, 92, 95, 99, 102
Tower, John, 20
Track and field, 61, 70-71, 98
Trainer's Association of the United States of America, 87
Travis, Larry, 100
Tucket, Glenn, 20
Turner, Ted, 121
Tutorial programs, 74-75

U
Ultimate goals, 79
Unitas, Johnny, 83
University of Alabama, 10
University of Arkansas, 128
University of Cincinnati, 16-18, 86, 119
University of Connecticut, 20
University of Delaware, 26
University of Florida, 14, 100
University of Georgia, 87, 90
University of Iowa, 26
University of Kentucky, ix, 9-13, 15, 47, 125-126
University of Maryland, 10, 141
University of Miami, 136
University of Mississippi, 12
University of Nebraska, 14-15, 20
University of North Carolina, 16, 19-21, 25-26, 29, 44, 46, 129
University of Oklahoma, 13-16, 126-127
University of Oregon, 15-16
University of South Carolina, 128
University of Tennessee, 12, 15
University of Texas, 14
University of Virginia, 20
University of Washington, 20
U.S. Navy, 1, 10

V
Van Leer, Blake, 170
Varitec, Jason, 136
Varsity Restaurant, 65
Vikings (Minnesota), 22
Volleyball, 99, 117, 138

W
Waddell, Ewell "Judge," 8
Walker, Hershel, 44
Walker, Leroy, 98-99
Walsh, Bill, 18, 21
Walz, Roger, 11, 12

Ward, Charlie, 130
Wardlaw, Edna, 65
Wardlaw, William A., Jr., 65
Wardrup, Leo, 155
Wardrup, Phyllis Callison. See Rice, Phyllis (Wife)
Wardrup, Tom, 154
Warmack, Bobby, 15-16
Wartburg Central High School, 1-5, 7-8
Washington, Booker T., 166
Washington Redskins, 23
Weaver, Doug, 26, 31, 47, 81
Weaver, Jim, 29, 129
Weitnauer, John, 94
W. Henry Maddox III Foundation, 161
Whisenhunt, Ken, 44
White, John, 125, 130-131
Whitley, Frank, 42
Wiggins, Harold, 159
Wilkinson, Bud, 13, 14
William, John, 133
William and Mary University, 20
Williams, Doug, 23
William Wardlaw Building, 65-66, 94
Wilson, George, 87
Wimbledon, 97
Windegger, Frank, 20
Windsor, Bob, 13
Women
    basketball team at Georgia Tech, 98, 117, 138
    as coaches, 63
    gender equity in athletics and, 48-49, 62-63, 73, 89, 96
    tennis team at Georgia Tech, 98
Woodruff, Robert, 123
Woolum, Gary, 12
World War II, 147
Wrege, Julie, 98
Wrestling, 73, 99

Y
Yates, Charles R., 61, 71, 123, 137
Yates, Dan, 137
Young, Andrew, 103
Yunkus, Rick, 47

Z
Zeigler, Jack, 137
Ziegler Tools, 42
Zolke, Scott, 99